THE JAPANESE COLONIAL LEGACY IN KOREA

1910 – 1945

A New Perspective

The Japanese Colonial Legacy in Korea

1910 – 1945

A New Perspective

George Akita & Brandon Palmer

Foreword by
Kevin M. Doak
Georgetown University

MERWIN ASIA

PORTLAND, MAINE

MERWIN ASIA

MerwinAsia
59 West St., Unit 3W
Portland, ME 04102
USA

Distributed by the University of Hawai'i Press

Library of Congress Control Number: 2014916958

978-1-937385-70-5 (Paperback)
978-1-937385-71-2 (Hardcover)

Printed in the United States of America

The paper used in this publication meets the minimum requirements of the American National Standard for Information Services—Permanence of Paper for Printed Library Materials,
ANSI/NISO Z39/48-1992

Contents

Acknowledgments

Having worked on this book for ten years, Akita has incurred debts from many. In Japan, Professor Hirose Yoshihiro (広瀬順晧); Surugadai Daigaku (駿河台大学); Horiuchi Hiroo (堀内寛雄); Section Chief Kensei Shiryōshitsu (憲政資料室); Kokuritsu Kokkai Toshokan (国立国会図書館); Takazawa (née Tominaga) Izumi (富永泉); and Waragai Kyōko (藁谷京子). In Hawai'i, emeritus professor of history, University of Hawai'i at Manoa, Yong-ho Choe (崔永浩); Dean, School of Asian and Pacific Studies, University of Hawai'i at Manoa, Edward J. Shultz; Alberta Joy Freidus, Minako Itō, Ikumi Matsufuji-Flynn, and David Flynn.

Palmer wishes to thank the College of Humanities at Coastal Carolina University for its financial assistance for this work, as well as his colleagues in the History Department for their unstinting assistance. Palmer understands that his work touches a sensitive nerve with his Korean friends and acquaintances; he asks they understand that the overall intent of this study is not to offend the Korean spirit. He hopes that this study will open a fruitful, and friendly, dialogue about Japan's colonial record. And finally, he expresses his appreciation to his parents, Bruce and Sylvia; his wife, Sunny; and daughters, Hailey and Braxton, for their love and understanding.

I, Akita, would like to acknowledge gratitude to Dr. Hisaharu Yagi (八木久治) and Mrs. Mutsumi Yagi (八木むつみ) who contributed greatly to my development as a scholar for allowing me to stay at a minimal rent for over twenty years in the quarters above the Yagi Clinic, which had been used by their son Naoto and his family. Naoto has now succeeded his father at the Clinic. Dr. Ruth Ono, Ph.D., who has provided a subsidy for this study, was a Vice-president for Administration of the Queen's Medical Center in Honolulu, happened to be in Tokyo and introduced me to Dr. and Mrs. Yagi. (Dr. Roy O. Kamada my cardiologist in Honolulu also has "kept me alive" for many a troubled year. The details will be forthcoming in one of the volumes of the Yamagata Aritomo study).

THE AUTHORS AND THE PUBLISHER GRATEFULLY ACKNOWLEDGE THE GENEROUS SUPPORT FOR THIS PUBLICATION FROM:

MAGISTRATE JUDGE (RE.) BERT S. TŌKAIRIN
IN MEMORY OF HIS BELOVED WIFE
THELMA T. (NITTA) TŌKAIRIN

MR. SANEO AND MRS. SHIZUKO OKADA

THE ALFRED AND RUTH ONO FOUNDATION

Foreword

Kevin M. Doak
Georgetown University

Throughout his long and illustrious career as a leading historian of modern Japan, George Akita has maintained an admirable commitment to open historical scholarship. By "open historical scholarship," I mean he consistently has eschewed the extreme claims and passionate argumentation that are all too often characteristic of a younger generation of historians in favor of a traditional modesty that only asserts what the historical documentation will support. Here, teamed up with his intellectual progeny Brandon Palmer, he presents us with a striking and important example of what such open historical scholarship can produce. *The Japanese Colonial Legacy in Korea* explores one of the most contentious, ideological, and emotional topics in modern historiography—the experience of colonial Korea under Japanese governance—but it does so with a refreshing candor, sound judgment, and evidence-based argumentation. It could not be a more timely book.

One of the great tragedies in contemporary politics in East Asia is the recent rise in tensions between the Republic of Korea and Japan—the region's two great democracies who by any reasonable expectation ought to be closing the gap between them in solidarity against common threats to their democratic culture in the region. And yet, since around 2006 and intensifying after the August 10, 2012, landing by President Lee Myungbak on the disputed Takeshima (Islands), animosities have arisen between the South Korean and

Japanese peoples (*kokumin*), particularly in the form of nationalistic (*minzokuteki*) pride by the former and a sense of disillusion if not disdain by the latter. What this recent sad turn of events suggests is that ethnic nationalism (*minzokushugi*) is not yet dead in the Republic of Korea (ROK), even as countervailing democratic and globalizing values are also on the rise there, too.

It is out of this confusing maelstrom of emotions and accusations that the calm, reasoned voice of Akita and Palmer calls us. Based on a careful use of historical evidence—and a searing critique of those historians whose disregard for careful historical scholarship has contributed to emotional hyperventilation in the Japan-ROK relationship—they courageously challenge the "nationalist (*minzokuteki*) historical paradigm" that threatens cooperative relations between these two important Northeast Asian democracies. In doing so, Akita and Palmer identify the problem precisely. Ever since J. A. Hobson's *Imperialism: A Study* (1902) defined imperialism as the result of a nation overflowing its "natural borders," a "naturalized nationalism" in the form of ethnic nationalism (*minzokushugi*) has been deemed by some as the best antidote to the dangers of imperialism. At the same time, the lessons of Bosnia and Rwanda—if not the Nazi ideology of ethnic nationalism decades earlier—have reminded us all of the horrors that arise from an ethnic nationalism thought to be merely a force that liberates from imperialism. In short, modern man still faces the same old dilemma in political affairs: the Scylla of ethnic nationalism or the Charybdis of imperialism. While Akita and Palmer take pains to assure us that they have no intention of justifying the darker side of imperialism, they are clearly conscious of the horrors of ethnic nationalism and opt for the promise of a modernity that can liberate us all from the idols of the tribe. I think history shows they have made the better choice.

Let me offer an anecdote that illustrates the values at play here. Although Akita asserts that "the Filipinos were probably the most anti-Japanese people in the years after Japan's defeat" (pp. 48-49), there is more than one side to that story, too. A few years ago I met an elderly Filipina, Josefa M., who attends my local church in Virginia. During the war, she was married to an important officer in the Philippine Army whom the Japanese military was looking for. She told me that they arrested her and held her prisoner, pressuring her to reveal his whereabouts. She knew that if she did, her husband would be executed. She boldly asked them, "would you tell, if you were me?" At any rate, she really didn't know where in the hills her husband was hiding with his troops. One Japanese officer drew his sword and threatened her with execution on the spot. She calming replied, "Fine. I only have one last request. Please send my body to my parents so they will know what happened to me and can take care of my children." Hearing this story, I was impressed with the courage of this young military wife during wartime. And I asked her, "You must really hate the Japanese?" But she said, "No, I don't hate the Japanese. There are good people and bad people in every nation (*kokumin*)."

And that, I think, sums up the point of Akita and Palmer's *The Japanese Colonial Legacy in Korea*. There are good people and bad people in every nation (*kokumin*)—in Korea and in Japan.

The Japanese Colonial Legacy in Korea

1910 – 1945

A New Perspective

Introduction

Let me, Dr. George Akita, first begin by pointing out some guidelines I have followed in this study. The reader will see long, direct quotations from the sources used, following one after another. This practice, I am aware, bores the reader. Still, in this instance, I ask for the readers' indulgence. I am dealing with highly sensitive, emotion-laden subject matter of which I am still woefully ignorant. Moreover, because of my specialty as a political historian of modern Japan, and possibly because of my ethnicity, the issues of bias and negative preconceived notions on my part may understandably be raised. It is to avoid this that I have tried as much as possible to let the Korean speaking and English speaking specialists do the talking. It also is not my (or Brandon Palmer's) objective to offend the sensibilities of Koreans or those who espouse the pro-Korean narrative; nor is it my intention to place Japan on a pedestal.

In no way should this work be interpreted as a denial or an effort to question the historicity of the suffering of the Korean people. The historical record is clear that Koreans from all social classes and geographic regions experienced discrimination and hardships caused by Japanese policies and administrators. I do not dispute those facts, nor do I seek to explain them away. This study, instead, seeks the middle ground based on the historical record to examine the multifarious ways that Japan impacted the Korean nation. The details and analyses that follow will sustain, I believe, that Japan's colonial record was moderate when compared to other colonial empires.

I have written most of the contents so all italics, unless otherwise indicated, *are mine*. The reader will also note the frequent use of "I," "mine," "my" throughout the manuscript. When these pronouns are used, they refer to me. I ask the reader to forgive what appears to be egocentrism on my part.

None of the foregoing is meant to belittle or besmirch Brandon Palmer's most valuable contributions. Indeed, were it not for him, I would still be a blissfully confirmed stalwart on the side of the espousers of the "patriotic historical narrative." And crucially, he continues to contribute mightily by enlightening me on Korean history and subjects Korean by digging deep into his well of knowledge on those matters. I must not forget to mention that he is as well a really fine chap. For all of this and more, I am grateful. As senior author, however, I take full responsibility for all errors of commission, omission, and judgment.

Revisionism Defined

There is good reason to clarify the word, "revisionism." I am aware that "revisionism" has a negative image (or connotation) in Japan. Indeed, I once published a work: *Taikoku Nihon: Amerika no Kyōi to Chōsen: Rebijyonisuto no Shikō to Kōdō* (大国日本 アメリカの脅威と挑戦—-リビジョニストの思考と行動) [Japan as a Great Power: The Threat and Challenge to America: The Ideas and Conduct of the Revisionists].[1] In it I dissected and analyzed the so-called "Japan bashers" who saw the growing strength of Japan's economic and fiscal powers as a threat to America's standing in the world. I remind the reader, however, that I was careful to distinguish among hardcore, moderate, and those who predicted war with Japan. My

1. Tokyo: Nihon Hyōronsha, 1993.

goal, in short, was *also* to write a revisionistic study, that is, to "revise" the "revisionists" of the time.

This is a revisionist work. I mean by revisionism that there is a study, concept, principle that is accepted as being "true," but requires, or literally "call outs," for at least a second look, or better yet, a scholarly rebuttal. This "truth" may be based on ideology, on nationalism, on emotional or passionate conviction, or simply on the human tendency of "we see what we want to see." There is also that so-called scholarly study based upon scholarly methodology and apparatus (footnotes, indices, bibliographies).

There are four triggers that should raise alarms about a generally accepted notion or work. The first is the "black vs. white" and "us vs. them" premises that underscore it; that is, moral judgments are implied, and sometimes, openly justified. The second is "neatness" of the presentation that ignores the fundamental reality of imperfect human beings acting in an imperfect world. The third is the aggressiveness by which the arguments are pushed forward. The fourth is a "truth" or a generalization that is postulated by a single word or generalization unaccompanied by evidence.

The alarm about generally accepted, even highly praised, works and sources can be set off in a person with a high level of skepticism, untainted by cynicism. The correctives are a reliance on published and unpublished primary sources (letters, diaries, official and unofficial *ikensho* (memorandum) and/or studies rich in documentation, including Doctoral dissertations, Master's theses, student papers, newspaper articles, and reviews. In other words, it is wise to seek and use *every sliver of* evidence to buttress the revisionist study. Clearly, all of this entails diligence, persistence, and time. Persuasive revisionism cannot be hurried.

With this definition in place, I am now prepared to proceed with my detailed reexamination of Japan's wartime actions. The examination can begin by looking at the *New York Times* Editorial of 3

January 2013. The editors make two charges in the piece against Japan's overseas actions between 1910 and 1945. The first is Japan's "brutal" wartime rule over Korea, China, and other Asian countries; and the second is that Japan's new Prime Minister Abe Shinzō (安倍晋三) is bent on "whitewashing this fact." The second indictment uses the word "aggression" in describing Japan's wartime conduct.[2]

Let it be stated: far be for me it to deny the *New York Times*' right to make the accusation. Nor is it my place to reject its unrivaled status as the source of "All the News That's Fit to Print" or to refute its confidently proclaimed, self-congratulatory assertion in a television advertisement that it is, "The Greatest Newspaper in the World." Still, its non-pareil status compels us to recognize that its sweeping, one-word accusation of Japan's actions against her Asian neighbors could become the accepted understanding of Japan's overall wartime conduct. There is a danger in this, and it therefore calls out for a scholarly rebuttal of the methodological fallacy inherent in it.

In the first place, the *Times* falls into the trap of what Rhee Yong-hoon (李栄薫), in a study of South Korea's textbooks, denigrates as being filled with "factless generalization."[3] Rhee cannot be

2. "Another Attempt to Deny Japan's History," *The New York Times*: Editorial, 3 January 2013. On 4 January 2013, the *Times'* wholly owned *The International Herald Tribune* repeated the charge. Earlier, on 15 August 2012, the *Associated Press* also used the word "brutal" to describe Japan's actions in Asia. See also, Martin Fackler, *New York Times* foreign correspondent in Japan who writes that the contemporary "conflict" between South Korea and Japan is ". . . rooted in grievances going back to Japan's brutal colonization of the Korean Peninsula from 1910 to1945, and its attempts to extinguish the Korean culture," which appeared in the *Honolulu Star-Advertiser*, 23 March 2014.

3. *Daikan minkoku no monogatari: Kankoku no "kokushi" kyōkasho o kakikaeyo* [The Narrative of Republic of Korea: "National History Textbooks of South Korea Must Be Revised], trans. Nagashima Hiroki(永島広紀) (Tokyo: Bungei Shunjū, 2009). I am grateful to Sakurai Yoshiko (櫻井よしこ), a noted commentator in Japan on a broad range of political, economic, social, and foreign policy questions for sending me a copy of Rhee's book.

dismissed out of hand. He is a professor specializing in economic history at Seoul National University, South Korea's premier center of higher education. His background has enabled him to base his conclusions on manifold evidence—and here we paraphrase a comment made famous recently by a former United States President: "It's simple arithmetic."

Moreover, related to the point just raised, the *New York Times* approach is a dispiriting blow for those of us endeavoring to be true to our scholarly craft.[4] Specifically, the *Times'* interpretation would characterize our study on Japan's colonial policy on Korea as being utterly without merit, and a total waste of the most precious commodity available to human beings: time.

There is no doubt in my mind, that the "aggression" indictment characterizing Japan's post-1930 overseas conduct covers a litany of sins, including "brutality" against the Koreans from 1905 to 1945. Still, since a detailed repudiation of the "aggression" charge will take us too far afield from the original goals of this study, I shall leave the refutation to another study that is now being written.[5]

Anti-Japanese Sentiment in South Korea

Junbeom Pyon, a Korean, and Yuka Tsukagoshi (塚越由郁), a Japanese, have each addressed anti-Japanese sentiments among the Korean population. It is a topic that is emotionally laden and difficult to pin down. Even granting that they do not confront the issue of quantifying the number of South Koreans who are anti-Japanese, I assume that most of them are sympathetic with the description presented by the two. They assert that despite all of the specific complaints that the Koreans frequently repeat regarding Japanese

4. See, George Akita, *Evaluating Evidence: A Positivist Approach to Reading Sources on Modern Japan* (Honolulu: University of Hawai'i Press, 2008). This work takes up the very serious problems involved in writing history and the extreme care needed to recognize and to cope with these difficulties.
5. "MacArthur's Misguided Attempt to Reform Japan."

misconduct in Korea—inspired by "the tendency (if not eagerness) of politicians in South Korea to play the anti-Japan card," *nothing* will stop the Koreans from continuing to demand apologies from Japan. The words of the two are brutally frank:

> The *root* of anti-Japanese sentiment in Korea is *wounded pride*. Koreans feel *humiliated* and *insulted* that they, [from] a *highly civilized society*, were invaded by the Japanese, whom they believed to be *barbarians* . . . Koreans *hate* the Japanese because Koreans cannot accept that the "*great people*" of Korea were invaded by the people to whom the Koreans taught Confucianism and Buddhism.

To their credit, the authors present concrete proposals that both countries could adopt to "make possible a genuine and enduring partnership."[6] Alas, their optimism, at least for now, appears to be a forlorn hope. There is an apparent resurgence of anti-Japanese attitudes within Korea, much of it related to a territorial dispute. Allow us a short digression to exemplify this point.

On 15 August 2012, a popular South Korean singer, Kim Jang-hoon (김장훈, 金章勳), led a group of forty amateurs in a relay swim to the cluster of islets known as Dokdo or Takeshima in the East Sea. These islets are claimed by both Japan and Korea and have been the source of recent diplomatic spats between the two nations. The aim of the relay was to call attention to the sixty-seventh anniversary of Korea's independence from Japan's colonial rule. This action followed on the heels of ROK President Lee Myung-bak (이명박, 李明博) becoming the first Korean president to set foot on these islets.[7]

The Associated Press's exegesis of the territorial dispute is pertinent to our study:

6. "Turn Japan—ROK Relations into a 'Real' Partnership," *Pac Net Newsletter* 14 (19 March 2007), published by Pacific Forum CSIS.
7. Hilary Whiteman, "South Korean Singer Swims into Island Dispute with Japan," *CNN*, 15 August 2012.

> The anniversary of Japan's surrender in 1945 revives long-running territorial disputes in Asia as well as memories of Japan's *brutal* colonial occupation of many neighbors that ended only at the close of the war.[8]

The Associated Press cannot be faulted for regarding Japan's colonial policy as having been "brutal," given the persistence among Anglophone specialists on Korea to make negative assessments on the subject.

Western Criticisms of Japan's Colonial Policies

Mark R. Peattie, in his "Introduction" to *The Japanese Colonial Empire, 1895–1945*,[9] makes statements that echo those made by the proponents of the "nationalistic narrative." He writes:

> . . . the iron-fisted rule of General Terauchi Masatake [寺内正毅]. [p.17]
>
> . . . the period of "military rule" [*budan seiji* (武断政治)] in Korea was draconian and vindictive. [p.18]
>
> . . . [Korea was under] an openly oppressive military administration. [p.19]
>
> . . . [under Terauchi there was a] ruthless political, educational, and social transformation. [p. 20]

His judgment on *bunka seiji* that followed the 1 March 1919 Movement is almost as dark:

> Certainly, the *feeble* administrative and social reforms of the decade of "cultural rule" [*bunka seiji*]. [p. 21]
>
> even the *pretentions* to liberal reform in the Japanese colonial empire did not outlast the 1920's. [p. 21]
>
> [the governors-general of Taiwan and Korea were] "highly authoritarian." [p. 25]

---

8. Mari Yamaguchi, "Asian Island Dispute Flares on WWII anniversary," *Associated Press*, 15 August 2012.

9. Edited by Ramon H. Myers and Mark R. Peattie (Princeton, NJ: Princeton University Press, 1984).

> . . . at the steely insistence of the Japanese army, the rule of military commanders continued unbroken. [p. 26]

The passage of time has not softened his position on Japan's rule over Korea. Eleven years after his Introduction, he notes that:

> . . . the Koreans . . . *seethed* as one people under the harshest colonial rule . . . each insult [dealt] to [the] Japanese [immigrants in the United States] was more than matched by the *contempt* that the Japanese dealt out on a *regular basis* to Koreans and Chinese in the Japanese homeland or under Japanese control abroad.[10]

It would be a mistake to regard Peattie's words as part of a one-dimensional rant on Japanese rule over Korea. He is too fine a scholar to be so dismissed. This is evident already in his Introduction (1984). He asserts that:

> . . . one must give Japanese colonial administrators high marks as a group . . . the competence and quality of the average Japanese colonial bureaucrat is remarkable . . . they were nevertheless imbued with a vigorous sense of public service . . . and they took their jobs seriously. [p. 26]

He also anticipates important conclusions propounded by present-day revisionists:

> . . . the surveys and registration programs were *scrupulously honest* and *not originally intended to redistribute land to Japanese at the expense of Korean cultivators.* [p. 31]

Peattie also takes note of "the flexibility of colonial authority in applying control measures, rather than simple brutality [that] were effective in structuring the Korean mass media to conform to Japanese policies" [pp. 41-42].

---

10. Mark R. Peattie, "A Historian Looks at the Pacific War," *Hoover Essays, No.13* (Stanford: Hoover Institution on War, Revoltution, and Peace, Stanford University, 1995), 2 and 4.

And then, there are the closing sentences in his Introduction that in poetic cadences call for the study of the Japanese colonizers, those, as Hildi Kang shows, who even under the "Black Umbrella" contributed to positive accomplishments of Japanese colonial policies.[11]

> For the Japanese in their colonies were not a faceless elite of uniformed oppressors, no more than they were all marble exemplars of progress and civilization, but were earnest administrators and calculating speculators, wealthy landlords and tenant farmers, teachers and ruffians, housewives and prostitutes, doctors and adventurers, who collectively embodied Japanese visions and prejudices, plans and passions, knowledge and ignorance, altruism and greed. When contemporary scholarships begins to populate the Japanese colonial landscape with living, acting individuals, Japanese colonialism will at last begin to take on a humanity, if not a humaneness, which it does not yet possess. [p. 52]

In striking contrast to the approach suggested by Peattie, we have the broadside delivered by Andre Schmid in his, "Colonialism and the 'Korea Problem' in the Historiography of Modern Japan: A Review Article."[12]

Schmid deserves to be credited for his work. He has utilized Korean newspaper articles and editorials and is therefore a pioneer filling a gap in our understanding of Japan's colonial policies.[13] In the Review Article, Schmid is unsparing in his critique of Mark Peattie's "Introduction" for what he sees as Peattie's attempt to soft-pedal Japan's rule over Korea. He is also very critical of Peter Duus'

---

11. Hildi Kang, *Under the Black Umbrella: Voices from Colonial Korea, 1910–1945* (Ithaca, NY: Cornell University Press, 2001).
12. *The Journal of Asian Studies* 59.4 (November 2000): 951-976.
13. Schmid is associate professor in the Department of East Asian Studies at the University of Toronto. He received the John Whitney Hall Book Prize of the Association for Asian Studies for his, *Korea Between Empires, 1895–1919* (New York, Columbia University Press, 2002).

The Abacus and the Sword: The Japanese Penetration of Korea, 1895–1910.[14] Simply put, his one-sided attacks diminish the credibility of his paper.[15]

The litany of negative charges against Japan's Korea policies continues beyond these scholars. Jun Uchida contributes to this approach by recording the memories, in the form of oral and written testimonies of eighty-seven former Japanese settlers. This is a significant and worthwhile contribution, especially when used in tandem with the voices of Koreans compiled by Hildi Kang. Still, the premise of his article is that the Koreans were the "products of *injustice, prejudices, and violence* they *suffered* under Governor-General's rule."[16]

We begin the next phase of this study by accepting the definition of history as a study of changes over time, and on this premise we introduce the many facets of the "nationalistic" or "patriotic" narrative to be followed later by "revisionistic" studies that compel a rethinking of Japan's rule over Korea.

---

14. Berkeley: University of California Press, 1995.

15. It is not, therefore, surprising that in a "Communications to the Editor" Mark Peattie and Ramon Myers, the co-editors of *The Japanese Colonial Empire, 1895–1945*, mount a vigorous rebuttal of Schmid's criticisms. See, *The Journal of Asian Studies* 60.3 (August, 2001): 813-815. Schmid responds, 815-816.

16. "A Sentimental Journey: Mapping Interior Frontier of Japanese Settlers in Colonial Korea," *The Journal of Asian Studies*. 70.3 (August 2011): 707. Uchida is assistant professor, Department of History, Stanford University. Unlike Schmid, he praises Duus, a senior scholar at Stanford, for providing "valuable profiles of settlers." fn. 2, 707.

Chapter One

The National Historical Narrative

The historiography of Japan's colonial rule of Korea (1910–1945) is undergoing a gradual transformation. The nationalist historical narrative, which consists of works that focus on Japanese abuses and Korean victimization, dominated Western and Asian academic works from the early 1950s to the mid-1990s. Beginning in the mid-1980s, a handful of studies by Korean and American scholars adopted "modernization" as a methodology to examine Korean history, and by so doing, they examined the multifarious ways Korean society, particularly in the economic realm, advanced during the colonial era.[1] These studies, known as the colonial development theory, do not challenge or deny the suffering of the Korean people; they merely expand the analytical framework to include the ways that Koreans benefited.[2] A third field of study that recently emerged,

1. Chŏng Chae-jŏng, "Looking at the Economy and Society of Korea under Japanese Rule: Beyond the 'Theory of Development' and 'Theory of Exploitation,'" in *Korea under Japanese Rule: Past and Current Research Results and Issues for Future Research*, ed. Matsuda Toshihiko (Kyoto: International Research Center for Japanese Studies, 2009), 39-49.
2. See Yun Hae-dong (윤해동, 尹海東), et al., eds, *Kŭndae rŭl tasi ingnŭnda: Han'guk kŭndae insik ŭi saeroun p'aerŏdaim ŭl wihayŏ* (근대를 다시 읽는다: 한국 근대 인식의 새로운 패러다임을 위하여) [Another reckoning of modern times: A new paradigm for modern Korea] (Seoul: Yŏksa Pip'yŏngsa, 2006) and Pak Chi-hyang (박지향, 朴枝香), et al., eds., *Haebang chŏn-husa ŭi chae insik* (해방 전후사의 재인식) [A rediscovery of history before and since liberation] (Seoul: Ch'aek sesang, 2006).

colonial modernity, moves beyond the rigid interpretations of nationalism and colonialism found in Korean historiography by analyzing the transformation of traditional Korean society into the modern age; works based on this approach examine Korean receptivity of social, economic, and technological innovations (through a Japanese-imposed filter) rather than victimization. Still, the national historical narrative persists as a viable and staunchly supported concept within academic circles in Korea and Japan, as well as among many Western scholars.

The inspiration for and genesis of this study came from a revisionistic study on Korean conscripts and volunteers in Japan's armed forces; it focused primarily on Japan's colonial mobilization policies as enunciated and acted on by those in the highest echelon of the Japanese government. By expanding widely on this narrow window of revisionism, we conclude that Japan's policies in Korea were embedded in realism, moderation, mutualism, and proportionality in its application and thus formed a foundation for South Korea's postwar developmental miracle.

THE NATIONAL HISTORICAL PARADIGM

The national historical narrative exaggerates Japan's abuses of individual Koreans, spotlights Korean victimization, and glorifies all forms of anti-Japanese resistance. Koreans accuse the Japanese of perverting Korea's natural historical development; introducing institutionalized prostitution to Korea; harboring a historical desire to dominate Korea; perverting Korea's historical development; and suppressing Korean nationalism.

A standard version of this paradigm is articulated by Kim Il Myŏn (金一勉), a resident of Japan of North Korean lineage. His litany of charges against Japan's "genocidal policies" includes the conscription of Korean youths, forced sexual slavery of women, and encouragement of drug addiction among the general populace. To these indictments he adds the cultural assimilation policies of the Government General of Korea, Chōsen Sōtokufu (朝鮮総督府) (GGK) that included forcing Koreans to use the Japanese language, adopt Japanese surnames, worship at Shintō shrines, and pledge allegiance to the emperor.[3]

Adherents of this paradigm castigate Japan's activities in Korea from the 1870s onward. For them, Japan's interests are framed in terms of Japan's centuries-long historical greed and desire to control Korea. Japanese greed, in the late 1800s, led Japan to eliminate China's influence from the peninsula, assassinate Queen Min (who dominated Korean politics) in 1895, and manipulate King Kojong to institute pro-Japanese reforms. Following the Russo-Japanese War (1904–1905), the Japanese established a protectorate over Korea. During the five-year protectorate (1905–1910), the resident-general, Itō Hirobumi, abolished the Korean army and actively suppressed armed resistance. In 1909, Itō, who is greatly maligned by Korean historians, was assassinated by An Chung-gŭn, who is hailed as a national hero within the national historical paradigm. Then, in 1910, Japan formally colonized Korea.

The periodization of Japanese rule, within the nationalist paradigm, is broken into three distinct periods. The 1910s are labeled as a decade of military rule (*budan seiji*), the 1920s and early 1930s as a period of cultural rule (*bunka seiji*) when Japan's iron fist was loosened, and the mid-1930s to the end of World War II as a militarization of Korea as Japan became embroiled in wars with China and then the United States. Koreans view these periods in terms of what

3. Bob Tadashi Wakabayashi et al., "Comfort Women: Beyond Litigious Feminism," *Monumenta Nipponica* (hereafter, *MN*) 58.2 (Summer 2003): 226; Kim Il Myŏn, *Tennō no guntai to Chōsenjin ianfu* (天皇の軍隊と朝鮮人慰安婦) [The emperor's military and Korean comfort women] (Tokyo: San'ichi Shobō, 1976), 7-21. This work caused a sensation (in Japan) when published. He continues to publish on comfort women: *Yūjo, karayuki, ianfu no keifu* (遊女・からゆき・慰安婦の系譜) [A record of prostitutes and Korean comfort women] (Tokyō: Yūzankaku Shuppan, 1997).

Japan demanded from them: In the 1910s Japan demanded Korean land; in the 1920s Japan demanded Korean rice; in the 1930s and early 1940s Japan demanded Korean labor and lives.[4]

Historical remembrance within this paradigm focuses on the oppression of the Korean nation, the exploitation of Korean workers, the discrimination against Korean students, and the victimization of the Korean populace at the hands of racist and brutal government authorities, be they police, teachers, businessmen, or bureaucrats. Each individual account of suffering at the hands of a Japanese overlord has been extrapolated into national suffering. The nationalist paradigm, in summary, tells how the Korean nation fell victim to Japanese imperialism, suffered during the colonial era, struggled against Japanese domination, and finally emerged as a divided nation. This narrative is told in public museums, school curricula, historical monuments, guidebooks, media, and so forth.[5] This paradigm criticizes the colonial regime on every front and refuses to acknowledge that no Korean benefitted in any way from the colonial experience.

The national historical paradigm has been influential in academic circles on both sides of the Pacific. In Japan, Pak Kyŏng-sik (朴慶植) (1922–1998), a Korean resident in Japan, states that Koreans suffered "inhumane slave-like labor conditions" and were victims of "colonial semi-feudal fascist oppression" and extortion.[6] English-language textbooks on Korean history continue to propagate themes based on these accusations. Shin Yong-ha, honorary pro-

4. Kang Tŏk-sang, *Chōsenjin gakuto shutsujin: Mō hitotsuno wadatsumino koe* (朝鮮人学徒出陣もう一つのわだつみのこえ) [Korean students go to war: Another voice of the sea] (Tokyo: Iwanami Shoten, 1997), v.

5. Guy Podoler, *Monuments, Memory, and Identity: Constructing the Colonial Past in South Korea* (New York: Peter Lang, 2011), 15-19.

6. Pak Kyŏng-sik, *Chōsenjin kyōsei renkō no kiroku* (朝鮮人強制連行の記録) [The record of the forced displacement of Koreans] (Tokyo: Miraisha, 1965) and *Nihon teikokushugi no Chōsen shihai* 2 (日本帝国主義の朝鮮支配–下) [Japanese imperialistic domination of Korea, Volume 2] (Tokyo: Aoki Shoten, 1975), 163.

fessor at Seoul National University, claims that the goal of Japanese imperialism was to "reduce Koreans to the status of slavish, inferior subjects."[7] Furthermore, the Korea Historical Research Association, which has seven hundred members in Korea, states that the "plunder of Korean land" forced Korean farmers to live in "semi-feudal subjugation by tacitly recognizing quasi-feudal exploitation. . . ." The association also claims that Japanese authorities implemented "heinous laws" as a means of "fascist domination that mercilessly suppressed" the independence movement and the Korean masses.[8]

If this were not enough, the terminology found in these books consists of intemperate language; one work calls the Japanese efforts to amalgamate the Korean and Japanese royal families through marriage as an "obscenity conceivable only . . . [to those with a] deformed conscience,"[9] while another text postulates that "Koreans lived under the most ruthless colonial rule ever known in history."[10]

7. Shin Yong-ha, *Modern Korean History and Nationalism*, trans. N.M. Pankaj (Seoul: Jimoondang Publishing Company, 2000), 260.
8. Korea Historical Research Association, *A History of Korea*, trans. Joshua Van Lieu (London: Saffron, 2005), 216, 235.
9. Wanne J. Joe, *A Cultural History of Modern Korea: History of Korean Civilization* (Elizabeth, NJ: Hollym, 2000), 806. *The Korea Times* picks up the bludgeon to declare without qualifications in an editorial dated 30 May 2010 that the "centennial year of Japan's forced annexation of Korea" is "the starting point for all modern Korean tragedies." Cited in *The Daily Yomiuri,* 3 June 2010.
10. Shin Yong-ha, 238. For other expressions of the nationalist historical paradigm, see, Yi Ki-dong (이기동, 李基東), "Ilbon cheguk gunŭi Hangukin changgyodŭl" (일본 제국군의 한국인 장교들) [Korean officers in the Japanese army] *Sin Tong-a* (신동아) no. 299 (August 1984), 452-499. C.I. Eugene Kim and Han-Kyo Kim, *Korea and the Politics of Imperialism, 1876-1910* (Berkeley: University of California Press, 1967), 203-204. Kang Man-gil, *A History of Contemporary Korea* (Kent, UK: Global Oriental, 2005), 140-141. Joung Yole Rew (Yu, Chŏng-nyŏl), *Japanese Colonial Government of Korea: Empire Building in East Asia* (P'aju, South Korea: KSI, Han'guk Haksul Chŏngbo, 2008), 240. Akita does not read Korean. All quotations and citations in Korean are by Palmer.

When Korean history is studied without regard to global colonial practices, statements and examples such as these make Japan's rule look excessively abusive and exploitive. When Korean history, however, is placed in a wider global context—which is one of the goals of this book—Japan's colonial practices are shown in a more moderate light.

The national historical paradigm is no straw man; it remains a powerful force in South Korea and within some Western circles. For example, *The Asia Pacific Journal: Japan Focus*, a journal that publishes essays by leading scholars in Japanese studies, on 15 February 2010 ran one piece that translated four articles from the Korean-language *Hangyŏre* newspaper. The piece, titled "Remembering and Redressing the Forced Mobilization of Korean Laborers by Imperial Japan," covered a range of horrible experiences suffered by Korean laborers. It focused on human rights abuses, the untimely deaths of laborers in coalmines, and the abandonment of colonial laborers on Sakhalin after the war ended. The article included an introduction by William J. Underwood, who has worked as a professor in Japan at several universities from 1997 to 2008 and is currently employed by the State of California. Underwood served as the editorial coordinator for *Japan Focus* from 2005 to 2010, and wrote over a dozen articles for the journal. All of his articles focused on Japan's obligation to provide compensation for Korean and Chinese laborers mobilized in Japan during World War II.

There is no doubt, however, that the nationalist historical paradigm is being questioned by distinguished specialists on modern Korea. Carter J. Eckert states that the nationalist historical paradigm has "so dominated intellectual life in Korea that [it has] obfuscated, subsumed, or obliterated virtually all other possible modes of historical interpretation."[11] Henry H. Em, professor at Yonsei University,

11. Carter J. Eckert, "Epilogue: Exorcising Hegel's Ghosts: Toward a Postnationalist Historiography of Korea," in *Colonial Modernity in Korea*, eds. Gi-Wook

adds that the paradigm has eliminated complexity, plurality, and difference in historical studies.[12] Yet, the persistence of the national historical narrative cries for a reexamination of this paradigm. And an appropriate start is to look at the words and actions of two Korean Americans; the one a scholar and the other a Foreign Service officer of the United States State Department.

The Expositions of Wonmo Dong and Andrew Hak Ou

Wonmo Dong (童元模) begins his doctoral dissertation (1965) with the laudable position that he will "treat the entire problem without reference to those moral sanctions which could either justify or condemn the Japanese colonization of Korea or the Japanese preference of assimilation as the basic principle of colonial government."[13] Yet he adheres closely to the nationalistic historical paradigm, which is not surprising given the prominent position it has held in the historiography of Japan's Korea colonial policy. How does Dong support his adherence to the patriotic narrative? First, he does so by asserting that Japan's colonial policy changed little from 1905 to 1945. He states, "The development policy of the Terauchi administration changed, *if any*, only slightly after . . . Saitō [Makoto

---

Shin and Michael Robinson (Cambridge: Harvard University Asia Center, 1999), 366.

12. Henry H. Em, *The Great Enterprise: Sovereignty and Historiography in Modern Korea* (Durham: Duke University Press, 2013), Introduction.

13. Wonmo Dong, "Japanese Colonial Policy and Practice in Korea, 1905-1945: A Study in Assimilation" (Ph.D. diss., Georgetown University, 1965), v. I was struck by the coincidence that his "mentor" Joseph S. Sebes, a Jesuit, was a fellow student in my first year (1951-1952) at Harvard graduate school. I remember him as a progressive with a skeptical turn of mind. Dong has retired, but we have not been able to verify his present (2015) status. He has been most recently listed as Affiliate Professor, Center for Korea Studies, University of Washington. We are grateful to Mr. David Flynn for providing information on the statuses of those we have cited.

(斎藤実)] [and] . . . Mizuno [Rentarō (水野錬太郎)] . . . arrived in Korea in 1919." And, Governor-General Koiso Kuniaki (小磯国昭) "promised to do his best to abolish existing discrimination." But, "*Like all his predecessors* . . . Koiso did not live up to his pledge."[14] He also states that "the colonial government failed to adjust its policy with regard to political participation and recruitment of Koreans"[15] until 1945. Earlier in his dissertation he asserts that following the March First Independence Movement, Japan "brought about *some* changes . . . [however they] were much more limited in scope than have often been exaggerated by some other authors." He then cites one foreign writer as a representative opinion to support his findings. To his credit, he acknowledges that the Saitō-Mizuno educational policy was "basically a conciliatory approach."[16]

Second, Dong emphasizes the militaristic aspect of Japan's Korea policy. He states the "militarism, which had prevailed among Japanese administrative circles since the Meiji Restoration, was a factor not to be ignored . . . military factors played a definite role in . . . the creation of a colony in Korea in 1905."[17] Third, he links the top-down military system to the existence of an "authoritarian state" in Japan, which may be translated as "the concentration of power in a leader or an elite not constitutionally responsible to the people."[18]

And fourth, Dong asserts that "[m]ost Japanese colonial theorists" with "some knowledge of . . . Western Colonialism of the 19th Century admitted . . . that the principle of assimilation in colonial politics" tended to "take little account of the peculiar conditions and institutions in a colony, and . . . that it is a type of colonial relation-

14. Ibid., 445 and 476. The August 1919 Organic Regulation of the Government-General removed the restriction that only a general or admiral could be appointed as Governor-General.

15. Ibid., 487.

16. Ibid., 153 and 380.

17. Ibid., 74.

18. Ibid., iv.

ship which is most likely to fail."[19]

Andrew Hak Ou, on the other hand, is a foreign service officer who deserves greater space and attention because of his unique background, his activities and ideas on Japan's colonial policy, and his recent position in Japan as a prominent official voice on U.S.-Japan relations as first secretary, Political Section, United States Embassy, Tokyo, Japan. As a representative of the American federal government, it is ironic that he would be a proponent of the pro-Korean nationalist historical narrative.

Ou's parents were born in Yawata, Fukuoka Prefecture, Japan.

> Ou was born and raised in Seoul, Korea and completed his secondary schooling in Nairobi, Kenya before moving to Washington DC to attend Georgetown University's School of Foreign Service. After he obtained his Bachelor's degree in International Politics, [Ou] worked in the Japanese government and education sectors for four years. He then completed a Masters degree in East Asian History at the University of Hawaii and East-West Center in Honolulu, where he wrote his thesis on Japanese cultural assimilation policies in colonial Korea. [Ou] also studied at Waseda University and Seoul National University, and speaks Japanese and Korean. He joined the State Department in September 2001, and has served in Jamaica, Hong Kong, and the Korea Desk in Washington DC before his current posting in Tokyo, Japan. As the second U.S. representative to the Baker-Katō Diplomatic Exchange Program, [Ou] worked at the Japanese Ministry of Foreign Affairs from 2008 to 2009 covering Japan's relations with India and Pakistan. As of July 2009, he has been covering Japanese domestic politics at the U.S. Embassy's Political Section.[20]

---

19. Ibid., 18.
20. Flyer to publicize Ou's speech at the University of Tokyo, International Relations Institution of Students (東京大学学生国際交流機構) http://ut-iris.org/page/event_464.html.

Howard H. Baker, Jr, U.S. ambassador to Japan (2001–2005) and Katō Ryōzō (加藤良三), Japanese ambassador to the United States (2001–2008) (and now commissioner of Nippon Professional Baseball) established the exchange program under which diplomats from each country would be placed in the other country's foreign affairs ministry starting in 2005. This program is based on the agreement between Secretary of State Colin Powell and Japanese Foreign Minister Kawaguchi Yoriko (川口順子).[21]

That Ou is an official voice of U.S. policy on Japan is made clear by the flyer distributed by Professor Stephanie Weston, former consul at the U.S. Consulate in Fukuoka, who arranged the opportunity for Mr. Ou to speak to her students.

> Mr. Ou [who] is responsible for monitoring Japanese domestic politics [hewed closely, naturally enough, to the official line by giving] his impressions about the state of U.S.-Japan relations during the transition from the Liberal Democratic Party's rule to that of the Democratic Party of Japan. He emphasized that the change in Japan's leadership has not damaged the strong working relationship between the two allies. He also made a case for the continued Marine presence in Okinawa, and welcomed student questions about the U.S.-Japan relationship and the role of U.S. forces in Japan.[22]

We now refer to his M.A. thesis, dated August 2001, titled "The Japanese Policy of Cultural Assimilation in Colonial Korea under Governor-General Minami Jirō (南次郎)." In his thesis, Ou is unequivocal in declaring that assimilation meant that Japan attempted to rob Koreans of their national culture and identity: he emphasizes

---

21. Department of State Washington File: Text: U.S., Japan Agree to Launch Diplomatic Exchange Program. http://usinfo.org/wf-archive/2004/040701/epf408.htm.

22. 2010 Consulate Activities | Consulate of the United States Fukuoka, Japan. See http://fukuoka.usconsulate.gov/fukuoka/e/f-20101124-01.html.

how Koreans were "prohibited from speaking their own language . . . forced to learn Japanese" and compelled to "change their Korean names to Japanese ones" as well as to "worship at Shintō shrines" against their will. He adds that "all were policies that were either newly created or intensified during the administration of colonial Korea's most notorious ruler, Governor-General Minami Jirō." These "regulations . . . subjected Koreans to some of the most severe restrictions they ever faced under Japanese rule."[23] He extrapolates from this that the assimilation policies "more importantly . . . negatively affected relations between Korea and Japan during the postwar period and continues to influence the mutual feelings of the people of the two nations to this day."[24]

There is little doubt as to where he had absorbed the bitterness that inheres in the nationalistic narrative of martyrs by his dedication of the thesis "To my parents and grandparents, whose histories I have tried to learn." Those lessons he learned may be the reason for his stating that "Even today, Koreans persist in calling the thirty-five years from 1910–1945 the 'darkest period' (*amhūk shidae*) [暗黒時代] of their history and many view it as a shameful part of the past that they would rather forget."[25] The basic theme and details, however, undoubtedly parallel Wonmo Dong's doctoral dissertation.

> However, a more constructive approach to dealing with a crippling past would be to develop a more positive sense of identity and a truly post-colonial form of nationalism that

23. Andrew Hak Ou, 1. He also describes Minami as "one of the most feared and despised figures in colonial Korea." See page 38.
24. Ibid., 2 and 42. He adds that the suffering of the "comfort women" also hinders the amelioration of the relationship between Korea and Japan. See page 2, fn. 3.
25. Ibid., iv and 7. See also page 41. It would be enlightening to compare these memories with those of Hildi Kang's father-in-law and his friends who lived under Japan's colonial rule. She was surprised enough by the lack of bitterness that she was compelled to record: "Where were the atrocities I had come to expect?" See her collection of oral histories in *Under the Black Umbrella*, xi.

> no longer uses antipathy toward Japan as its raison d'être. By coming to terms with their deep-rooted animosity for the perpetrators of their pain and *rebuilding their ties with Japan*, Koreans can adopt a more positive belief in their country and promote their own culture and rich tradition as a nation.[26]

For all this positivity, Ou does not move beyond the nationalist historical narrative. Instead, he returns to the nationalistic theme posited in his Introduction and reminds the reader in his last few words that the Japanese "painfully imposed" their culture on the Koreans during the colonial era.[27]

Seven years later, in 2008, Ou, then a Baker-Katō Diplomatic Exchange Program Fellow, and slated to begin work at the Japanese Ministry of Foreign Affairs in September while assuming a position as Political Officer at the U.S. Embassy in Tokyo, gave a talk titled, "The Impact of Korean-Japanese Relations by (sic) the Japanese Occupation" at Lakeland College Japan. Lakeland College is a fine liberal arts college, founded in 1862 in Sheboygan, Wisconsin. Its Tokyo branch is located in Shinjuku. According to the flyer publicizing his speech on September 24, 2008, here are his concluding remarks:

> From 1936 to the end of Korea's colonial history in 1945 . . . a coherent campaign of cultural assimilation . . . subjected Koreans to some of the most severe restrictions they ever faced under Japanese rule. Perhaps more importantly, the Japanese attempt to take from Koreans their sense of cultural identity negatively affected relations between Korea and Japan during the postwar period and continues to influence

---

26. Ibid., 98. Compare this with the more negative concluding sentence of his "Introduction": "Finally, I return to the underlying question behind my study—how the assimilation policies of the Minami period influenced *the continuing reality of lingering tensions* between Koreans and Japanese." See page 2.
27. Ibid., 99.

> the mutual feelings of the people of the two nations to this day.[28]

As of July 2012 a copy of the whole speech was not available for further analysis. It is significant, however, in that his basic theme of oppression of Koreans by Japan from 1936 to 1945 remains unchanged. The pro-Korean, and quite nationalistic, wording of this flyer most assuredly was approved, if not written by, Ou, since it appeared *before* he spoke. As an official representative of the American government, the tone of this speech is most curious.

Revisionism and Colonial Conscription

We believe that our précis of the nationalist historical narrative is accurate and equitable. I (Akita) admit, however, that until I had read Palmer's graduate student paper on "Koreans in the Japanese Army during the Second Sino-Japanese War: The Korean Special Volunteer System, 1937–1943,"[29] I was fully convinced that the nationalist historical narrative was correct.

I had co-authored with Professor Yong-ho Choe[30] the introduction to *The Clan Records* (1995), a translation of five short stories set in colonial Korea by Kajiyama Toshiyuki (梶山季之), a widely read novelist. Kajiyama was born and raised in Seoul (1930–1945), where his father, from Hiroshima Prefecture, was an engineer in

28. Lakeland Lectures. Andrew Hak Ou of the U.S. Embassy speaks. http://www.h-net.org/announce/show.cgi?ID=164032.

29. It became part of his doctoral dissertation, "Japan's Mobilization of Koreans for War, 1937–1945" (Ph.D. diss., University of Hawai'i, 2005).

30. Choe is professor emeritus, Department of History, University of Hawai'i at Manoa. He continues his research and writing on modern Korean history. He grew up in the Korea under Japanese rule, and has painful memories of that period in his life. We once shared, cheek-by-jowl, a small office and have agreed to respectfully disagree—given our conflicting views on 1910–1945 Japan-Korea relations. I suspect, however, that we may be close in our understanding of modern Korean history.

the GGK.[31] In the introduction we used terms such as, "extremely harsh military rule," "extreme brutality," and "heavy-handed rule" to characterize the nature of GGK's rule.[32] At that time I did not question the terminology being used because I passively accepted that the Japanese were guilty of these charges levied against them.

Even as I was becoming increasingly convinced of Palmer's revisionism, I came across Hiroko Rokuhara's (六波羅弘子) "Local Officials and the Meiji Conscription Campaign."[33] I was primarily drawn to it given my four-decades long research on Yamagata Aritomo, the drafter of Japan's Conscription Law. Rokuhara's work is very enlightening, being well-researched and detailed, with the added fillip of translation of terminology not found elsewhere. I noted that the Korean and Japanese conscription experiences had similarities, such as draft evasions and official attempts to ameliorate the hardship of conscripts. I saw, however, dramatic differences between Palmer's and Rokuhara's descriptions of the reactions in Korea and Japan to conscription; so much so that those who hold to the nationalist historical narrative would be hard put to use the conscription of Koreans as a plank to sustain their narrative.

The Japanese conscription system preceded that of Korea's by seventy years, and in Rokuhara's telling, had a riotous and sometimes bloody beginning. "Two months after the proclamation of the Conscription Act" (1873), in a dire precursor of things to come, the inhabitants of a village in Mie Prefecture "took up bamboo spears and persuaded the people of neighboring villages" to jointly protest the Act. A riot, fortunately for the authorities, was averted. Villagers

31. Kajiyama's mother was born in the rural village of Kahuku, on the island of Oahu, Territory of Hawai'i before returning to Japan at age nine and being raised by relatives in Hiroshima.

32. *The Clan Records: Five Stories of Korea*, trans. by Yoshiko Dykstra, with an introduction by George Akita and Yong-ho Choe (Honolulu: University of Hawai'i Press, 1995).

33. *MN* 60.1 (Spring 2005): 81-110.

in Okayama Prefecture, however, were angered when the term, "*ketsuzei*" [血税] (blood tax) appeared in the "*Chōhei Kokuyu*" [徴兵告諭] (instructions relating to conscription) issued by the "*Dajōkan*" [太政官] (Council of State) on the same day as the Conscription Law's proclamation. The villagers rioted on the belief that the term meant selling the blood drawn from men of conscription age. They were soon joined by inhabitants of other villages. A force of three hundred ex-samurai failed to quell the riots, and it took the Osaka garrison to do so. Twenty thousand people were charged with participating, of whom fifteen were sentenced to death and sixty-four sent to prison.[34] Unrest, however, continued to simmer. In 1883, inhabitants of a village in Osaka tried to destroy the house of the

34. Hiroko Rokuhara, 84-85. See also, Simon Partner, "Peasants into Citizens?! The Meiji Village in the Russo-Japanese War," *MN* 62.2 (Summer, 2007): 179-209. His primary source is the well-known diary of Aizawa Kikutarō (相沢菊太郎), village head of Aihara in Kanagawa Prefecture. His secondary sources go back to the 1950s when the influence of Japanese "Marxist" historians was strong. He states that he tried to "read between the lines of the diary" to analyze the situation of the "poorer members" of the village, especially tenant farmers. Since one of his primary aims was to explore the "suffering and possible resistance brought about by the war" he obviously sides with the tenant farmers against the landlords such as Aizawa. While I am uncomfortable with the "reading between the lines" methodology, Partner's translation sheds some light on the actions and reactions of the village elders on conscripts, and their families. Japanese scholars have long known of the diary's existence and have published its contents. See, for example, Ogi Shinzō (小木新造), "*Aru Meijijin no Seikatsushi: Aizawa Kikutarō no nanajūhachinenkan no kiroku* (ある明治人の生活史―相沢菊太郎の七十八年間の記録)," *Chūkō Shinsho* 714 (Tokyo: Chūō Kōronsha, 1983). Aizawa was an extraordinary person who left an equally extraordinary diary. He began to write it at age nineteen (1885) and continued until ten days before his death at ninety-six (1962), never pausing for a day. It is a rich record of the livelihood of the inhabitants of Aihara, Sagamihara, Kanagawa Prefecture, including sericulture; as well as reactions of villagers to such great historic events as the promulgation of the Meiji Constitution (1889), the Great Kantō Earthquake (1923), and postwar agricultural reform.

"*kochō*" [戸長] (register chief).[35]

In glaring contrast, the Korean conscription experience was uneventful, to such an extent that one of the most comprehensive college-level history books on Korean history says nothing about riots against conscription, but limits itself to but two statements that do not indicate resistance: one, that the "war's continuous drain on Japanese manpower ultimately required the general conscription of Koreans after 1943," and two, "While thousands of Korean men found themselves in military service, by far the greater Korean contribution to Japan's war effort was made by ordinary Koreans mobilized to work in factories and mines in Manchuria, northern Korea, and Japan."[36]

Palmer's discussion of the GGK's establishment and implementation of the volunteer and conscription systems goes a long way toward explaining the quiescent Korean reactions. In Palmer's telling, there is no hint of genocidal acts against Koreans by the supposedly all-powerful, authoritarian Japanese regime. He asks his reader to shed the notion that the GGK was omnipresent and omniscient. He adds that the notion that the GGK held "absolute power" over Korea should be replaced by one that is more nuanced.[37] There is no other way, he continues, to explain the GGK's widespread,

35. Hiroko Rokuhara, 90. Roger F. Hackett writes that the inclusion of *eta* [穢多], (outcastes) in army units set off riots in Hiroshima, Himeji, and Kyoto. He adds that "opposition to conscription was the primary cause of at least fifteen major peasant uprisings." *Yamagata Aritomo in the Rise of Modern Japan, 1838–1922* (Cambridge, MA: Harvard University Press, 1971), 68. See also E. Herbert Norman, *Soldier and Peasant in Japan: The Origins of Conscription* (Vancouver, Canada: University of British Columbia, 1943; 1965 ed.), 48 and 49.

36. Carter J. Eckert, Ki-baik Lee, et al., *Korea, Old and New: A History* (Seoul: Ilchokak, 1990), 322. This textbook is authored by several of the most respected scholars of Korean history. It is published by Ilchokak on behalf of Harvard University, which holds the copyright to the book.

37. Brandon Palmer, 4, 17, 20, and 124.

expensive, and varied attempts *to gain* Korean cooperation and acceptance.

One example is that the GGK did not aggressively push for the widespread use of the Japanese language until the *late-1930s* and, in fact, the Japanese and Korean publics as well as bureaucrats had expected that the compulsory educational system, set to be established in 1946, would precede the conscription system. Only wartime conditions altered the timeline. These actions reveal that the GGK wanted to, and did, come to terms with the reality that the Koreans were not passive or powerless members in the colonial relationship. The GGK's actions were impelled as well by the powerful grip of memory. Palmer declares that GGK concerns over a rebellion during Japan's war against the Allied Powers similar to the March First Independence Movement "prevented the use of blatant coercion."[38] Finally, the GGK's approach to and actions taken to implement the volunteer and conscription systems are vital signposts of Japan's self-interested conservative colonial policies, but one that had its genesis long before the March First Independence Movement.

Hildi Kang's *Black Umbrella* and "Revisionism"

It may be quirky to begin our foray into revisionism with the study already much cited, and one that lies within the nationalist framework. Hildi Kang's introduction to Japan's colonization of Korea, she says, came from the systematic study of history works on the subject and the "passionate stories of martyrs." And her choice of the book's title, *Under the Black Umbrella*, indicates her strong bent toward the anti-Japanese narrative. The book is a compendium of the interviews of fifty-one elderly Koreans living in the San Francisco area. There is enough here to sustain the nationalistic narrative: a young man who was jailed, tortured, and unendingly harassed; another who was waterboarded; still another who was whipped; and

38. Ibid., 25, 130, 137, and 188.

some who spoke of discrimination in pay and promotion, and others who were denied ration cards. Yang Sŏng-dŏk, speaking of Japan's assimilation policies, conveyed the typical Korean viewpoint:

> This was just a tactic to make Koreans into Japanese. They didn't do this blindly, you know. They had very sinister plans. The purpose of changing names was obviously to make us sound Japanese. . . . This was all part of their long-range plan to eliminate any vestige of Korean consciousness.[39]

Yet, Kang is a scholar who admits to the limitations stemming from the small number of interviews as well as the pitfalls of relying on memory. Most admirably, she lets the interviewees speak for themselves and most of the time does not allow herself the luxury of "the satisfying purity of indignation," so well put by President Barack Obama in his Nobel Prize acceptance speech.

Kang also writes of the epiphany experienced as she noticed how the family of an interviewee "chuckled" and "smiled" on learning her father-in-law's recollections of his early years in Korea. It struck her that all his stories were based on what "took place under Japan's onerous rule." This made her wonder, "Where were the atrocities I had come to expect?"[40] We then knew of her scholarly integrity, given that she let the interviewees speak for themselves and she basically limited herself to straightforward commentaries—with the result that her study would differ from the norms established in the "passionate martyrs' narrative." Kang's interviewees portray Japan's colonial rule as marked by complexity, nuances, contradic-

---

39. Hildi Kang, 119.

40. Hildi Kang, xi. Kang is a Caucasian married to a Korean-American professor in the University of California system. She may be retired. Her biography posted on the Internet lists her "last" position as: "Research Fellow, Korean Studies Center, University of California, Berkeley." Her husband is Dr. Sang-Wook Kang, Lawrence Livermore Laboratory (Retired), a member of OKSPN (Overseas Korean Senior Professionals Network).

tions, and normalcy; as well as one under which ordinary Japanese and even the police are sometimes seen in a positive light.

We build upon her statement in which she states that "[i]nterview after interview began with sentences such as, 'Nothing much happened to me.'" In the Introduction to her book, she notes that she excluded replies that were "uneventful or redundant." She also points out that some respondents "said that nothing much happened to them." It may be ungracious, but the high frequency of comments such as "[n]othing ... happened to me" and "*most people adjusted to Japanese rule*" support our contention that more than "some people ... led close to normal lives." Furthermore, we suspect that if Kang had provided the count for the "uneventful or redundant" replies out of a very limited population of interviewees, this number would add support to our contention. Let us now look at the record she provides, remembering that she selectively omits uneventful responses.[41]

In Part I, which deals with the years from 1905 to 1911, Kang says that three elders who were born and raised in these years, "for the most part lived their lives according to their own choice." Complexity also is evident in Kang's vignettes on the police and their conduct. The first recollection confirms the standard view of the police, that the "Japanese people were not bad. We got along. It was the police that bothered us. I just stayed out of their way." After this, things do get complicated. One, who was nine at the time, recounts the beginnings of the March First Movement and the bloody reprisals conducted by the soldiers. He says that the police, too, began to arrest the demonstrators, but that "the Police Commander . . . spoke kindly," especially to the older men, and "unfastened the ropes that bound them and sent them home." He tells Kang, "It was the policemen who were kind." Another tells Kang that since his father was more highly educated than the Japanese leaders, "*the Japanese police chief, the most powerful man in town, always bowed low to*

41. Ibid., xi-xiii, 5, and 13. Italics in original.

[his] father"; and still another says that, "I don't remember any harassment by the Japanese police or government officials."[42]

Another Korean interviewee who lived in Shanghai recalls that since her father was suspected of harboring independence thoughts, the secret police sent a police detective to permanently watch him. The family began to feed the policeman and developed a friendship with him. The female interviewee's judgment on this friendship between the watcher and watched is moving: "[a]fter all, we were all humans."[43]

It is striking that other recollections in Kang's book are the memories of positive, even friendly, interactions between Koreans and Japanese. Said one, "I never felt any animosity toward the Japanese. It just didn't occur to me that they were persecuting us." And another, "The teachers used respectful language" when addressing us; and still another, "I had close friendships with my Japanese classmates." The litany continues, one student who attended a primary school in Shanghai stated, "I don't recall a single incident of being mistreated by the Japanese"; while another added, "I do not believe the [Japanese school] principal looked down on us Koreans as inferior. He was . . . very interested in educating Koreans"; and a young Japanese male teacher is said to have influenced greatly his three female charges, that he went out of his way to prepare them for the high school entrance exam; and "[a]fter forty years . . . [they] were delighted to have [a] reunion" in their hometown.[44]

To these we add the experiences of Professor emeritus Yong-ho Choe. He remembers that the principal of his school was an "ogre" (*oni* [鬼]), but that the female teacher was an "angel" (*tenshisama* [天使さま]). He remembers her name well: Nishimura Sumiko (西村すみ子). It is a measure of his character that in the mid-1980s,

---

42. Ibid., 4, 5, 19, 20, 58, 59, and 64. Italics in original.
43. Ibid., 107-108.
44. Ibid., 26, 39, 44, 45, and 107.

he took the trouble to go to Kokura (小倉) in Kyushu to pay his regards and express his respects to her. He regrets, he says, that he has so far failed to visit her again.[45]

Truth be told, there was enough goodwill on both sides under trying circumstances to turn Choe's hope into reality. One interviewee recalled that "[i]n about four or five years, I was promoted four times, and got a raise each time. So I must say, I was treated the same as my Japanese coworkers and not discriminated against"; while another says that his superior was *not* "*a typical Japanese*" and "disliked discriminatory practices against the Koreans, and so . . . treated everybody the same." Others recalled that "We became good friends" with the children of our Japanese neighbors; and others said that they "had become friends" with Japanese wives; and one added that "my best friends were Japanese."[46]

Without becoming didactic or treacly, two of the most moving reminiscences are linked by a common thread of humanity. The one, already cited, is the recollection of the Shanghai housewife who befriended Japanese detectives because "we were all humans." The other is the experience of an ambitious young Korean, Hong Ŭlse, who made his way to Japan where he began to work for the *yakuza* [やくざ], the Japanese mob organization. His boss, from his description, was probably a street-stall keeper (*tekiya* [的屋]) who consistently showed him kindness, such as paying for his tuition, praising him, and raising his salary. Hong once turned down his raise, but his boss, unknown to Hong, saved the money, and later gave him a bank book with the raise untouched. Perhaps his boss's advice was even more valuable. "I don't want you to end up the way I did [a failed student] . . . Before it is too late, you must leave this business . . .

45. It should be added that Professor Choe has good reason to be angry at Japanese rule. His father was a Christian minister, and as such, was arrested by the police and brutally tortured. Still, he says, "We should let bygones be bygones and move on."

46. Ibid., 67, 116, 132, 136, and 145.

you must study more and get a higher education."[47] The intimate and human side of colonialism should not be ignored.

Kang's narrative of the person-to-person interactions between Koreans and Japanese is, to us, her most valuable contribution. Almost as illuminating is the fact that the Japanese, according to one of Kang's interviewees, built a modern infrastructure. This contribution sometimes is dismissed with a shrug: "Yes, they did so, but it cannot outweigh their cruelty and oppression against us." The following is an example of this dichotomous attitude: My father "hated the Japanese [for] coming [to Korea] . . . to me, they weren't all that bad." Our village always flooded in the rainy season and the "Japanese came and built reservoirs . . . I must say their organization impressed me . . . They built things that worked."[48]

This last quote segues into an area of debate between adherents of the nationalist historical narrative and scholars of the colonial development theory. There is no question that the Japanese brought modern technology and innovation to Korea in the form of railways, telegraph lines, schools, universities, libraries, department stores, hospitals, theaters, factories, and so forth. The GGK also made strides to improve public health and sanitation. However, supporters of the nationalist historical narrative argue that these improvements were done only for the benefit of the Japanese. Said another way, Japan sought a modernized Korea so it could better exploit and control the Korean society and economy. On the other hand, studies originating from the colonial development theory note the short and long term ways in which Korean benefitted from the colonial public and private investments.

Nationalistic Koreans also frequently mention the wage disparity between Korean and Japanese workers and bureaucrats as an example of Japanese discrimination. The salaries of employees in

47. Ibid., 30-31.
48. Ibid., 10.

Japan were almost universally higher than wages in Korea. However, it is doubtful that any Japanese worker would have taken a salary cut to work in Korea; Japanese citizens expected wages comparable to those in Japan proper to work in Korea. Such unequal wages continue to this day. South Koreans and Americans working for MNCs (ranging from Samsung to Nike to Chevron) in third world countries are paid more than their local counterparts for comparable work. Furthermore, expatriate Americans, particularly those associated with the military, enroll their children in schools designed exclusively for English-speaking students—yet another practice for which the Japanese colonialists are criticized.

Japan in Taiwan and the Philippines

The dichotomous narrative in Korea that ignores Japanese successes, but loudly criticizes the negatives of colonialism is not as extreme in Taiwan. Steven Phillips characterizes the Taiwanese perception of Japan's regime as exhibiting "honesty, competence, predictability, and efficiency." Yet, he also stresses that the Taiwanese everyday life was negatively affected by "a brutal police state, second-class citizenship, [and] economic exploitation."[49]

Harry J. Lamley, professor emeritus of History at the University of Hawai'i takes a more sanguine position. He writes that Japan's *kōminka* [公民化] (imperialization) seems to "have been generally unsuccessful in the long run" because "[f]ew Taiwanese were transformed into 'true Japanese,'" given their resentment over "harsh and demanding *kōminka* measures." Yet, he continues, when the post-1937 *kōminka* movement is measured against the realistic standard of rapid acculturation (assimilation), the policy seems to "have been relatively effective under controlled conditions." In fact, he says,

49. Steven Philips, "Between Assimilation and Independence: Taiwanese Political Aspirations under Nationalist Chinese Rule, 1945–1948," in *Taiwan: A New History*, ed. by Murray A. Rubinstein (New York: M.E. Sharpe, 1999 & 2007), 277 and 282.

Taiwanese and aboriginal inhabitants engaged in "very few hostile" acts; that they "served faithfully in the Japanese armed forces as a rule"; and that "[b]y early 1945, even the middle-aged and elderly prepared to fight [for Japan] to the bitter end."[50] Moreover, we call attention to an achievement by Japan in Taiwan that has been given scant notice by non-Japanese specialists.

This achievement is the total eradication of opium addiction in Taiwan. This was the result of hard working people, including Gotō Shimpei (後藤新平), whose career included mayor of Tokyo and adviser on sanitation in the Taiwan Government General (TGG), and To Sōmei (杜聡明), a Taiwanese professor of medicine. To Sōmei was venerated and trusted by the Taiwanese so much that when he was assigned as the attending physician for the leader of the anti-Japanese movement, who subsequently died of illness in a TGG hospital, not a single rumor emerged that the death was the result of a plot or conspiracy. This contrasts with the rumors that followed the death of the last Korean king, Kojong. When the TGG created the Opium Rehabilitation Center for addicts, in a "master stroke" it appointed To as the head, an appointment that was greeted with jubilation and anticipation among the Taiwanese that guaranteed its success. When the last addict, a young woman of twenty-six, was released, it signaled the eradication of opium addiction in Taiwan.[51]

We cannot leave the topic of Japan in peripheral areas without

---

50. Harry J. Lamley, "Taiwan under Japanese Rule, 1895–1945: The Vicissitudes of Colonialism," in *Taiwan: A New History*, ed. by Murray A. Rubinstein (New York: M.E. Sharpe, 1999, 2007), 242-243. Italics in original. He believes that if there had been no war and Japan remained in Taiwan, the *kōminka* movement may have been successful within a generation. This statement was made to me before my interest in the assimilation of colonies, and is recalled as being one that I had not expected to hear and therefore, remembered.

51. Liu Mei-shū (劉明修), *Taiwan tōchi to ahen mondai* [台湾統治と阿片問題] (Tokyo: Yamakawa shuppansha, 1983), 154-155; fn. 22, 156-157, and 235. Liu's respect for his mentor at Tokyo University, Itō Takashi, is evident by his Japanese name, Itō Meishū.

mentioning the following anecdote. The Filipinos were probably the most anti-Japanese people in the years after Japan's defeat. I was returning to Hawai'i from Japan by ship via the Philippines in 1948. Those of us with Japanese features were ordered to stay on the truck transporting the passengers to an American base and have other servicemen make purchases at the PX (post exchange) for us. This was because of the real possibility of bodily harm at the hands of the Filipinos. Despite this animosity, in the summer of 2010, Jeffrey Satō, a registered nurse at Kaiser Permanente Moanalua Medical Center and Clinic whose parents lived next door to me for forty years, related that he provided physical therapy to an elderly Filipino gentleman whose given name was Hirohito. His curiosity more than piqued, he asked how his patient received his given name. The reply was that his parents were so gratified by the modern infrastructure created by the Japanese in their region—paved roads, a sanitation system, as well as public security—that they gave him the only Japanese name they knew.[52]

52. Privacy concerns prevent using his surname. Sir Francis T. Piggott was a lawyer who came from England as an adviser to Itō Hirobumi on constitutions. He wrote that Itō was the "most capable" of the Meiji leaders. He was so impressed by Itō that he named his son, Julian Itō Piggott. Sir Francis T. Piggott, "The Itō Legend: Personal Recollections of Prince Itō," *Nineteenth Century and After*, XLVII (January 1910), 174-176. Balance requires that we take notice of the position of respectable scholars who stress that assimilation policy was not everywhere successful. David L. Howell concludes that the Japanese effort to assimilate the Ainu was a failure. He so concludes even though he admits that the Ainu are now monolingual in Japanese and are largely ignorant of traditional Ainu culture, some thirty thousand people continue to identify themselves as Ainu. For a discussion of these failed policies see "The Meiji State and the Logic of Ainu Protection," in *New Directions in the Study of Meiji Japan*, ed. Helen Hardacre and Adam L. Kern (Leiden: Brill, 1997), 631-634.

Chapter Two

The Principles Governing Colonial Rule

The second area of analysis to shift the gaze away from the nationalist historical narrative toward our revisionistic position is to introduce the principles on colonial policy articulated by the highest-level decision makers in Japan from the earliest days of modern Japan's overseas ventures. These principles were enunciated by Yamagata Aritomo (山縣有朋) (1838–1922) and were reiterated by other leaders that included Ōkuma Shigenobu (大隈重信) (1838–1922), Hara Kei (Takashi) (原敬) (1856–1921), and Hasegawa Yoshimichi (長谷川好道) (1850–1924). It is possible that these postulations were given voice by others earlier than Yamagata but, as soon explained, his had greater weight. But first, it is useful to provide a brief description of the document that set down these prescriptions.

Home Minister (*Naimu daijin*) Yamagata (1885–1889) on May 25, 1886, wrote to Shinagawa Yajirō (品川弥二郎) (1843–1900), a close friend from Hagi in Chōshū and minister plenipotentiary to Germany. He added a *besshi* [別紙] (enclosure), and explained that the contents were his "personal views" (*ikko no iken* [一己の意見]) on policies Japan should adopt vis-à-vis Okinawa, Gotō, and Tsushima. His "personal views" explanation cannot be taken at face value, given that he was the Home Minister on an officially authorized inspection tour of these areas and accompanied by an entourage of officials from the Finance, Justice, Education, and Agriculture-Commerce ministries. We concede that his personal views exhibit a degree of colonialist rhetoric that was common for that time, but they are illuminating in light of Japan's subsequent actions in Okinawa, Taiwan, and Korea. Yamagata sent copies of this missive to other Cabinet members. The *besshi* is therefore a *fukumeisho* [復命書] and was designated as such by Yamagata. The *fukumeisho* are detailed reports of official fact-finding missions dispatched from Tokyo to outlying areas.[1]

It should be noted that Yamagata's policies were not aimed at a specific colony itself but were concerned with integrating a non-contiguous prefecture acquired in 1879. Still, as can be shown, the gradualist and moderate principles enunciated were later applied to colonial Taiwan and Korea. The penultimate goal according to the thrust of this 1886 position paper is the assimilation (*dōka* [同化]) of Okinawans as Japanese.

What, then, did Yamagata consider the bedrock principles that would guide Tokyo's actions? In the first instance, given the dangerous realities of nineteenth century dog-eat-dog international rivalries, his initial concern was to make Okinawa a bastion to protect Japan's southern flank against foreign incursions (in much the same way that Tsushima's proximity to Korea would guard Japan's western flank). Let it be stressed that the singular responsibility of political leaders everywhere is to prevent the extirpation of the nation or the entity they govern.

We need to look no further than the thirteen colonies' Declaration of Independence on this, for it reiterates references to the "security and safety" of the colonies and colonists. The new government to be established by the colonists would lay "its foundation on such principles and organizing its powers in such form, as to them shall

1. The letter and *besshi* will be published in Shōyū Kurabu, ed., *Shinagawa Yajirō Kankei Monjo* [品川弥二郎関係文書] vol. 8 (Tokyo, Yamakawa Shuppansha, forthcoming).

seem most likely to effect their Safety and Happiness." It continues by stating that it is a peoples' right and duty "to throw off such [a despotic] Government, and to provide new Guards for their future security." And still again, the King of England by his actions has "exposed [the colonies] to all the danger of invasion from without, and convulsions from within." Japan was no different.

In the second place, Yamagata believed that a vibrant, productive economy was inextricably linked to the making of newly acquired lands a Japanese stronghold. Here is a concrete example of *fukoku kyōhei* [富国強兵] (rich country, strong military), an enduring Meiji era national policy. Yamagata pointed out that the viability of any economy depended on concentrating on products favored by the topography. For Okinawa this meant raising sugar cane, cattle and horses, growing millet, producing cloth (*nuno* [布]), and digging coal. As envisaged by Yamagata, and this is absolutely crucial in understanding Japan's colonial policy, the sale of these products would be for the "*mutual benefit*" (*hoeki* [補益]) of Japan and Okinawa. Here we have the clearest expression of "mutualism." Moreover, this mutually advantageous arrangement would have the added dividend of providing the Okinawans a strong incentive to defend themselves and Japan. However, the Okinawans' lack of a martial tradition slowed the process. Yamagata, therefore, realistically proposed to start modestly with a small contingent of conscripts that would gradually be built up to an all-Okinawan force which would become a part of the Japanese garrison in Okinawa.

The lack of a martial tradition, Yamagata pointed out, was the result of the Okinawan Kingdom's willing acquiescence to its vassal relationship vis-à-vis its suzerain, Qing China. A further consequence, he wrote, was the absence of a sense of patriotism among the Okinawans. Yamagata's remedy to overcome the related obstacles of the lack of a martial tradition and sense of patriotism was to educate the Okinawans in Japan's traditions. And he regarded *education as "the fundamental aspect of our Okinawa policy*." Here again, as in the case of conscripting Okinawans as soldiers, he stressed starting modestly. Yamagata's stances on these two instances represent the Meiji government's fundamental approach to reform, political change, and colonialism: gradualism (*zenshin shugi* [漸進主義]). Put another way, there would be no force-feeding of reforms in Japan's colonies.

This slow, gradualist transitioning of Okinawa into Japan proper meant starting modestly with a small core of elementary school students.[2] He proposed, therefore, sending to Japan the best Okinawan elementary school students. There, they would be taught standard Japanese and be provided with a general knowledge of Japan's political institutions and history. They would graduate after mastering these subjects and return as elementary school teachers. The reasoning underlying this proposal, though unstated, is that the most effective teachers of Okinawans would come from the growing cadre of fellow Okinawans.

At first blush Yamagata's emphasis on education and on teaching standard Japanese to Okinawans appears to have produced but meager results. In 1899, 76.3 percent of Okinawans were illiterate, the highest percentage in Japan. In 1904, the rate was still over 20 percent, which relegated Okinawa to the bottom among the prefectures.[3] Yet, only thirteen years separate 1899 from 1886 with

---

2. Students in prewar Okinawa, if they chose and were able, could go only as high as *chūgakkō* (中学校) (middle school). Yakabi Osamu (屋嘉比収), "Kindai Okinawa chishikijin no senjika no genron: Iha Fuyū to Shimabukuro Zenpastsu" (近代沖縄知識人の戦時下の議論), *Hongō* [本郷], no. 86 (March 2010), 16.

3. Richard Rubinger, "Who Can't Read and Write?: Illiteracy in Meiji Japan," *MN* 55.2 (Summer 2000): 179,184. Rubinger uses data from conscription exams since they provide a comprehensive national overview of illiteracy patterns over an extended stretch of time. The data used present results of tests given to all males who reached the age of twenty. He admits, however, that there are problems in using conscription exams to measure illiteracy. See pages 170-173 and 193-195.

Okinawans starting from a low baseline. Moreover, a distinction must be made between conscripts and the movers-and-shakers of Okinawan society. Steve Rabson points out that the leaders of Okinawan society were "enthusiastically taking up the cause of language 'standardization,'" and as early as 1903, Okinawa's leading newspaper voiced resentment that they, who were "truly Japanese," were being placed on the same level with Taiwanese and Ainu.[4]

Yamagata then turned his attention to governance and fiscal reforms. His unshakeable premise was that necessary changes, including those governing Okinawa, must be based on respect for the Okinawans' traditional ways and customs. He applied this principle to the judiciary system, saying that the establishment of the new system must start at a point *proportionate* to the level then existing in Okinawa. In this way, the legal issues would be effectively adjudicated. Judiciary reform also must not be hastily pushed forward from Tokyo; the pace, he believed is best left in the hands of prefectural officials who are more intimately involved in the peoples' lives.

In a related reform, he points out that Tokyo had tried to modernize Okinawa's tax system but that the people "strenuously opposed" the attempt, making tax collection extremely difficult. The central government, therefore, reversed itself and reinstated the traditional collection system, even with all its problems. Still, he reports, the people were "comfortable" with their system, so for the time being, traditional tax collectors were used as much as possible. This change "eliminated the peoples' doubts, making them amenable to tax collection." Here we pause to emphasize a striking aspect of Meiji Japan's reform efforts: the willingness to realistically admit a failing, and to change course to ensure a better result for all con-

4. "Meiji Assimilation Policy in Okinawa: Promotion, Resistance, and 'Reconstruction'," in *New Directions in the Study of Meiji Japan*, ed., Helen Hardacre and Adam L. Kern (Leiden: Brill, 1997), 647 and 649.

cerned, as happened again in Korea. Yamagata closes with the wish that at the appropriate time, these same policy principles be adopted for Tsushima and the Gotō Islands since the result would be the strengthening of Japan's western flank against foreign incursions.

Ōkuma Shigenobu's Korea Policy

Ōkuma Shigenobu's Korea policy contains a plank that reinforces Yamagata's stress on economic development and that the resulting benefits should accrue to both parties:

> If our policy toward Korea is to be attended with permanent results, it must be carried out first of all along the lines of economic advancement. . . . Truly profitable dealings between individuals are always mutual; and this is true also of nations. . . . [W]e can never achieve greatness for our country at the expense of our neighbors, especially of Korea.[5]

Ōkuma's proposition was one that Yamagata could applaud, yet, the article offers another opportunity to return to the methodological pitfall regarding bifurcated "black and white" historical judgments. Ōkuma founded a major political party, one that often fought against the "oligarchic" Meiji government that included Yamagata and its more conservative rival party. He was an education pioneer who established what is now Waseda University, a prestigious liberal, private university, and after his death was widely hailed as a people's politician. Yet this liberal politician in 1915 presented Yüan Shih-kai's government with the infamous Twenty-one Demands that

---

5. "Japan's Policy in Korea," *The Forum* 37.4 (April-June 1906): 577-580. The article only appeared in English, probably an effort to justify Japan's 1905 creation of a protectorate over Korea. I am indebted to Professor Nagai Jun'ichi (長井純市) of Hōsei University for sharing a copy. In his translation, Nagai renders "mutual benefit" as (*gokeiteki* [互恵的]). "Ōkuma Shigenobu no Chōsen Kaihatsu Kōsō" (大隈重信の朝鮮開発構想), *Nihon Rekishi* [日本歴史] 695 (6 April 2006): 74.

would have effectively brought China under Japan's control.

Yamagata—the putative autocrat, militarist, imperialist—for his part had this criticism of Japan's China policy: I note that "there are those who are apt to be overly confident of Japan's military power. This is evident in their belief that coercion is only way that we can deal with China. [They forget that] in the real world, matters cannot be resolved simply by the use of power."[6] This quote is critical to combating the incorrect portrayal of Yamagata as a militarist, a point we will return to later in this book.

The danger of black vs. white interpretation is also illustrated in a recent and timely article by Hans Martin Krämer that not only casts additional light on education, a central tenet of assimilation, but shows how, at this late date, there is still the need to rethink the bifurcated interpretations of all aspects of modern Japanese history, including Korea's nationalist historical narrative. Krämer begins by showing that immediately after the Pacific War, leading education specialists were convinced that prewar Japanese education, especially in the 1930s, was "fascistic"; and that in this period ultranationalism permeated Japanese society. He brings up the corollary that it was a commonplace belief after the Pacific War that SCAP's (Supreme Commander for the Allied Powers) reform agenda created a "democratic, egalitarian Japan." It may be added that this is still a widely accepted notion.

He rebuts these assertions by showing that between 1925 and 1945, "lively debate on educational reform" took place in Japan. He notes that a major topic of this debate was to provide "equality of opportunity" for all Japanese through widespread public education as a way "to make maximum use of its human resources."[7]

6. Ōyama Azusa (大山梓), "Taishi seisaku ikensho" (対支政策意見書) (Position on Japan's China Policy) in Ōyama Azusa, *Yamagata Aritomo Ikensho* [山縣有朋意見書] (The Position Papers of Yamagata Aritomo) (Tokyo: Hara Shobō, 1966), 340-341.
7. Hans Martin Krämer, "The Prewar Roots of 'Equality of Opportunity':

Krämer is on target, and his claims echo one of Yamagata's central convictions. This point is emphasized by Richard Staubitz, who writes that Yamagata's preoccupation with creating the local government system in 1889 was to draw the "energies of the masses of the people into national political life."[8]

To be sure, all authoritarian, totalitarian regimes mobilize the masses for states' ends. In Japan's case, nothing nefarious was involved. Yamagata and the Meiji Genrō aimed to build a lasting government and nation that, even if imperfectly, balanced the needs of all people. James Fallows provides an insightful perspective in Japan's case. Fallows, a liberal, has been a Rhodes Scholar, chief speech writer for President Jimmy Carter, and editor of the *Atlantic Monthly*. In the late 1980s he spent two years in Japan as a Japan Society Fellow. It is highly unlikely that he has read Staubitz or Yamagata, but these two would approve of his stance. He asserts that Japanese society works, and that it works because it has discovered "the right way to elicit its people's best efforts." And for Fallows, the ordinary people's efforts count because "there are so many of them." Still, he continues, this effort must also be "voluntary" since "it's too hard to supervise everyone all the time." Fallows adds that Japanese society works because it has succeeded in giving individual members a sense that they "can control their [own] destiny."[9]

HARA KEI ON KOREA

Hara Kei (Takashi) is another weighty voice speaking out on

Japanese Educational Ideals in the Twentieth Century," *MN* 61.4 (Winter 2006): 523 and 544. Krämer is associate professor of Japanese Studies at Ruhr University Bochum.

8. "The Establishment of the System of Local Self-Government (1888–1890) in Meiji Japan: Yamagata Aritomo and the Meaning of 'Jichi' (Self-government)" (Ph.D. diss., Yale University, 1973), viii.
9. *More Like Us: Making America Great Again* (Boston: Houghton Mifflin Company, 1989), 5, 13-14, 25-35.

Japan's Korea colonial policy. He was the powerful Home Minister in the second Saionji Kinmochi (西園寺公望) cabinet (August 1911–December 1912) when he gave the following remarks. He is stereotypically regarded as a conservative and even a reactionary, so he is another example of the pitfall of rushing to place people in a box. His views on Korea, however, are genuinely liberal and are in stark contrast to those of the generally acclaimed progressive, Ōkuma. Moreover, Hara's views also reveal a commonality with those of the so-called anti-liberal, Yamagata, who even today is considered Hara's *bête noire*, the one who stood in Hara's way until almost the eve of the creation of the Hara-led, Seiyūkai Party Cabinet in 1918, the first of its kind in modern Japan.[10]

In 1911, Hara gave his views on Korea to Inoue Kakugorō (井上角五郎), a member of the Diet's House of Representatives. Hara in this conversation stressed assimilating the Koreans, a point reminiscent of Yamagata's primary goal in dealing with newly acquired Ryūkyū. He insisted that Korea could not be merely regarded as a colony in the accepted sense of the word since the Koreans could and should be assimilated (*dōka*). To underscore his point, he asserted that Japan should treat the Koreans differently as the Chinese are in Taiwan.[11]

---

10. Najita Tetsuo, *Hara Kei in the Politics of Compromise, 1905–1915* (Cambridge, MA: Harvard University Press, 1967). This is the only monograph in English on Hara's political career. It is readable and useful. He stresses the conflict between the Yamagata-led bureaucratic clique (*batsu* [閥]) and Hara's Seiyūkai. Itō Yukio (伊藤之雄), a Kyoto University professor who loves "dogs, sake, and people" published "Yamagata Aritomo: Guchoku na kenryokusha no shōgai" (山県有朋：愚直な権力者の生涯), *Bunshun Shinsho* 684 (2009). Itō persists in creating a dichotomy between Hara and Yamagata, the latter he now says he has come to increasingly like (*dondon suki ni natte itta* [どんどん好きになっていった])., see page 475. While I am pleased by Itō's change of heart, a critique of this dichotomous relationship must wait a while longer.
11. A possible clue as to why Hara differentiated the Koreans from the Chinese is found in one of Ōkuma's opening statements. He declared that there is evi-

Hara then echoed a major point in Yamagata's *ikensho* by telling Inoue that it was extremely wrongheaded, as some were suggesting, that the Koreans' education should be different from that offered to the Japanese. In his opinion, the solution was to offer them the same education by raising their Japanese-language competence. He then followed with a radical statement by telling Inoue that once the Koreans became competent in Japanese, it would be desirable to have them participate in the *fu-ken* administration in Korea; and that furthermore, in the future, he saw no problem in having Koreans in the Imperial Diet. In sum, Hara declared that he could not think of any obstacles to treating Korea on par with Hokkaido and Okinawa, both of which had become parts of Japan. He concluded his conversation with Inoue by saying that the latter should keep in mind these statements, but that the time was not ripe to make them public.[12] It is noteworthy that these words were spoken only a year after Korea became a colony.

Wonmo Dong, who is generally skeptical of Japan's aims in Korea, nonetheless correctly intuited Hara's open-mindedness, asserting that, "Particularly in term of political assimilation of the Korean colony, Hara showed great liberality in approving the possibility of Korean political participation in the Japanese political system."[13]

---

dence that, "the race peopling the southern part of the peninsula of Korea is of the same stock as that whence we of Japan have sprung . . . [that the Koreans] are Kin to our own race." He dismissed those in the north as being "similar to the Tartar family." See Ōkuma, 571.

12. Hara Keiichirō (原奎一郎), ed., *Hara Kei Nikki* [原敬日記], Fukumura edition, vol. 3 (Tokyo, 1965), 114, 24 April 1911. See also, Hara's reply to interpellation by Baron Fujimura Yoshirō (男爵藤村義朗), 21 July 1920, in *Hara Kei Zenshū* [原敬全集], ed., Tanaka Tomoyoshi (田中朝吉), vol. 2 (Tokyo: Hara Kei Zenshū Kankōkai, 1929), 515-516. The volumes are for available for purchase.

13. Wonmo Dong, 246-247.

Hara was still waxing positively about Korea after his short visit there. He wrote that to "assimilate" the Koreans would not be difficult; and that in fact, the Koreans are "enthusiastic about becoming Japanese." He substantiated this conclusion by dividing the Koreans into three groups. He asserted that those in the upper reaches of society were on the surface expressing bitterness, but were inwardly overjoyed by the prospect of assimilation. Similarly, Hara thought the lower classes were happy with Japan's policies. A third, but small group of people in the middle (class) was not satisfied, largely because they had lost their livelihoods. Regardless, he did not consider Korean opposition to be worrisome.[14]

Hasegawa Yoshimichi's "Recommendations"

There was, however, a small fly in the ointment in all of Hara's positivity. Inoue Kakugorō had earlier warned Hara that his Korean friends were dissatisfied with Governor-General Terauchi Masatake's policies, which they considered insensitive and heavy-handed.[15] And indeed, Hara's assessment of the colonial situation was overly optimistic. The dissatisfaction with Japanese rule in Korea spilled over with demonstrations against the GGK on March First 1919 with heartbreaking consequences for the Koreans.

The nationalist historical paradigm points to the March First Independence Movement as the apex of Korean resistance to the colonial regime. This paradigm interprets the motivation of each demonstrator as though their sole motivation was Korea's independence—nothing more and nothing less. While many demonstrators sought independence; for example, a Declaration of Independence was signed and most cried "Mansei" as they marched in the streets. Yet, an accounting needs to be made for the many participants who used the demonstrations to voice their grievances against the colo-

14. *HKN*, 31 May 1911, 130-131.
15. Ibid., 24 April 1911, 114-115.

nial regime in an effort to seek reform. There was a "festering resentment of ordinary people all over Korea at the constant, unending intrusions into their everyday lives by nosy, controlling rank-and-file *kempei* police." In the rural areas, complaints against the colonial regime included the "proscription on communal graves listed, no bans on slash-and-burn cultivation, freedom to gather forest products, [and a] repeal of taxes on alcohol and tobacco."[16]

The demonstrations started peaceably and quickly spread throughout Korea. The number of participants reached over 2 million. The GGK issued an order for demonstrators to cease and desist, and when they did not, the colonial regime resorted to violence to suppress the movement. By mid-April the demonstrations had ceased, but Korean and Japanese clashes continued until the end of the year. Official statistics on the number of demonstrators arrested as well as casualties reveal the scope of the tragedy: according to official Japanese sources, 12,522 people were arrested, 553 were killed and 1,409 injured; conversely, Korean sources claim that 46,948 demonstrators were arrested, 7,509 killed, and 15,961 injured. In addition to the human tragedy, property damage, including destruction of schools and churches, was immense.[17] Frank P. Baldwin, Jr. lists five sources showing the number of Koreans killed and wounded. He admits to gaps in the statistics but concludes that, "Japanese accounts understate the Korean losses to a very large degree."[18]

---

16. Matsuda Toshihiko, *Governance and Policing of Colonial Korea, 1904–1919* (Kyoto: International Research Center for Japanese Studies, 2011), 177.
17. Richard Devine, "Japanese Rule in Korea after the March First Uprising: Governor General Hasegawa's Recommendations," *MN* 52.4 (winter 1997), 524. Devine was associate professor in the Faculty of Comparative Culture, Sophia University, at the time of publication. He now resides in the Society of Jesus House in the Sophia University grounds, and is immersed in sculpting human figures that are highly regarded among fellow sculptors. We had a long telephone conversation in mid-June 2012. I was pleased to have been able to inform him of his sterling contribution to understanding Japan's role in colonial Korea.
18. "The March First Movement: Korean Challenge and Japanese Response"

Before proceeding to discuss the "Recommendations," the document deserves a brief introduction. The "Recommendations" or "*Sōjō zengosaku shiken*" [騒擾善後策私見] is found in the *Saitō Makoto kankei monjo* [斎藤実関係文書] and Kensei Shiryōshitsu [憲政資料室] collections at the National Diet Library. The report is undated but is filed under the year 1919, and was likely written after the March First Movement. I and my colleague, Professor Hirose Yoshihiro (広瀬順晧), compared Devine's translation against a photocopy of the original. The purpose was not to question its accuracy, but to get the feel for this vitally important document.

Hasegawa's use of *shiken* may be likened to Yamagata's *ikko no iken*, in that the recommendations were more than a compendium of his personal views, but were backed by the authority of the GGK. The "Recommendations," duplicated by a scribe, is written on sheets with *Chōsen Sōtokufu* [朝鮮総督府] printed at the margins. And, as Devine points out, it was customary for the outgoing governor to leave a written report of his views for his successor.[19]

Hasegawa's "Recommendations," as a whole, were moderate; so it may surprise those who know of his less than charitable 1905 view of Koreans when he was the commanding general of forces in Korea:

> I cannot help but believe that in dealing with [the Koreans masses], who are nearly barbarians in their level of knowledge, in their want of any conception of the state, and in their worship of the strong, it will not be effective to use means that do not rely on force . . . [20]

(Ph.D. diss., Columbia University, 1969), 232-236. Some care should be exercised in reading Baldwin's narrative since he leans toward the "patriotic paradigm" with its highly negative perception of Japan's colonial rule.

19. Richard Devine, 524. Let the record show that the translation is praiseworthy, although there is a minor slip. Devine renders (ハ) as "eight" years when it should be "as for." Still, Hasegawa contributes to the confusion by giving "nine" and "ten" years as the period of Japanese rule. Akita is indebted to KS section chief Horiuchi Hiroo (堀内寛雄), for a photocopy of the document.

20. Peter Duus, 196.

Still, a little perspective may mitigate the tone of Hasegawa's harsh judgment. The international opinion of Korea in the early 1900s was decidedly unfavorable with regard to Korea's turbulent domestic conditions. Western politicians and travelers similarly disparaged Korean public health, lack of industry, corruption, and cronyism. A year earlier, Horace Allen, the American minister in Seoul and long-time friend of Korea, declared:

> [The Koreans] must have an overlord as they have had for all time . . . I [am not] opposed to any civilized race taking over the management of these kindly Asiatics for the good of the people and the suppression of oppressive officials, the establishment of order and the development of commerce.[21]

Hasegawa's "Recommendations" may be arguably one of the most telling documents in Japan's colonial history. It is distinguished by four markers that were also seen in Yamagata's *ikensho* on Okinawa. First, he proposed that the GGK make a specific admission of consequential errors of judgment, both by omission and commission. Second, it displays the expeditious willingness of the colonial regime to change to cope with these errors; that is, the GGK establish concrete, visible measures to address the perceived problems. The GGK, in short, followed Confucius' admonition: "When you have faults, do not fear to abandon them." Third, the Tokyo government overlooked the author's "disgrace" and "failure" as a governor-general and a swift official imprimatur was granted to the "Recommendations." And fourth, Yamagata's *ikensho* on Okinawa and Hasegawa's "Recommendations" for Korea show that Japan attempted to adhere to certain principles, norms, and actions that were realistic and moderate with an unblinking eye toward maintaining proportionality.

Jon Meacham of *Newsweek*, as befitting a professional word-

---

21. Ibid., 189. Allen later characterized the Japanese as "the civilized race." Letters to Joseph Choate, ex-ambassador to London, 18 December 1905, in Peter Duus, 206.

smith, struck a similar chord, only better, when speaking of the Gulf oil spill: "No reasonable person can expect institutions to get everything right all the time. By the same token, no reasonable institution should expect people to believe it infallible. Learning, adjusting, admitting error—these are the marks of a mature human being, and of a mature institution."[22] Moreover, the Tokyo government may have realized that it shared part of the onus for its overly roseate analysis of the Korean situation. Hara, in a speech on 22 January 1920 to the 42nd session of the Diet, still insisted that the previous year's demonstrations stemmed from what was "unexpected" by Japan; this is because the Koreans "misunderstood" Japan's aims in Korea.[23] Shortly afterward, in a reply to an interpellation on 19 February 1920 by Baron Satake Yoshinori (男爵佐竹義準), he conceded that the March 2 (sic) uprising took Japan by surprise since the government had no indication that such would take place.[24]

How, then, did Japan and the GGK deal with the unexpected? Hasegawa outlined a clear path in his "Recommendations" with a straightforward, subject-by-subject manner of presentation of Japan's principles of colonial rule that first discussed the mistakes and problems committed by the GGK and followed by his recommended solutions. But in the document's "preamble" he encapsulated the GGK's missteps and his proposed remedies.

The first principle of colonial rule, according to Hasegawa, is that the colonies are to serve as bastions of *defense* against foreign incursions. Yamagata for his part, expanded this principle to define Japan's security in terms of the "line of sovereignty" (*shukensen* [主権線]) and the "line of [national] interest" (*riekisen* [利益線]). Roger F. Hackett explains that the former referred to the "territorial limits of the nation," and that while the "line of [national] interest" was not

22. Jon Meacham, "Trial, Error, and the Gulf of Mexico," *Newsweek*, 7 June 2010, 2.

23. *HKZ*, vol. 2, 319.

24. Ibid., vol. 2, 377-378.

spelled out, it could mean an area "beyond the territorial boundary . . . in which Japan *should seek dominant influence*" or a "buffer zone of protection, a strategic area, which, if in unfriendly hands, would threaten the nation's security."[25]

The second of these principles is that the GGK did not stress economic exploitation, but rather economic development as an approach that would, in Devine's words, be of "mutual benefit" to Japan and Korea. Hasegawa does not use "*hoeki*" as did Yamagata, but his intent is unmistakable, given his declaration that the "prerequisite for insuring the very existence of our empire is the strengthening of the bonds that bind [Japan and Korea] based on 'harmony' (*konzen* [渾然]) and 'conciliation' (*yūwa* [融和])." He later stresses that the GGK's greatest regret vis-à-vis the March First Incident was that in nine years following Korea's annexation, it had failed to persuade "knowledgeable" Koreans that Korea's economic development lay at the heart of Japan's Korea policy, and that the benefits would flow to both Koreans and Japanese;[26] and as seen earlier, Ōkuma Shigenobu could not have been more explicit by declaring that economic development was the key to Japan's Korea policy and that Korea and Japan had much to gain by working together.

The third of the principles is that Hasegawa, as did other Meiji

25. Roger F. Hackett, 138. We prefer the "line of [national] interest" over his the "line of advantage" since the latter suggests a positive, aggressive move to secure an "advantage" over potential enemies. This is not the place to be fully involved in a discussion of how these concepts were and are still being applied by other Powers. As an example, the Monroe Doctrine was enunciated to prevent European Powers from expanding their influence and control in the western hemisphere, and may be defined as the United States' "line of sovereignty." Over time, however, the "line of [national] interest" has been pushed farther and farther away from the western hemisphere so that, first the Philippines in 1900, and today, Japan, Korea, and Taiwan are encompassed within its fold, not to mention Iraq and Afghanistan.

26. The translation is mine, but Devine correctly grasps the strength of Hasegawa's sentiments. Richard Devine, 529-530.

leaders, placed great store in the crucial role of education. On this point, however, he went beyond Yamagata and called for Korean and Japanese students in middle school and above to study together (*kyōgaku* [共学]) as a necessary step to bring about the assimilation (*dōka*) of Koreans. It should be added that Yamagata and Hasegawa were dealing with Okinawans and Koreans who were on different levels of Japanese-language ability when they made their respective points on the importance of education. In fact, the Korean elite regarded themselves as being culturally more advanced and sophisticated than the Japanese.

It should be noted that despite Hasegawa's roseate view that *kyōgaku* would facilitate the assimilation of Koreans, things did not turn out as well as hoped. One of Hildi Kang's informants recalls that even when Japanese and Koreans students studied side-by-side, Koreans did not socialize with their Japanese counterparts. Furthermore, when the Korean students protested against having to live together with Japanese in the student dorms, school officials relented and permitted separate halls for each group.[27] This incident, however, shows another instance that Japanese rule was not relentlessly arbitrary, discriminatory, and oppressive. It also shows that Koreans resisted some of the moderate policies put in place by Japanese bureaucrats.

Hasegawa also shared with his Meiji cohorts the belief in and the efficacy of gradualism (*zenshinshugi* [漸進主義]). He believed, for example, that the Korean students' grasp of nationalism [or patriotism] (*kokka shisō* [国家思想]) was yet a work in progress.[28]

---

27. Hildi Kang, 54-55.
28. Devine translates the term as "national thought." Richard Devine, 535. I use nationalism interchangeably with patriotism given that Yamagata linked education with infusing the Okinawans in patriotism. Here again, the Korean elite's pride that their Confucian bureaucratic tradition trumped the Japanese warrior history led to its sense of cultural superiority and sophistication over the latter.

Still, since its absorption was a vital part of the gradual (*zen o ōte* [漸を追ふて]) Japanizing Korean society, to expect quick results was shortsighted.

It is at this juncture that Hasegawa articulates the fourth and unexceptionable principle of Japanese colonial rule—one that is overlooked by many political historians on modern Japan, but a precept that was agreed upon by Japan's mainstream leadership; to wit, he recognized that the universal affliction stemming from despotic government (*sensei seiji* [専制政治]) impedes (*sosoku* [阻塞]) the concerns of the lower ranks from reaching those in power.[29] Hasegawa then proceeded from this generalized statement of the Meiji leadership's baseline conviction that the GGK could now posthaste narrow the distance between it and the Koreans. It cannot be questioned that the Meiji leadership was paternalistic. Yet, if the Meiji leadership and GGK were autocratic and despotic and eager to suppress the masses, Hasegawa, an army general and part of the leadership, hardly could have been expected to deliver such an admonition.

Hasegawa first pointed out that adherents of Ch'ŏndogyo (天道教), which played a significant role in the March First Movement, did not act as a religious organization. Therefore, "it would be impossible to disband [it]."[30] He then wrote that while it is true that the GGK had the power to disband it as a subversive group, to adopt this option would merely drive its members underground and thus make it a greater source of misery for the GGK. His recommended solution was to recognize it as a religion, and then to strictly regulate

---

29. Richard Devine, 532. (Translation of the terms is mine.)

30. Ibid., 538. Hildi Kang describes it as a "religious movement" combining elements of "Confucianism, Buddhism, and Taoism," that called for the "equality for the peasants," for the improvement of "village conditions," and the "reform of the corrupt government." One of her interviewees claimed that it was "very chauvinistic" and "rejected all western things." See Hildi Kang, 10.

it, and lead it to a more positive direction.[31] Obviously to "strictly regulate it" is not as heavy-handed as to "suppress it." This sort of moderate approach to suspect organizations typified the GGK's modus operandi.

Hasegawa applied the same approach to the issue of speech and press. He admitted that the restrictions against both had been "overly severe." He suggested that moderating the restrictions would enable the GGK to hear what the Koreans had to say; and when they were wrong, guide them to change. When this was done, he concluded, the pathway would be opened "for communication from bottom to top and from top to bottom."[32] Hasegawa then offered a solution to achieve effective communication: the GGK should increase by two or three the number of vernacular newspapers from the single one that was permitted to exist at that time.

Hasegawa's next proposal to narrow the gap between the GGK and the Koreans was highly significant; he urged that the Koreans be given voting rights in the House of Peers. This step would give the Korean public, as well as the Japanese citizenry, the sense that they were indeed, "constituent members of the empire."[33] Here is planted the seed for the movement toward the enfranchisement of Koreans, a possibility reiterated in Japan in the House of Peers interpellations on the conscription of Koreans in the early 1940s.

The Hara Kei government took Hasegawa's recommendations to heart as witnessed by his lengthy reply to Baron Satake Yoshinori's interpellation that includes an almost point-by-point presentation of Hasegawa's recommendations.[34] In this reply to Satake, Hara makes

---

31. Ibid., 526.

32. Ibid., 539.

33. Ibid., 538. Beyond the two major newspapers that came into being, "hundreds of popular magazines and more specialized political publications" came into existence. Eckert et al., 283.

34. In other Diet sessions, Hara described Japan's post-demonstration's policies as reforms aimed at the welfare and security of Koreans in the spirit of "fair play

the eye-catching statement that since representatives from Okinawa are "already members of the Diet . . . the Koreans will follow."[35] And he leaves no doubts among his listeners in a later session of the Diet by declaring that the Hara government "holds on to the hope that Korea would reach our level [of modernization] as speedily as possible . . . And if Korea's local self-government system becomes viable as we hope to see it be; then [at that point] Koreans will send representatives to the Diet and participate in both Upper and Lower Houses (*jōge ryōin* [上下両院])."[36]

It may be worth noting that Korean men living in Japan had the right to vote as long as they met age and residency requirements that also applied to Japanese men. In fact, from 1930 on, Koreans could vote in *hangul* (the Korean script). Equally interesting, Koreans had the right to run for political office in Japan. There were dozens of Koreans and Taiwanese who ran for office in the Lower House in the 1930s and 1940s, but only Pak Ch'un-gŭm (朴春琴) actually won a seat in the 1932 and 1937 elections.[37] Furthermore, after 1932 three Koreans and one Taiwanese received lifetime appointments to the Upper House. In April 1945 "Koreans and Taiwanese received the right to vote for and send representatives to the national Diet . . ."[38] However, the war ended before these elections took place. We concede that granting suffrage was a wartime concession to placate colonial subjects. Yet, two points should be

---

and impartiality" (*isshi dōjin* [一視同仁]), based upon just and upright (*kōmei seidai*[公明正大]) ways. Speech to 42nd session of the Diet, 22 January 1920, *HKZ*, vol. 2, 319; also, reply to Baron Sakatani Yoshirō (阪谷芳郎), 27 January 1920, *HKZ*, vol. 2, 356.

35. *HKZ*, vol. 2, 384. (19 February 1920).

36. Reply to Baron Fujimura Yoshirō's interpellation, 21 July 1920, *HKZ*, vol. 2, 515-516.

37. Takashi Fujitani, *Race for Empire: Koreans as Japanese and Japanese as Americans during World War II* (Berkeley: University of California Press, 2011), 24 and 28.

38. Ibid., 66.

raised: first, the enfranchisement of Koreans had been discussed in tandem with Korean military service long before the war grew desperate for Japan; and second, had Korea remained a Japanese colony after the war, the constitutional changes granting suffrage would have remained in effect.

Admiral Saitō Makoto (斉藤実), who succeeded Hasegawa as governor-general (1919–1927), escaped an assassination attempt by bomb soon after his arrival in Korea. Despite this anti-Japanese display, he proceeded to implement some of the reforms Hasegawa had advocated. Saitō adjusted the wages of Korean bureaucrats, reorganized and expanded the police force, abolished the unpopular gendarmerie system, opened provincial governorships to civil officials, instituted educational reforms, and permitted the printing of vernacular newspapers and journals. Another reform forbade Japanese educators, judges, and other civilians from carrying swords, as was befitting their appointment by the emperor. One of Hildi Kang's interviewees remembers a teacher who came to school "resplendent" in a black uniform that was decorated with "gold ornaments on his collar, shoulder, chest, and sleeves" and had "a saber at his waist"—the interviewee's reaction to his intimidating vision was: "Wouldn't you be frightened out of your wits if you were just ten years old and standing before such a magnificent uniform and long sword?"[39] These moderate reforms contributed to a time of cultural nationalism in Korea during the 1920s and early 1930s. Finally, the GGK's sensitivity to the necessity of reforms both large and small is an indication that these reforms were more than superficial and insincere as some advocates of the passionate narrative would have it.

Frederick Starr (1858–1933) was the first anthropologist [hired to be] at the University of Chicago (1892–1923). After he retired, he spent much time at "work in Japan and Korea." He was "on his fourteenth visit" when "he died in Tokyo." After the March First

---

39. Hildi Kang, 52.

Movement he met Governor-General Saitō Makoto and he recorded his impressions of Saitō as one who "spoke with apparent honesty and earnestness of his work and seem[ed] *sympathetic* with Korean aspirations."[40]

Reforms Based on Hasegawa's "Recommendations"

A measure of the impact of these reforms is provided by two 1936 police surveys of Korean attitudes cited by Wonmo Dong. We admit to a certain wariness in using statistics, especially those based upon government sponsored polls, a cautiousness reinforced by Mark Twain's assertion: "The remark attributed to Disraeli would often apply with justice and force: 'There are three kinds of lies: lies, damned lies, and statistics.'"[41] We recognize that the conditions under which the surveys were conducted are not known, and that the potential for bias is great. Still, these numbers, when used in conjunction with the studies of revisionists, none of whom have an especial predisposition to favorably portray Japan's rule over Korea, may shed light on the complexities involved.

The first poll cited by Wonmo Dong, on "independence thoughts," showed that of those polled, 8.1 percent always thought of independence; 11.0 percent wanted independence at a favorable time; 32.6 percent had given up the thought; and 48.3 percent did not care one way or another. Of interest is that among intellectuals, 47.2 percent had given up the thought, and 28.1 percent did not care; among students, the percentages were 33.6 percent and 50.6 percent, respectively. The results of the survey also showed that 9.3 percent of intellectuals reported that they always thought of independence, while 15.4 percent wanted independence at a favorable

40. Robert Oppenheim, "'The West' and the Anthropology of Other People's Colonialism: Frederick Starr in Korea, 1911–1930," *The Journal of Asian Studies* 64.3 (August 2005): 677 and 688.

41. http://www1c.btwebworld.com/quote-unquote/p0000149.htm.

time. Among students, the figures were 5.6 percent and 10.3 percent, respectively. Interestingly, 6.5 percent of farmers/laborers always thought of independence and 68.3 percent did not care, whereas religious leaders were fairly evenly divided on these issues at 27.1 percent and 25.2 percent, respectively.[42] The results of another survey, on attitudes toward the Japanese government, showed that overall, 11.1 percent were opposed; 14.9 percent called for reform; 37.7 percent were satisfied; and 36.1 percent showed no interest in the issue. Among intellectuals, the numbers were 10.7 percent, 24.9 percent, 44.9 percent, and 19.5 percent; and among students, 9.9 percent, 12.7 percent, 40.7 percent, and 36.7 percent, respectively.[43] It is noteworthy that Koreans felt safe enough to respond and openly state they "always thought of independence" and that the Japanese were willing to tally the responses as such.

Michael L. Sprunger correctly notes that the inclusion of colonial peoples in the national polity (*kokutai* [国体]) via assimilation, *ipso facto* meant granting the rights and privileges of Japanese citizenship, including representation in the Diet, all of which were guaranteed by the Meiji Constitution and sanctioned by the emperor. This was the central principle of assimilation that significantly moderated the acts of the authorities who acted in the emperor's name in Tokyo and the colonies.[44] The reason was that the Meiji leadership, including politicians in the provinces, the central and local bureaucrats, the press, the educators high and low, and part of the informed Japanese public firmly supported the Meiji Constitution and the laws that were based

42. Wonmo Dong, Table 37, 341.

43. Ibid., Table 39, 345.

44. The extension of Japan's laws to the colonies, according to Sprunger, was by *chokurei* [勅令] (imperial decree) that were usually requested by colonial governors. Japanese laws were extended to Korea by being either combined with or applied by a *seirei* [政令] issued by the governor-general. Michael L. Sprunger, "Grafting Justice: Crime and the Politics of Punishment in Korea, 1875-1945," Ph.D. diss. submitted to the History Department, University of Hawai'i, July 2011, 108-109.

on it. There was a realization that Koreans needed to be incorporated into the Japanese polity and citizenry, but at the appropriate time for both Koreans and Japanese. That time never came.

THE ŌTSU JIKEN

Support for the aforementioned generalization is found in the complex series of events that played out from the genesis to the denouement of the *Ōtsu Jiken* (大津事件). The *Ōtsu jiken* had its genesis when Tsuda Sanzō (津田三蔵), a policeman assigned to guard duty along the route to be taken by the Russian crown prince, drew his sword and slashed the crown prince's head at Ōtsu, Shiga Prefecture, on 11 May 1891. The whole nation was panic-stricken over the fear that Russia would extract revenge by waging war and therefore undo all the progress made by Japan to enter the modern world. The press and the Meiji leaders offered abject apologies, and the emperor paid an unprecedented visit to the injured crown prince.[45]

The following discussion is based on two sources; one, an article written by Barbara Teters, an American scholar;[46] the other, the documents submitted to the Meiji political leaders by one of

45. Barbara Teters, "The Ōtsu Affair: The Formation of Japan's Judicial Conscience," in *Meiji Japan's Centennial, Aspects of Political Thought and Action*, ed. David Wurfel (Lawrence: University Press of Kansas, 1971), 38, 39, 45-50. I have read the parts of Kaneko Kentarō (金子堅太郎); Shunpo-kō Tsuishōkai (春畝公追頌會), *Itō Hirobumi den* [伊藤博文傳] vol. 2, (Tokyo: Tōseisha, 1943) dealing with the *Ōtsu jiken* and found that Teter's account is accurate. See, pp. 755-772.

46. Teters was a faculty member at Iowa State University when this book was published. She received a bachelor's from the University of Michigan, and a master's and doctorate in political science from the University of Washington. She was professor and chair of the department of political science at Mississippi State University from 1973 to 1978, and vice chancellor for academic affairs at the University of Arkansas at Monticello for two years. She joined Southern Illinois University Edwardsville as provost in 1981, and retired in 1986. We regret to say that she passed away at age eighty-four in Spokane Valley, Washington on 1 January 2011.

the most gifted, multi-faceted bureaucrats of the Meiji period. In my discussion of Teters, I follow her narrative to trace the details of the *jiken* for two reasons: first, the article is one of the few in the English language that has had a lasting impact on my development as a scholar; and second, she was one of the earliest non-Japanese specialists to deal open-mindedly with the subject of judicial independence in Japan. In short, she showed how the Japanese had internalized the concept of judicial independence in less than a generation following the Meiji Restoration. We say this even as we recognize that the groundwork for judicial independence can be traced to the Tokugawa Period (1603–1867) and even earlier.

The *jiken* in the meantime had been moving to the legal issue of Tsuda's punishment, i.e., which of the Criminal Code's stipulations would be appropriate for the crime Tsuda had committed. The government argued for the death penalty on the basis of Article 116 of the Criminal Code, which called for the death penalty "for anyone who committed violence against the emperor, empress, or crown prince."[47] Against this, Supreme Court Chief Justice Kojima Iken (児島惟謙) and the Supreme Court justices asserted that Articles 292 and 112 were applicable since they "provided for the death sentence for premeditated murder." If, however, the action did not result in death, the sentence would be reduced "by one or two degrees." Such being the law, Tsuda could only be given a life sentence.[48]

Kojima's unquestioned contribution to the rule of law is his legal rationale for arguing against applying Article 116 in Tsuda's case; and his fervent, consistent efforts to rally the Supreme Court justices to his reasoning.[49] In brief, Kojima argued that the application

47. Barbara Teters, 47.

48. Ibid., 49 and 51. Tsuda died of pneumonia in a Hokkaido Prison less than five months after he slashed the Russian crown prince. Ibid., 45.

49. Kojima could not participate in Tsuda's trial that was "conducted by a special court in accordance with provisions of the law" covering cases such as this. Ibid., 52.

of Article 116 "to the monarchs of foreign countries" would be "a violation of Japan's sovereignty." The passions aroused by Tsuda's dangerous act must not blind the justices to the fact that the law is imbedded in the soul of the nation and that personal feelings should not sway justices. Such being the case and even granting the immensity of the peril confronting the nation, the justices should not be deterred from basing their decision on the law; for this would safeguard the very essence of the law.[50] Kojima's arguments held sway, and on 27 May 1891, the Supreme Court justices by an overwhelming vote of six to one, sentenced Tsuda to life imprisonment.[51]

The names of the Supreme Court justices are known, and can be judged by history for their roles in this precedent-setting case. There is, however, a coterie of bureaucrats, names unknown, who deserve a place of honor in Japan's development of the rule of law. These were the bureaucrats of the Justice ministry who vehemently opposed their superior, Justice minister Yamada Akiyoshi (Kengi) (山田顕義), in a spirited three-hour oral battle, and not yielding an inch.[52]

This confrontation in the Justice ministry is but one example of the complexity of the relationships between the bureaucrats and their official and political superiors and among bureaucrats throughout in the central and local governments.

This complexity is completely ignored by one of the most overrated foreign "Japan specialists," Karel van Wolferen. In one of his latest "contributions" to Japan's modern political history, he confidently asserts in *Chūō Kōron* [中央公論], a "progressive" journal of opinion, that "Yamagata Aritomo is the central figure in the creation of modern Japan's bureaucratic system." Van Wolferen opines that:

50. Ibid., 53; also 56-57.

51. Ibid., 38.

52. Ibid., 41 and 48. Miyoshi Taizō (三好退蔵), the *Kenjisōchō* [検事総長] (Public Prosecutor-General) also argued against Yamada's position that Article 116 was applicable. Ibid., 49.

> Yamagata did not want the purity of a supposedly harmonious Japanese nation . . . to be spoiled by contentious politicians. . . . Yamagata introduced arrangements to make sure that they never could have the power they were officially supposed to exercise. . . . His measures allowed a political system to evolve in which military bureaucrats would eventually hijack the country in the 1930s for ill-considered purposes.

The essay continues by stating that what the party then in power, the *Minshutō* [民主党] (Democratic Party), "must try to do is nothing less than to break with the tradition of governance established by . . . Yamagata Aritomo" and that the "basic institutions for democracy . . . must now be built almost from scratch."[53]

These statements are not surprising coming from van Wolferen, who in the late 1980s and early 1990s enjoyed much praise, especially among foreign residents in Japan, for his best-selling work, *The Enigma of Japanese Power: People and Politics in a Stateless Nation* (1989). In it he postulates that Japan's political structure and system is one in which no part is responsible for its actions, even as the bureaucracy wields the most power. The bureaucracy, according to him, controls the economy; it enacts most of the laws; elected politicians blindly approve what the bureaucrats decide upon; the Cabinet merely rubberstamps what has been determined by the bureaucrats; the Supreme Court justices, while themselves bureaucrats, must approve what the bureaucrats have decided upon. The voters are powerless against the bureaucrats' decisions, having been brainwashed by the educational system not to question anything, or trying to be creative. These are astonishing, uninformed, illogical

---

53. Karel van Wolferen, "Nihon seiji saisei o meguru ken'ryoku tōsō no nazo (日本政治再生を巡る権力闘争の謎)," trans. Inoue Minori in *Chūō Kōron* (中央公論), (April 2010), 183-184. English translation available at "Japan's Stumbling Revolution," *The Asia-Pacific Journal* 15.2 (12 April 2010). See Japanfocus.org.

statements that ignore much of modern Japan's concrete achievements in all areas, including the precedent-setting blow struck by Supreme Court justices for judicial independence in the *Ōtsu jiken.*

CABINET MEMBERS' ACTIVE ROLE IN POLITICS

We rebut van Wolferen's assertion that the cabinet's meetings simply serve to rubberstamp what had been predetermined by the faceless bureaucrats. One of *Ōtsu jiken's* lessons, contrary to van Wolferen's conjecture on the cabinet's role, is that the words and actions of cabinet members reveal that they are active actors, even if the reader may not agree with the proposals and justifications for their actions.

Mutsu Munemitsu (陸奥宗光), the Agriculture and Commerce minister (*Nōshōmu daijin* [農商務大臣]), not incidentally from Kii (one of Tokugawa's three collateral domains (*shinpan* [親藩]), and now Wakayama Prefecture) had been imprisoned for planning a revolt against the Meiji government. He had the temerity to urge that the Meiji Constitution be respected by proposing that a life sentence instead of death for Tsuda was appropriate. He was quickly silenced by Inoue Kaoru (井上馨) of Chōshū who was not in the cabinet but still one of the most powerful figures in the Meiji State and who argued vehemently for Tsuda's political and expedient execution.[54]

Justice Minister (司法大臣) Yamada Kengi, knowing that he could not sway the Supreme Court justices, threatened to declare martial law;[55] while Foreign Minister (外務大臣) Aoki Shūzō (青木周蔵) drafted a proposal for *ex post facto* execution for acts of violence against foreign chiefs of state or members of their families. This proposal was rejected when Itō Miyoji (伊東巳代治), the Privy Council's (*Sūmitsuin* [枢密院]) chief secretary (書記官長) strenuously opposed it.[56] Miyoji was from Hizen (now Nagasaki Prefecture), and one of the four drafters of the Meiji Constitution and thus an Itō Hirobumi

54. Barbara Teters, 47.
55. Ibid., 49.
56. Ibid., 50.

disciple. It is likely that by taking this position, he followed the lead of Itō Hirobumi who was at this time the Privy Council president (*gichō* [議長]).

Another outsider, Enomoto Buyō (榎本武揚), a former very high-ranking Tokugawa vassal, was sent to see the Russian ambassador to inquire about his possible reaction to the possibility that Tsuda might be sentenced to life. When the ambassador expressed indignation and demanded that Tsuda be executed, Enomoto quickly replied that the suggestion that Tsuda would be given a life sentence was his personal opinion.[57] Whether he was trying to protect Itō Hirobumi is not known. Still, his reply reveals that there were those in the highest level of the Meiji government who did express agreement with the Supreme Court justices.[58]

Prime Minister Matsukata Masayoshi (松方正義) for his part rebutted Kojima's strong adherence to the law by stressing that legal arguments were irrelevant when the very existence of the nation was at stake. He argued, not without some logic, that, "The nation's existence comes before that of the law"; that "[i]f there is no nation, there will be no law."[59] The Home minister, Saigō Tsugumichi (西郷従道), younger brother of the renowned Saigō Takamori (西郷隆盛) of Satsuma (now Kagoshima Prefecture), excitedly raised the specter of war, declaring that while he was ignorant about the niceties of law, he envisaged the Russian fleet steaming into Shinagawa harbor and the resulting destruction of Japan. Such being the possibility, he then asserted, who dares to say that the law protected the nation; to the contrary, it destroyed the nation.[60]

Inoue Kowashi (井上毅) deserves our closest attention. He was the director-general of the Cabinet Legislation Bureau (*Hōseikyoku chōkan* [法制局長官]) during the first Itō (1885–1888), the Kuroda

---

57. Kaneko Kentarō, *Itō Hirobumi den*, vol. 2 (Tokyo: Tōseisha, 1943), 763-764.
58. Barbara Teters, 57.
59. Ibid., 48.
60. Ibid., 57-58.

Kiyotaka (黒田清隆) (1888–1889), the first Yamagata (1889–1891), and the early days of the first Matsukata cabinets (until June 1891). He was from Kumamoto (熊本) Prefecture in Kyushu, a domain (*han* [藩]) that chose to stay neutral during the Restoration Wars, and as a consequence, lost its place on the highest levels of the Meiji government. Still, such was the force of his intellect, and his repute as a Confucian scholar who was as well highly versed on matters Western that he was respected throughout the Meiji government, including, by Itō Hirobumi, who chose him to become one of the four drafters of the Meiji Constitution.

Given his reputation, I choose to devote lengthy and detailed space to his words and actions in dealing with the *Ōtsu jiken*. First, however, important distinctions must be noted between Inoue and Kojima. Inoue belonged among the innermost circle of the Meiji government. Moreover, more than Kojima, his actions and views covered a wider spectrum of the most significant issues facing Japan. Still, it bears attention that both represent undeniable evidence that the concept and practice of judicial independence as well as respect for written law was by 1891 already deeply imbedded in the psyche and spirit of a very large segment of Japanese society.

For our purpose, Inoue's role in the *Ōtsu Jiken* begins with a letter dated 13 May 1891 that he wrote, but was co-signed by Tanaka Fujimaro (田中不二麿), a privy councilor, and sent to Itō Hirobumi. In it Inoue went directly to the main question at hand—the appropriate punishment for Tsuda: if Japan were to err in this matter, it would earn the "derision" of the intelligentsia (*yūshikisha* [有識者]) of the nation, and also "leave a stain for posterity." He sustained his position that Article 116 was not applicable for the following reasons.

> 1. An imperial prince is not the emperor, but only a member of the imperial family. International law maintains that "An attack on the person of the ruler is an attack on the state." But since the imperial prince is not the ruler, an attack upon him does not constitute an attack on the state.

> 2. Article 116 of Japan's penal code [criminal code] itself is not applicable to foreign rulers, much less to members of foreign imperial families.
>
> 3. Therefore, [Tsuda] should be punished for attempted assassination. If we purposely pervert [*mageru* (曲げる)] the criminal code in this instance, we shall in perpetuity lose the right to try foreigners under our laws. [The meaning, though unstated, is clear; that is, if we cannot apply to our own subjects our own laws rigorously and fairly, how can we expect that foreigners will feel that they can get real justice under Japanese law in Japan?].[61]

It is pertinent to note that another of Inoue's distinctions is his fine hand in writing with brush dipped in India ink (*sōsho*) (草書). Here, however, he wrote in pencil, thus imparting his sense of urgency and gravity. On 24 May 1891, Inoue Kowashi sent a lengthy position paper to Itō Hirobumi.[62] His positions and reasoning stress the legal issues, the potential for handing to anti-government political parties fodder for use later against the government, national honor; and sensitivity to Western reaction:

> Even a person with only a rudimentary knowledge of law [*hōritsu* (法律)], would be skeptical if the government applied [Article 116] to Tsuda.
>
> No country in the world has a law that would permit the application of criminal sanctions to acts committed against other than those in that nation's imperial/ruling family. (All laws of this nature in every country limit punishment to acts committed only against members of the imperial family). If we apply this article to a member of the imperial family of another country, this means in effect that Japan has two sovereigns. Just as there are not two suns in the sky, the

61. Inoue Kowashi denki hensan iinkai (井上毅傳記編纂委員会), *Inoue Kowashi den* (井上毅傳), *Shiryōhen daini* [史料篇第２] (Tokyo: Kokugakuin daigaku toshokan, 1968), 341.
62. Ibid., 381-382.

> people do not have two rulers. If we apply Article 116 to Tsuda, the governments and people of other countries will laugh at the Japanese for not knowing their own criminal code and for insulting the dignity of their own judges. Westerners [*seiyōjin* (西洋人)] will come to the conclusion by this one incident alone that Japan today is truly not a constitutional state [*kenpōkokuhōchikoku* (憲法国法治国)].
>
> Although Tsuda's act is a blot on our national honor, to wrongfully apply Article 116 in this instance is a greater stain on our national honor.

Up to this point, Inoue stressed the possible impact that a wrong decision might have on foreign opinion. He then switched to the domestic impact of the *Jiken*.

> The case is already providing grist for the mill for political commentators. The *Jiyūtō* [自由党] and *Kaishintō* [改進党] are covertly overjoyed for being given this issue (but they cannot press the government at this juncture because of the gravity of the situation).
>
> I happened to hear the rumor that the application of Article 116 is based upon a special imperial command [*tokushi* (特旨)]. We have been granted a Constitution by the Emperor. Can we therefore at this point say that there are reasons for the Emperor, by special imperial command, to have [the government] do something outside the law [*hōritsugai* (法律外)]? If this is true, public opinion will attack the government on the ground that the government is hiding behind the Emperor for stating that it was the Emperor who gave the special command to apply Article 116.

Inoue then warned that Itō Hirobumi [himself] would be the prime target, because no one will be fooled by saying that this wrongful application was based upon the judges' misjudgment. As part of his argument, Inoue cited Article 23 of the Constitution: "No Japanese subject will be arrested, detained, tried or punished unless according to the law." He further cautioned Itō against acting for political expediency [*seiryaku* (政略)] and strongly urged that Itō act according to the Constitution and the penal code since this matter is inextricably tied to Japan's very existence as a constitutional state [*kokka rikken no sonpai* (国家立憲の存廃)]. In other words, Inoue stated that if this case were mishandled, Japan's international prestige would be lost and that the seeds of a revolution would be planted. In short, Japan could be speeding toward a state of destruction.

Inoue concluded by writing: "Since this is a matter of great urgency compounded by my deepest sense of anxiety, I have left my sickbed to write this position paper."[63] He was the Education minister (*Monbu daijin* [文部大臣]) in the second Itō Hirobumi cabinet (8 August 1892 to 18 September 1896), and was involved in the attempt to modernize Japan's educational system. He served merely for a little over a year (7 March 1893 to 29 August 1894). We assume that his failing health was the reason. Inoue, in spite of his demanding public life, was not physically well in the last years of his life.

For his part, Ienaga Saburō (家永三郎), a renowned progressive scholar, disagrees firmly with the foregoing conclusion and contends that the *Ōtsu jiken* should not be a showcase for proving its role in the strengthening of an independent judiciary. Indeed, he reasons, the lesson from the *Jiken* is that Japan could not break free from the shackles of the immense power in the hands of the executive.[64]

---

63. Ibid., 382. He died of pulmonary tuberculosis in March 1895.

64. *Ōtsujiken nisshi* [大津事件日誌], Kojima Iken (児島惟謙), Ienaga Saburō (家永三郎), henchū (編注), Tōyō bunko, 187, Tokyo: Heibonsha, 1982, 274-275. A scholarly study that minutely dissects Kojima Iken's professional career undistorted by the lens of ideology is Ichikawa Kunitoshi, Ichihara Yasuhisa, Yoshida Eiji, *Kojima Iken (Korekata) no Kōseki* (児島惟謙の航跡) [Kansai Daigaku Hōgaku Kenkyūjo, Kenkyū Sōsho, No. 14]. (Suita-shi, Osaka-fu, 1996), i-vi, 1-283. See especially, 85-118, "Ōtsu jiken 'Ikensho' ni kansuru shomondai." We note two different publication dates, 1995 and 1996. The correct date is 1996. The authors also give Kojima's given name as Korekata. By coincidence, my research assistant's father's given name is Kenzō (謙三). He

It is relevant to note that Ienaga was not always the progressive he became after the war as the champion of the forces fighting against the textbook revision system. The details of the thirty-two-year-long court battles will not be related here. It is enough to point out that before his *hensetsu* [変節] (apostasy); he avidly supported Japan's war; venerated (*sūhai* [崇拝]) the imperial institution; and volunteered for the army officer training school. He was rejected for health reasons. He is lauded by some Koreans today for his stand on textbook revision, and was nominated twice for the Nobel Peace Prize by, among others, Noam Chomsky, Herbert Bix, John Dower, and Bruce Cumings.[65]

THE *ŌTSU JIKEN* AND JAPAN'S KOREA POLICY

What relevance does the *Ōtsu jiken* have to Japan's policies in colonial Korea (1905–1945)? This is our position: The *jiken* sheds light on, that is, expands our understanding of, Japan's moderate Korea policy. We acknowledge the existence of the strong antipathy against this position held by those who adhere to the nationalist historical paradigm. We present an expression of the nationalist historical narrative to frame support for our proposition.

Mark Caprio's *Japanese Assimilation Policies in Colonia Korea* examines Japan's assimilation policies in colonial Korea by delving into the vibrant debate between Japanese politicians, journalists, academics, and businessmen about Japan's assimilation of the Korean people. Caprio claims that cultural assimilation was doomed to failure whenever rhetoric was not put into practice; in fact, for

---

confirmed that 謙 may be read as "kata." University of Hawaii's Library has listed both books cited here under Kojima Iken.

65. See「日本の良心」家永三氏、教科書歪曲と３２年間 ("Japan's Conscience" Mr. Ienaga Saburō's 32-year Battle against Textbook Distortions). http://japanese.joins.com/article/297/115297.html?sectcode=&servcode=, and ウィキペディアフリ百科事典家永三 (Saburō Ienaga from Wikipedia, the free encyclopedia).

him, the fatal flaw of Japan's policy was its failure to convince the Japanese people to accept Koreans as imperial subjects. Caprio correctly notes that Japan's assimilation policies, as conceived of from the beginning, sought a gradual, cautious change to Korean culture. The GGK knew that "[r]adical change would disrupt the Korean social structure in a harmful way." Furthermore, Japanese assimilation practices did not seek to make Koreans a clone of themselves.[66]

Marie Seong-Hak Kim[67] deconstructs Caprio's severe critique of Japan's assimilation policy in Korea. In her article, she starts with a general description of colonial assimilation policies that reiterates the nationalist historical narrative:

> The imposition of an alien language on colonized subjects . . . brought about strenuous resistance to forcible acculturation; measures to incorporate the natives into political participation, if any, did not ensure political and civil equality. Assimilation was a corollary of imperial policy to obliterate the national identity of the colonized people and at the same time separate them systematically from the colonizers. Japanese colonial rule in Korea . . . *seemed to* combine the worst kinds of assimilation. Koreans were required to undergo cultural and even spiritual assimilation while subject to stark discrimination as an inferior people.[68]

---

66. Mark E. Caprio, *Japanese Assimilation Policies in Colonial Korea, 1910–1945* (Seattle: University of Washington Press, 2009), Chapter 3, especially 102-104. Caprio is Professor of Korean History at Rikkyō University in Tokyo.
67. Kim is Professor of History, St. Cloud State University in Minnesota and attorney at law. She began as a specialist on sixteenth-century French history and was a fellow at the Collegium de Lyon (École Normale Supérieure de Lyon) in 2011–2012. She was born in Korea and attended Ewha Women's University in Seoul.
68. Marie Seong-Hak Kim, review of *Japanese Assimilation Policies in Colonial Korea, 1910–1945*, by Mark E. Caprio (Seattle: University of Washington Press, 2009), in *The Journal of Japanese Studies* 37.2 (Summer 2011): 434-439.

She notes that Caprio regards assimilation as "the core agenda in Japanese colonial policies in Korea" but that it failed because the Japanese did not match their high sounding rhetoric with practice.

For a moment at this point, her analysis of Caprio gets somewhat confusing. It is unclear whether Kim is paraphrasing Caprio's description of Japan's assimilation policies or agreeing with the latter's description of Yanaihara Tadao's (矢原 忠雄) 1937 criticism of Japan's Korea policy, which stated:

> It is important then to ask what kept the Japanese on the path of seemingly blind pursuit of this ill-conceived and ill-executed assimilation policy, especially when other imperial powers in the early twentieth century had more or less abandoned the assimilation approach and embraced a more cooptative and accommodationist policy.

The rest of the article indicates that Kim was paraphrasing Caprio's arguments since she raises serious questions about Caprio's overly theoretical approach that results in ahistorical pronouncements. She writes, for example, that:

> . . . questions arise whether the author's formulation of the conception of assimilation in terms of the dichotomy of "political assimilation" and "cultural assimilation" is not *overly schematic*. Caprio largely equates political assimilation with the grant of suffrage, which took place—by necessity—gradually and partially, and cultural assimilation with the *decisive imposition* of the colonizer's language and education system, which entailed high-handed sweeping changes. But this framework seems too *topological*.[69]

69. Ibid

To this can be added that Hasegawa Yoshimichi urged "gradualism" in Korea reforms, a point that Palmer's recitation on Koreans in Japan's military also sustains. Moreover, Kim continues her criticism by describing Caprio's views as being "conceptually confining" and that "separating rhetoric and practice is not as clear-cut as the author seems to assume." She adds, "one wonders whether it would have been *more fruitful* if the author had considered factors *other than racial ideology* and attempted to explain Japanese colonialism against the backdrop of the European colonialism that was evolving contemporaneously with Japan's domination of Korea." Her analysis leads her to believe that "it may be a peremptory argument that assimilationist policy failed because of the Japanese belief in racial uniqueness and superiority. Caprio's emphasis on racial ideology steered the book largely toward cultural and geographical determinism." I believe that Kim makes this point to rebut Caprio's position.

Caprio's critique is that Japan did not "embrac[e] a more cooptative . . . policy."[70] The historical record, however, clearly reveals that the Japanese preferred "cooptation" over imprisonment or execution in Japan, and whenever possible, in Korea. The colonial authorities did not resort to the irredeemable alternative of death except when the colonized took to arms against the state. In Korea, this is exemplified by the instances of the conflict with the "Righteous Army" [*ŭibyŏng*] (義兵) and the tragic March First 1919 Independence Movement. Still, we submit that state authorities have the obligation to exercise this option for the greater good of "security and happiness" of others in the populace. The crucial caveat here is that the state that has this option must be a polity that is politically open and pluralistic; that is, there are options available to the populace to vent their dissatisfaction and opposition to state authorities in ways

70. Ibid.

that are not threatening to the existence of the state.

The final verdict on Tsuda was life imprisonment, a punishment proportionate to the crime. Our position is that the emphasis on and respect for proportionality stayed the hands of those in the GGK in dealing with Koreans even as we grant that individual bureaucrats at times did cross the line, a not uncommon occurrence everywhere. This point will be covered later in greater detail in our discussion of penal punishment.

Chapter Three

Japan and the Rule of Law

Japan at the time of the *Ōtsu Jiken* in 1891 had anti-government newspapers that were giving voice to opposition concerns; anti-government parties existed to noisily and sometimes physically thrash the authorities; elections were mandated and held as required and this showed that the trend was toward increasing powers in the hands of the parties, undergirded by their ineluctable role in compiling the national budget, thus compelling the government to compromise with them, which further increased their ranks in the Diet; and the judiciary without doubt was an independent branch of the government. All of these developments were anchored in and sanctified by the Meiji Constitution. They were gradually, and not reluctantly, extended to the colonies. It was this process that was crucial, and gave meaning, to assimilation of colonial peoples.

The struggle for judicial independence has been more than adequately covered. Since, however, this is a cornerstone of Japan as a relatively open and pluralistic polity, and its existence remains a key to understanding Japan's attitude and actions vis-à-vis the colonies, it behooves us to listen closely to the voices of two who stood at the forefront of the *Ōtsu Jiken.*

Itō Hirobumi in 1891 was arguably the most influential figure in Japanese public life, and as drafter of the Meiji Constitution is amply suitable to opine on this subject. The notation here cited is not specifically related to the *Ōtsu Jiken*, but it is worthy of notice that

Itō and Inoue Kaoru did not flinch when the Russian ambassador reacted angrily when informed by the two of the possibility that Tsuda would not be executed given the laws of Japan.

At the outset of this quote, Itō emphasized the rationale for the existence of the state in words familiar to readers of the American Declaration of Independence:

> The functions of the administrative are to carry out laws and to take such measures as may be found expedient for the maintenance of the public peace and order, and for the promotion of the happiness of the people; while the duty of the judiciary is to pronounce judgment upon infringements of rights, according to the provisions of the law. In the judiciary, law is everything, and the question of convenience is left out of consideration. . . . Such being the distinction between the nature of the administrative and that of the judiciary, were there only administrative officials and no judicial functionaries, the rights of individuals would be in danger of being made subservient to the ends of social convenience and would ultimately be encroached upon by power. Therefore trials must be conducted according to law; the law is the sole standard for conducting trials, which must always be conducted in a court of law.[1]

We know where the Supreme Court justices stood on the laws' primacy. What is less known is that their decision was not made in a political vacuum. Teters repeatedly makes the point that the justices as well as their countrymen were fully aware of the very existence of Japan was in jeopardy.[2]

Yet, Kojima stood firmly on the principle of the rule of law:

> [Whatever the feelings aroused by Tsuda's act] we must understand that the law is the spirit of the nation and judges

1. Itō Hirobumi, *Commentaries on the Constitution of the Empire of Japan*, trans. Itō Miyoji (Tokyo: Igirisu-Hōritsu Gakkō, 1889), 101.
2. Barbara Teters, 38-39, 42, 44-45, 51, 55, and 56.

> must not act on the basis of their personal feelings. . . . Therefore, no matter what the danger to the nation, those who are judges can only rely on the exact words of the law and so safeguard its spirit.[3]

Teters' judgment on Kojima's stand on law is unimpeachable:

> When the independence of the judiciary prevailed in spite of the awesome risk of war, it was likely to survive almost any test, and in the limited sense of the integrity of the judge or judges in deciding specific cases, it did so, its slight spirit remaining throughout even the tumultuous 1930s . . . the events of the sixteen days of crisis contributed greatly to Japan's legal modernization, since the existence of the modern state would be precarious at best without a professional judiciary. . . . Kojima's performance was no minor act of courage, and its consequences reach into the lives of individuals in post-World War II Japan.[4]

Judicial Independence in Japan in the 1930s

Professor, now emeritus, Richard H. Mitchell in two path-breaking studies shows that Teters is correct that the precedent set by Kojima and the Supreme Court served as the template for judicial independence in prewar Japan. The first study is focused on the Imperial Rayon Company corruption scandal, in popular parlance, the *Teijin* [帝人] *Incident* which concluded in December 1937. In this instance, the judges ruled in favor of the defendants who had been charged with illegal profiteering. Space constraints prevent us from going into detail, so we quote Professor Mitchell's basic conclusion:

> Their verdict ranks in importance with the famous *Ōtsu* case judgment, the benchmark for judicial independence . . . the *Teijin* case, . . . [is] another example of judges resisting

3. Ibid., 53.
4. Ibid., 38 and 60.

> outside pressures . . . during an emergency period (war in China began nearly six months before the judgment) and in the face of increasingly severe rightist pressures . . .[5]

We applaud Mitchell's conclusions but regret as well that he fails to acknowledge Teters' pioneering study on the *Ōtsu jiken.* In the second study, Mitchell examines the *Chian ijihō* (治安維持法) [Peace Preservation Law] that was enacted on 11 May 1925 to illustrate that the Japanese authorities have been unfairly tainted as being suppressive in dealing with those who opposed the law and the authorities who established it.[6] He stresses that while he does not want to "whitewash or excuse those who suppressed liberal ideas and democratic tendencies" the standard dark view had been based on the "self-serving complaints of Marxist scholars who have harshly condemned the entire prewar elite."[7]

Mitchell addresses the question of government attitudes and actions toward victims of thought control in three ways. First, he asks if police brutality reflected government policy and whether reports of brutality were "magnified." He answers "no" to the former, and "yes" to the latter. He asserts that "compared with the club-swinging, head-cracking approach . . . by German riot police in 1927 . . . [and] the techniques used by modernizing communist states, Japanese actions were mild."[8] Second, he then turns to an account of the mass trial of top Japan Communist Party leaders (25 June 1931–2 July 1932) and shows that presiding judge Miyagi Minoru (宮城実) of the Tokyo Appeals Court established the precedent of not sentencing anyone to death for violating Article 1 (1928 version) of the Peace Preservation Law. This policy remained unchanged until the end of

5. Richard H. Mitchell, *Justice in Japan: The Notorious Teijin Scandal* (Honolulu: University of Hawai'i Press, 2002), book jacket and p. 185. See also, review of Mitchell by James C. Baxter in *MN* 58.3 (Autumn 2003): 417- 419.
6. *Thought Control in Prewar Japan* (Ithaca: Cornell University Press, 1976).
7. Ibid., 13.
8. Ibid., 101.

the Pacific War.[9]

And third, Mitchell's analysis of "thought control" helps us to better comprehend the relationship between developments in Japan and assimilation:

> Thought control in Japan was different; . . . No mass application of terror, no Japanese executed in Japan under the provisions of the Peace Preservation Law [except for Ozaki Hotsumi] . . . no deportation or use of forced labor, . . . [These mild policies were based upon the] feeling that all Japanese were brothers under the emperor, and that no thought offender was beyond salvation.[10]

We submit that these two feelings were among the principles undergirding assimilation in Korea and the actions of the GGK. The actions of the colonial regime in Korea mirrored the activities of the police in Japan proper. The police force in Korea arrested and imprisoned nationalists and communists, but did not resort to a reign of terror to secure compliance to state policies. In fact, the state sought to convert and reform the recalcitrant, not eliminate them.

Sustaining Japan as a Modern, Open Society

It probably appears to most readers by now that I [Akita] am being overly sanguine in seeing Japan as a modernized, open society. Yet, support for this contention is shared by several sources, none of which has an overt ideological agenda.

Paul Miliukov (1859–1943) is described by Donald W. Treadgold (1922–1994) as "one of Russia's foremost historians and the most prominent leader of Russia's liberals." Miliukov admits that reading Karl Marx helped him shape part of his world view, but he insists

9. Ibid., 88, 104-113, and 128. Ozaki Hotsumi (尾崎秀実) is the only person who, on 7 November 1944, was executed for treason under the provisions of the law. The Pacific War by this time, and even earlier, was going badly for Japan.

10. Ibid., 191.

that he was never a "political radical," and was an anti-communist to the end.[11]

In his work *Russia and Its Crisis*, Miliukov writes that in 1903 he had heard a lecture by Iyenaga Toyokichi (家永豊吉). On the basis of this lecture, he compares the Russian and Japanese experiences in establishing their respective political institutions. He says that, "I think I have the key to the explanation of this similarity in parts and dissimilarity of the whole." He believes that the "process" by which both countries underwent "political unification and Europeanization" was similar. Yet, he continues, the "tempo" differed. By this he means that it "took centuries" for "political unification and Europeanization" to be achieved in Russia but only a "short space" of a few decades in Japan. The consequence for Japan is that "the ancient tradition of Japan . . . had no time to die out, and has kept enough of its vitality to be able to enter into some degree of combination with the elements of the new life and culture." Here we have Miliukov anticipating my unchanging emphasis on how the Meiji leaders had based their reforms on precedents stretching centuries into the past.

Miliukov concludes that the length of time it took for the process to work itself out meant that "no possibility of such a combination between new and old exists any longer in Russia."[12] While part of the narrative for Miliukov, the period between 1868 and 1903 appeared to be a "short space" of time; he also correctly "intuits" that Japan had built a foundation that stretched backward in time for centuries. Miliukov, however, confesses to puzzlement about one aspect of Iyenaga's talk, i.e., there is no reference to "any serious social or political struggle in his country." He then suggests that the lack of struggle perhaps means that "Japan is not so much democratized" as Russia, that Japan's public did not demand as much as

11. *Russia and Its Crisis*, Collier Books (London: Collier-MacMillan, 1962), with a Foreword by Donald W. Treadgold. "Foreword," 5-8. Treadgold himself was one of the most acclaimed American Russia specialists. He died in 1994.
12. Ibid., 402.

Russia's public. The other possibility; the one that he believes to be correct is that in Japan "much more is given" to the people than is Russia. His punch line is one that I ask the readers to take with them: "Japan [already] enjoys the elementary condition of progress—a free political life—which we [in Russia] are yet striving to attain." He praises the Japanese leaders for independently acting upon the "wise counsel . . . [of] the greatest of Russian statesmen, [Mikhail Mikhaylovich] Speransky" (1772–1839) that "patriotic battles" be held "not in the streets, not in the lecture-rooms of universities, not in annual sessions of Zemstvos, but within the walls of a national diet."[13]

Miliukov's reactions to Iyenaga's speech were anticipated in an address by T. M. Cooley, a former Chief Justice of the State of Michigan, and at that time a member of the United States Government's Interstate Commerce Committee and the author of *A Treatise on the Constitutional Limitations Which Rest Upon the Legislative Power of the States of the American Union*. He gave his speech at Johns Hopkins University (Baltimore, Maryland) on the evening of 17 April 1889, to commemorate the promulgation of the Constitution of Japan.

In the speech, he generalized about how governments made political concessions to its people and then contrasted the process elsewhere with what he saw happening in Japan. He noted that world history is full of examples of such concessions made to the populace by those who governed; that these are "won by the people in successful uprisings against their existing governments." He especially pointed to the Western world where in the nineteenth century, "every considerable advance has been at the cost of civil war." He then turned his attention to Japan:

> In all history I know of no recorded deed more noble or more commendable than that of the ruler of a great people who . . .

13. Ibid., 403.

> deliberately and without regret . . . lays down some portion of his authority, and invites his people to assume such share in the responsibilities of government as he believes them ready for.[14]

He follows this statement with the list of the preparatory steps taken by Japan's government, including the establishment of "local institutions . . . in which the people enter upon practical training for the higher duties of free government." This is *precisely the rationale* given by Yamagata Aritomo. Another thing that struck him is the "concessions of the privilege of participation in the legislative power to representatives of the people freely chosen." He continues: "What our ancestors only gained after a struggle with the rulers continued through many centuries." Cooley is here reiterating the proposition posited by Miliukov, who noted that Russia's "political unification and Europeanization" was a matter that took centuries, meaning that this was a commonly accepted interpretation of Europe's political history. He is particularly intrigued by the Bill of Rights in the Meiji Constitution that he notes is fuller and more detached than the Magna Carta, and he goes on to list all the rights, and ends with: "And then we have that great and vital principle, without which there can be no true liberty, that no subject shall be arrested, detained, tried or punished, unless according to law, and by the judges determined by law."[15]

FURTHER ANALYSIS OF IYENAGA

On 16 June 1889 Mutsu Munemitsu, Japan's ambassador to the United States (1888–1889), wrote a letter to Inoue Kaoru of Chōshū, a "founding father" of modern Japan. The contents are self-explanatory.

---

14. "On the Promulgation of the Constitution of Japan," *The Constitution of the Empire of Japan, with the Speeches Addressed to Students of Political Science in The Johns Hopkins University, Baltimore, 17 April 1889*, 25-29.
15. Ibid.

I have written two or three letters to you recently but have not received your replies. I am sure this is because of your hectic schedule. . . . I stressed that the reality is that once the national assembly is established, it is of the utmost importance that the cabinet must either (see to it that) it controls a majority (in the House of Representatives) or have a small group of steadfast and loyal representatives (beholden to it). In order to organize such a group, you will need to nourish supporters of considerable education and talent, especially those who are young. I have been trying to find those who would fit this description among Japanese students in America, but unfortunately, I have not been able to discover anyone who is particularly outstanding. Still, I have taken note of a student, Iyenaga (Toyokichi), at Johns Hopkins University in Baltimore who hails from the Yanagawa (han) [on the western edge of Fukuoka]. He was born as Tsuji (辻), and was a Niijima Jō (新島襄) disciple. I understand that he was a classmate of Tokutomi Iichirō (at Dōshisha). He is slated to receive next year his doctor of philosophy degree (ドクトル・ヲブ・ヒロソヒー) from Johns Hopkins University. He is quite fluent in speaking and reading English. I cannot now vouch for his character but from what I have observed, he is, first of all, not ostentatious but is conscientious and talented as well. Therefore, this young man's future is bright (he is between twenty-seven/twenty-eight to thirty years of age). This young man, however, has few funds with which to pursue his education, and he is paying for it entirely on his own (he does give an occasional speech as well as write newspaper articles and gives lectures [on Japan] when asked.) I believe that he is the kind of student who deserves some help, but given my own tightened private circumstances, I am limited to helping him purchase books. This is why I am reduced to asking you to help him in some way for two or three years at the rate of six hundred dollars a year. In any event, it will be very difficult [for Mutsu] to continue after that. I would appreciate a quick response from you on whether or not you will be

> able to support him. If you agree to help him, you will, of course, attach conditions, that is, he promises to work for you or someone you designate. I hope that you will be able to give full consideration to this matter. I realize that for me to ask you to render him this support will entail considerable expenditure of funds on your part. However, if you are able to help, I, of course, will be in your debt.[16]

Iyenaga Toyokichi was an outsider as a member of Tokutomi Sohō's (徳富蘇峰) Kumamoto Band (熊本バンド), an anti-Meiji government group; and as a student at Dōshisha University in Kyoto, he participated as a progressive in student movements.[17] He then attended school in the United States, graduating from Oberlin College, a fine liberal arts university in Ohio. (Edwin O. Reischauer, a postwar ambassador to Japan, some years later also graduated from Oberlin.) This was followed by his Masters and Doctorate at Johns Hopkins University.

Unlike Ienaga Saburō, however, he became a member of the Meiji government's elite Foreign Ministry, and later, in the United States, an ardent advocate of Japan's domestic and foreign policies.

So what we have here is the intriguing political phenomenon of two men with similar surnames whose life trajectories were both characterized by "*hensetsu*" who, however, moved in arcs that dif-

---

16. *Inoue Kaoru Monjo Fukuseiban Dai* 20 *Satsu* (井上馨文書複製盤 第２０冊), 154-158. The letter was copied from the microfilm version of *Inoue Kaoru Monjo* (Kensei Shiryōshitsu). Mr. Horiuchi Hiroo once again provided sterling help on this matter.

17. Iyenaga is not related to Ienaga Saburō of "textbook revisionism" fame, who writes that he had once heard that there was someone with the same surname. "Introduction" (*Jobun* [序文]) by Ienaga Saburō in *Iyenaga Toyokichi to Meiji Kenseishiron* [家永豊吉と明治憲政史論], edited and translated by Ōta Masao (Tokyo: Shinsensha, 1996), 1-2. I also wrote a second "Introduction," translated by Ōta Masao who lived briefly in Honolulu, pp. 3-6. Professor Masako Gavin (ギャビン真佐子), Bond University, Gold Coast, Queensland, Australia, is currently deeply into the life and works of Iyenaga. It already shows signs of becoming the definitive work on the subject.

fered from their respective beginnings. On the one hand, we have Iyenaga starting out as a "progressive" "anti-Meiji government" young student who later praised Japan's Meiji Constitution and became a government bureaucrat and later a "spokesman" for the Japanese government while residing in the United States.[18] And, on the other hand, as noted earlier, we have one who began before the War in the Pacific as an arch-conservative who praised Japan's wartime actions and who unreservedly exhibited obeisance to the emperor and then became a "darling" of the "progressive" camp after the war.

We now ask the reader to take note of three historical facts. The first is the earliness of the political developments praised by Cooley. His astonished reactions to Iyenaga Toyokichi's speech are dated 1889, a mere twenty-two years after the Meiji Restoration. The second is that a short two years later, in 1891, Kojima and Japan's Supreme Court justices struck their unqualified blow for judicial independence. The third is that Miliukov heard and enounced his positive analysis to Iyenaga's speech in 1903. More than a century later, China is still an authoritarian state; a subject to which we now turn our attention.

A Comparison of China and Japan

Japan's achievements in modernizing its polity are brought into sharper focus by comparing them with the pathways chosen by China. The manifold reasons for these choices are best left to China specialists. Here, we describe merely what China-watching journalists and China's former prime minister Zhao Zhiyang (趙紫揚) have said about the existing polity and the suggested remedies for reform of the polity. This approach will eliminate, we hope, any

18. An example of this is Iyenaga's high praise for the Government-General of Korea's "thoroughly reformed" Korean penal system, including the abolition of torture that according to him was also being praised by some foreigners. In Michael L. Sprunger, 96-97.

suspicion that we are engaging in China-bashing.

Hannah Beech and Austin Ramzy write about the Chinese authorities' reaction to the 2010 Nobel Peace Prize awarded to Liu Xiaobo (劉曉波): the Nobel Peace Prize awarded to Liu Xiaobo "may end up being a turning point in modern Chinese history, the moment at which China's people—and a world that has looked on enviously at its stellar economic record—realize the flaw in its development model." They then quote Ai Weiwei (艾未未) a human-rights advocate, "who was beaten so severely by Chinese police last year that he had to undergo cranial surgery," as saying: "Today, with China showing such a strong economic performance, there still hasn't been any change to the political structure, and [the government] avoids any discussion or recognition of different ideas. . . . The Nobel sends a signal to the young generation, to people who don't know the history, to remind them that the world is still concerned about China and common values."[19]

Melinda Liu and Isaac Stone Fish add an equally scathing denunciation in an article whose title explains their sense of outrage. We add two of their comments that are particularly apt: "most [political prisoners] disappear inside prisons, gulags, or 'black jails'—under 'house arrest' in squalid hotels or under lock and key in psychiatric institutions. In this dystopian world where prisoners have little legal counsel, medical care, or contact with the outside world, deaths behind bars are not uncommon." And, they quote Ai Weiwei: "What does it matter if China's economy grows when there are no basic protections for its citizens?"[20]

A reader takes away from the Beech and Ramzy interview of Ai a depressing feeling and at the same time an exhilarating high. Ai

19. Hannah Beech and Austin Ramzy/Beijing, "China's Eyes on The Prize," in *Time* 25 (October 2010): 40-43.

20. Melinda Liu and Isaac Stone Fish, "Portrait of the Gulag: Artist Ai Weiwei is freed. But China continues its harshest crackdown on political dissidents in decades," in *Newsweek International* 11 (July 2011): 48-51.

repeats several times that matters have not changed for the better: ". . . it's still the same machine. There's no judicial process or transparency . . . [the authorities] make sure you know that nothing can protect you, no law can protect you. They gave me the example of Liu Shaoqi (刘少奇) [the Chinese head of state who was persecuted during the Cultural Revolution and died in prison in 1969]. The constitution could not protect him, and today not much has changed." Ai stresses that "[w]e need clear rules to play the game. We need to have respect for the law."

Still, for all of his pessimism, Ai is hopeful about the future. The reason is the technological revolution of the internet that enables people to talk to each other. This means that the authorities cannot "completely censor the information and the knowledge available there." And the fact that the information can be circulated made him feel as if "a bullet [had been shot] out of the gun." At times he tweeted for twenty-four hours, and the words conveyed were "rich, real and spontaneous." He continues: "[The internet] really changes the landscape of the political situation." He sums up the whole of the situation in China with these words: "On the one hand [the power machine] is ruthless, but on the other hand it is so weak."[21]

We continue this theme by examining Clarissa Sebag-Montefiore's interview of Raymond Zhou, China's most famous movie critic. Zhou began his career as a movie critic when his salary in Silicon Valley was cut in half. He is now "the closest China has to a Roger Ebert-type personality" who also works as a reporter at the *China Daily*, a state-run paper. He states frankly that "there are many things that he cannot—or will not—write," given that he would become a non-person in the movie world. He argues that everything he writes is an honest opinion, but argues as well that he does not commit to writing "many things." "I don't have the freedom. [It's] like my

21. Hannah Beech and Austin Ramzy, "Ai Weiwei: The Dissident," in *Time* 178. 25 (26 December 2011): 105, 106 and 108.

hands are bound invisibly." He notes that criticism has been "stunted by corruption and bribes, state censorship . . ." Chinese do not read reviews because "the government, and filmmakers, work to ensure [that] only articles they endorse see the light of day." One bit of hope is the one pointed out by Ai Weiwei in his interview: "The young and tech-savvy are increasingly turning to online forums, where outspoken views are easier to come by." Another competent young man in technology supports the same notion: "For young people, the Internet is the most influential channel [to discuss movies] because anyone can get access to share and spread information."[22]

ADDITIONAL ANALYSIS OF CHINESE POLITICS

Bo Xilai (薄熙来) is a famous person in China and around the world. He is a Politburo member, and progeny of a founding father of modern China. A political tempest followed his dismissal as Chongqing's (重慶) Party secretary. Eric X. Li (李世默) is crucially concerned about which of two *extreme* ideological forces will emerge victorious in the wake of Bo's incarceration.

> On one side are the leftists, who believe China has lost its socialist way in its headlong pursuit of market economics and want the nation to go back to its past of a completely state-owned economy and dogmatic Leninist rule. On the other side are the liberals, who just cannot live with the fact that China is *succeeding* without multi-party elections and a Bill of Rights . . . [the cacophony resounding from the clash of these contending ideological forces deflect] our attention from the extraordinary progress China has gained in the last three decades and the *underlying consensus* that made it possible.

Eric X. Li is a venture capitalist so it is not surprising that he concludes that,

---

22. Clarissa Sebag-Montefiore, "Reel China: He's Beijing's answer to Roger Ebert" in *The Daily Yomiuri* (26 March 2012), based on a *Los Angeles Times* World Report.

> The quiet and steady currents of China's *mainstream*, along with the common sensibility of its leadership, will almost certainly continue to guide China on its path of pragmatism and moderation. The tide of history favors the large center.[23]

The five journalists mentioned above, for all their expertise are still outsiders looking in. For an insider's view, from one who was at the highest level of the Chinese government, we turn to Zhao Zhiyang who was "heir apparent to Deng Xiaoping" (鄧小平). He was purged as general secretary of the Chinese Communist Party and premier and sentenced to house arrest in 1989 for proposing "multi-channel dialogue and communication to persuade students to return to classes, and the avoidance of bloodshed at all costs." He so remained "until his death at 85 in 2005."[24]

During his incarceration "he secretly recorded his memoirs for posterity. *Gaige Licheng*, a transcript of about thirty cassette-tapes was smuggled out of China and, together with an English translation" published in June 2009 as *Prisoner of the State,* timed to coincide with "the eve of the 20th anniversary of the Tiananmen [天安門] crackdown."[25]

There is apparently an attempt to discredit *The Secret Journal.* Chan points to the "recent publications of Chinese 'secret' documents of dubious provenance," in "stilted and artificial language . . . [that] contrasts with the vivid, natural and unrehearsed style of

---

23. Eric X. Li, "Bo Xilai and the future of China" in *The Daily Yomiuri* (4 April 2012), from 2012 Global Viewpoint Network / Distributed by Tribune Media Services.
24. The content here is following Alfred L. Chan's (University of Western Ontario) review essay, "Power, Policy and Elite Politics under Zhao Ziyang": *Gaige Licheng* [改革歷程] (The Journey of Reform). Zhao Ziyang (Hong Kong: New Century Press, 2009); *Prisoner of the State: The Secret Journal of Zhao Ziyang*, Translated and edited by Bao Pu (鮑樸), Renee Chiang and Adi Ignatius (New York: Simon & Schuster, 2009). Reviewed in the *China Quarterly*, September 2010. Alfred L. Chan, 708 and 711.
25. Ibid., 708.

Zhao's tapes." To cope with the doubts cast upon Zhao's journal, the editors have "pledged to make the tapes readily available to open scrutiny," and to "await voice/speech expert confirmation" before pronouncing on its authenticity. China specialists inside and outside of China seem to have been drawn into the debate.[26] Chan argues that the hardliners were able to turn Deng against Zhao because the former, "of all the elders . . . was the most enamored with the method of dictatorship (of the proletariat) and the use of highly concentrated power to ensure stability and perpetuate communist party rule" Deng hated "those who took to the streets to make demands, and advocated summary and coercive methods to suppress such unrests."[27]

Zhao, for his part, is highly favorable in his view of Hu Yaobang (胡耀邦): Hu "undoubtedly sought democracy" and "would have pushed China's political reform forward along the path of modernizing the political system and democratization."[28]

Zhao gradually proceeded to complete the circle that Hu had begun to draw. The evolution in his views took some time to evolve, but not in a straight line (1986–1989). He started to believe in the "transparency of Party and state decision-making" that is, that the public needed to know; that "[d]ecisions on major issues should be made with ongoing consultation and dialogue with various social groups," and not only within the Party; that laws should be established to "guarantee . . . freedom of association, assembly, demonstrations, petitions, and strikes"; and that there is also the need for "greater press freedom" but "under management and leadership." In 1988, he began to see that, "[w]ithout an independent judiciary, the courts could not judge a case with a disinterested attitude, the

26. Ibid., 708-709;709, fn.2; 718.

27. Ibid., 712.

28. *Prisoner of the State: The Secret Journal of Zhao Ziyang*, Translated and edited by Bao Pu (鮑樸), Renee Chiang and Adi Ignatius (New York: Simon & Schuster, 2009), 255.

procurator could not exercise power independently, and even laws that were in place could not be carried out." Still, he believed that all the preceding would occur "under the Communist Party's . . . ruling position."[29] The ultimate changes in his belief system occurred after he stepped down in 1989. He records that:

> In fact, it is the Western parliamentary democratic system that has demonstrated the most vitality. . . . this system is not perfect; it has many problems. Yet relatively speaking, this system is best suited to a modern civilization, more adaptable to shifts in public opinion and most capable of realizing democracy. Moreover, it is more stable. . . . Why is there not even one developed nation practicing any other system? This shows that if a country wants to modernize, to realize a modern market economy, it must practice parliamentary democracy as its political system.[30]

Significantly, he does not mention at all China's neighbor Japan, which is a thriving parliamentary government.[31] Yet, he mentions Taiwan and Korea as being worthy of study for "gradually" making "the transition from their old systems to a parliamentary system."[32] These two Asian nations, of course, were former colonies of Japan, and one of our basic themes is that they benefitted in ways that enabled them to ascend economically and socially in the postwar years.

We close our discussion on Zhao with the three conditions he believes that China must adopt to achieve a parliamentary system. One,

---

29. Ibid, 256-260; 265-266.

30. Ibid., 270.

31. The word "democracy" is tossed around too loosely. Japan has never been a "democracy." It has been, since 1889, a constitutional monarchy with an emperor who has "authority" but cannot exercise political power. Yet Japan has all the traits mentioned by Zhao in his description of a "Western parliamentary democratic system." The United States, strictly speaking, also is not a "democracy" but a "republic."

32. Ibid., 271.

there should be multi-parties and a free press; two, the Communist Party should adopt democratic procedures and democratic means to reform itself, and three, the establishment of "reform of the legal system and an independent judiciary should take precedence."[33]

Zhao's aspirations for a parliamentary system went for naught when Deng allied himself with the Party elders who toppled Zhao. Instead, China adopted policies that turned China "*into a twenty-first-century economic powerhouse, with a renewed insistence on authoritarian autocracy*"—points emphatically underscored by Beech and Liu.[34]

If more evidence is needed that an independent judiciary is an indispensable component in a pluralistic, open society, one needs to look no further than the political instability confounding Egypt today. It is true that while this manuscript was being written (July 2013), the situation there evolved rapidly. On the one hand, supporters of the president Mohamed Morsi maintained that his decree to place himself beyond judicial oversight represented only a "temporary measure" that was to remain in force only until Egypt's Constituent Assembly enacted a new constitution and elected a new assembly. On the other hand, his opponents, with liberals and religious minorities forming the core, vigorously questioned his action, charging that Morsi's "ultimate goal" was the creation of a "rigid Islamic state no longer open to democratic freedoms." A scholar in the United States lent support to the anxiety of Morsi's critics by insisting that, "[Morsi] is not, and never has been, a moderate" and that he is instead, one who is determined to eradicate any group that disagrees with the Muslim Brotherhood's doctrines and actions. The overall view as of today is that Morsi's action has resulted in

33. Ibid., 271-272.

34. Ibid., 272-273. Italics in original; see also, "Epilogue" by Bao Pu, 275-281. I am grateful to Associate Professor Shana Brown and Assistant Professor Wen-sheng Wang (王文生), Department of History, University of Hawai'i at Manoa for providing the "characters" of names used in this segment.

demonstrations, and his eventual overthrow, that are reminiscent of the 2011 Tahrir Square protests.[35]

Jerome A. Cohen on China's Stagnant Legal System

The next voice belongs to Professor Jerome A. Cohen (b. 1930), without qualification, the most highly regarded scholar and specialist on China's legal and political systems. He is professor of law at New York University and a Senior Fellow for Asian Studies at the Council of Foreign Relations. He graduated from Yale (B.A.) in 1951, and earned his law degree at Yale in 1955. He then, as is the practice among bright law graduates, served as a law clerk for U.S. Supreme Court justices. He joined the faculty at the University of California in 1959, and subsequently moved to Harvard University's School of Law (1964–1981). He spent a year (1971–1972) as a visiting professor of law at Dōshisha University in Kyoto on a Fulbright grant.

He is currently visiting professor at the University of Hawai'i's William S. Richardson School of Law. In an interview with Michael Tsai of the *Honolulu Star-Advertiser* (13 January 2013), Cohen revealed that he was directly involved with the U.S. State Department and Chinese leaders to find a "face-saving solution" to free "the blind self-educated Chinese lawyer" Chen Guangcheng (陳光誠) that resulted in Chen being allowed to leave China. The quality of Cohen's scholarly integrity shines through in his admission *in print* that he still does not "fully understand [how] Chen escaped from house arrest and made his way to the American Embassy in Beijing." He further states that "[a]fter a series of stranger-than-fiction twists and turns, Chen was eventually allowed to leave the country." He admits that he still "isn't sure what strings were pulled

35. "The most important man in the Middle East: An exclusive interview with Egypt's Mohamed Morsi," *Time* cover story (10 December 2012): 30-39.

and by whom." Given his achievements, stature, and universal acclaim he has earned, he did not have to admit, not once but twice, his ignorance. This makes his comments about contemporary China's stagnant politico-judiciary system highly credible.[36]

His basic conclusion is literally a bombshell: "China's leaders are sitting on a volcano." He then told Tsai that he was a "*long a believer that greater rule of law* can help China realize its vast global potential," but regretfully notes that, "[m]any hopes for legal reform were lost in the last five years or so," and in language that Zhao would have applauded, states:

> Many people hoped to develop an independent court system and rule of law that would place government and the Communist Party under the rules of society. Instead, there has been a contrary and repressive spirit and paranoia among leaders, even as people are demanding a better legal system.

We close this section by noting that Cohen calls attention to a generally held, scary scenario; that is, the

> Chinese leadership diverting attention away from internal political strife and toward something external that can be used to mine nationalistic fervor. A conflict with Japan in the South China Sea, perhaps.

Cohen's position adds a dimension lacking in the *New York Times*' 3 January 2013 editorial; that is, the tensions in the region should not be viewed as a "one-way street" situation. Unfortunately, the Chinese also vehemently reject the "two-way street" proposition. To avoid distortion of the contents of the source that reveal China's preference for the "one-way street" interpretation, I cite it in verbatim:

> In a *harsh* statement Sunday, China accused Secretary of

36. Michael Tsai, "Attorney visiting UH shares insight on China," in *Honolulu Star-Advertiser*, 13 January 2013.

> State Hillary Rodham Clinton of presenting *a distorted picture* about its dispute with Japan over islands in the East China Sea, and it expressed "*resolute opposition*" to her position.
>
> The Foreign Ministry said Clinton "ignores the facts and confuses right and wrong" in a short description she gave of the situation at a news conference Friday in Washington.
>
> The *unusual objection*, released as Clinton prepares to step down as secretary of state, appears to have been prompted by a new phrase used by Clinton in what was an otherwise standard reference to the escalating feud between China and Japan.
>
> With Japan's foreign minister at her side, Clinton said that the Obama administration opposed "any unilateral actions that would seek to undermine Japanese administration" of the islands, known as Diaoyu in China and Senkaku in Japan.
>
> The reference to unilateral actions was interpreted in the Japanese media as meaning that the United States was unhappy with China's recent actions in the East China Sea, where the islands are located.[37]

The position taken by the editorial page of the *New York Times* also appears to have been contradicted in a later *Times* article. Jane Perlez writes that the Philippines will "challenge China's claims in the South China Sea before a United Nations tribunal." She goes on to cite two university specialists, one from each country, who predict that that action will be an exercise in futility, given that any negotiation mandated by the U.N. panel would require China's participation, to which China would not agree.[38]

---

37. Jane Perlez, "China Criticizes Clinton's Remarks about Dispute with Japan over Islands," *The Honolulu Star-Advertiser*, 21 January 2013, citing a *New York Times* dispatch from Beijing.
38. "Japan Makes Overture to China in Islands Dispute," *The New York Times*, 22 January 2013. See also, "Philippines Seeks UN help to resolve maritime row

JAPAN'S COLONIAL POLICIES IN A GLOBAL CONTEXT

As shown above, Korean nationalists claim that Japan's colonial record was uniquely malevolent and, as a result, the Koreans' suffering was unlike that of any other people. This claim cannot be taken at face value. A fruitful approach to scrutinize this claim, and to sustain our premise (that Japan's colonial policy was moderate), is to compare the colonial records of all major colonial powers with each other.[39] Japan did not act in a vacuum; Western powers had colonized nearly all of Africa and large swaths of Asia by the 1910s. In this global environment, Japan had adopted many its practices from other imperial powers. A brief exploration of the global environment during the Age of Imperialism provides valuable nuance to this book's argument by contrasting Japan's colonial record with that of the Western powers.

This discussion begins by noting that all colonial powers operated under a constant anxiety that their colonial subjects might rebel if the regime failed to act swiftly and forcefully at the first sign of resistance. The Sepoy Rebellion in British India in 1857 loomed heavily in the minds of imperial powers. Imperialists realized that they never had total control over their subjects; indeed, hegemony was "a process continuously negotiated, contested, defended, renewed, recreated, and altered."[40] A nervousness that their colonies might rebel contributed to abuses by the Dutch, Portuguese, Germans, British, French, Americans, and Japanese. Still, even a brief foray into the colonial policies and practices of Western Powers will be useful to determine whether the "Koreans lived under the most ruthless colonial rule ever known in history,"

---

with China," *Reuters*, 22 January 2013.

39. This segment is written by Brandon Palmer.

40. Gi-Wook Shin and Michael Robinson, "Introduction: Rethinking Colonial Korea," *Colonial Modernity in Korea*, eds. Gi-Wook Shin and Michael Robinson (Cambridge, MA: Harvard University Asia Center, 1999), 9.

as maintained by some Koreans.[41]

Indeed, a survey of global colonial practices yields numerous instances of forced labor, economic exploitation, and destruction of recalcitrant villages, with occasional forced relocation and racial segregation. With the exception of the Philippine-American War (1899–1902), this discussion does not address the wartime actions of colonial powers in their colonies. For example, this discussion does not look at the French colonial wars in Indochina (1945–1954) or Algeria (1954–1962), in which French forces killed hundreds of thousands of Indochinese soldiers and civilians in Vietnam and over a half million Algerian soldiers and civilians in Algeria; nor does it address the Indonesian War of Independence (1945–1949) in which Dutch forces killed 50,000 to 100,000 Indonesian soldiers in military action and another 25,000 to 100,000 civilians.

Numerous colonial states imposed forced labor requirements on their colonies, often requiring subjects to work on plantations or government projects. The process involved appropriating land for plantations from the rightful owner and then forcing the dispossessed owner to work on the plantation. These plantations, as well as the extraction of various natural resources, were central to the profitability of colonialism in Africa and Southeast Asia. Yet, sufficient cheap labor for the plantations, the mines, and elsewhere was often not always readily available. As a result, workers were in some instances compelled by military force and by other forms of coercion to work salaried jobs for a pittance so they could pay their taxes in cash. In most cases, the "labor's exploitation and conditions resembled slavery," despite the global abolition of the slave trade.[42]

The most infamous system of forced labor was in King Leopold II's Congo Free State (1885–1908). The Congo was the king's personal colony, and his primary objective was to maximize profits. To

41. Shin Yong-ha, 238.

42. *Encyclopedia of African History*, s.v. "Plantations and Labor, Colonial."

this end, his agents had free reign to collect rubber and ivory in any manner they wanted. Leopold's agents established a

> new system [that] encouraged widespread abuses and horrific violence against Africans. Individuals who did not meet their assigned quotas were beaten, whipped, and tortured. Mutilations became a common punishment to heighten fear and to set an example for others. Recalcitrant villages were burned, and women were taken as hostages until rubber or other goods were procured.[43]

In some areas of the Congo, heavy labor was conducted by chain gangs in conditions that were thinly veiled forms of slavery.[44] Under the Belgians, systemic levels of abuse that included murder, rape, starvation, and neglect—coupled with flight—led to a drastic decline in the Congo's population. In 1885, at the beginning of the Belgian colonization, the population was between 20 and 30 million, but had dropped to 8.5 million by 1911.[45]

The Dutch, for their part, instituted a system of compulsory labor in the Dutch East Indies (modern Indonesia) to collect cash crops such as coffee, tobacco, indigo, and sugar from 1830 to 1870, with parts of the system still in place as late as 1917. Known as the cultivation system (*Cultuurstelsel*), the Dutch colonial regime introduced taxes that mandated Javanese peasants "to devote one-fifth of [their] land or sixty-six working days in a year for the cultivation of cash crops for the government," but the Dutch and their Indonesian partners in exploitation confiscated as much as half of the harvest.[46] This system of forced labor, disguised as taxation, diverted

43. *Encyclopedia of African History*, s.v. "Congo (Kinshasa), Democratic Republic of / Zaire: Congo Free State, 1885–1908."

44. Georges Nzongola-Ntalaja, *The Congo from Leopold to Kabila: A People's History* (New York: Zed Books, 2002), 20-21.

45. Ibid., 22.

46. D.R. SarDesai, *Southeast Asia: Past & Present*, 5th ed. (Boulder: Westview Press, 2003), 96.

much needed land and manpower to harvesting cash crops, thereby causing a decline in food production. The result was periodic famines, including one in 1850 that killed upward of 300,000 people.[47]

French, Germans, Portuguese, and British likewise used taxes to impose forced labor on their African colonies. European regimes required taxes be paid in cash, thereby coercing Africans into wage labor. For all practical purposes, many of these forced laborers were slaves of the state or private investors.[48] The French, for instance, instituted systems of forced labor to harvest coffee in Madagascar that continued until after World War II; Portuguese systems of forced labor killed over 300,000 Africans in Angola; and the French in Mali used military conscription laws to funnel men into forced labor corps.

Colonial governments were frequently challenged by armed rebellions which they suppressed to restore peace in the colony. For example, the Japanese military, in an effort to subdue the Korean "Righteous Army" (*ŭibyŏng*) killed an estimated 17,600 Koreans from early in the colonial period.[49] Koreans accuse the Japanese army of also burning villages and summarily executing prisoners. These statistics should be compared to the actions of the United States, supposedly a benign colonial power, that it too was not exempt from committing horrific acts. The American military in the Philippines resorted to harsh measures from 1899 to 1902 to crush the Philippine insurrection. "The U.S. Army confiscated the property of prominent revolutionaries and harassed their relatives" and "also sanctioned crop destruction and the concentration of the civilian populations of certain villages in camps to cut the guerrillas

---

47. Ibid., 97.
48. Gerald J. Bender, *Angola under the Portuguese: The Myth and the Reality* (Berkeley: University of California Press, 1978), 139, fn. 14. An Englishman, who visited Angola in 1902, claimed that half the population "lived under some form of slavery."
49. Carter J. Eckert et al., *Korea, Old and New*, 244.

off from their supplies and shelter." Furthermore, the Army "tried and occasionally executed captured guerrillas, and Army provost courts . . . were given a free hand to try and punish suspects without evidence."[50]

During this little known Philippine-American War (1899–1902), Major General Arthur MacArthur, father of famed General Douglas MacArthur, "ordered increased attention to the destruction of the civilian infrastructure in the towns that supplied the guerrillas with food, information, and shelter."[51] The pacification of Philippine territory was "characterized by an unusual degree of ferocity" that included the relocation of populations in rebel territory into "protected zones" and concentration camps so that the military could eliminate those outside the camps.[52] The United States Army was so brutal in repressing resistance that the colonial regime faced a serious legitimacy crisis among the Filipino population. The Americans pursued moderate policies and shared power only after all resistance was crushed. General Franklin Bell "estimated before a Senate committee that 600,000 Filipinos died of disease in concentration camps or on the battlefields of Luzon alone" and that upward of "a million—one-seventh of the total population—were killed" in the process of pacification.[53] Still, even after the country had been pacified, the American colonial government "denied Filipinos full civil liberties" and "deployed police surveillance to track suspected subversives, both Filipino and foreign."[54]

European colonial powers, much like America, also utilized in-

50. Brian M. Linn, *The U.S. Army and Counterinsurgency in the Philippine War, 1899–1902* (Chapel Hill: University of North Carolina Press, 1989), 25.
51. Brian M. Linn, *Guardians of Empire: The U.S. Army and the Pacific, 1902–1940* (Chapel Hill: University of North Carolina Press, 1997), 14.
52. Brian M. Linn, *Guardians of Empire*, 14, and D.R. SarDesai, 158.
53. D.R. SarDesai, 158.
54. Alfred W. McCoy, *Policing America's Empire: The United States, the Philippines, and the Rise of the Surveillance State* (Madison: University of Wisconsin Press, 2009), 60.

ternment camps to subdue their colonies. In German South-West Africa (modern Namibia), the Germans forced the Herero people into concentration camps from 1906 to 1908. Prisoners in these camps were used as forced laborers despite malnourishment. Abuses, starvation, and disease in these camps resulted in the death of nearly half of the Herero population. After the concentration camps were closed, the Herero were either deported or dispersed, and the Germans established a social system much like the apartheid of South Africa.

Even the British used internment camps in several of their colonies to suppress resistance. An early example of concentration camps appeared during the Second Boer War (1899–1902) in South Africa. In order to weaken local support for the Boer settlers, British troops employed a scorched earth policy and destroyed fields, homesteads, and livestock, forcing tens of thousands of people to move into internment camps. Approximately 25,000 people died of disease and starvation in these camps. "Measles, pneumonia, dysentery and typhus were endemic" within the camps due to inadequate sanitation and medical care; "28,000 Europeans [Boers] died in the camps, 22,000 of them children, whose natural lack of resistance to illness was made worse by the poor diet offered by the army authorities."[55] Nobody counted the number of Africans who died. The British again used these camps during the Mau Mau Revolt in Kenya (1952–1960), calling it the "villagization policy." Common peasants were forcibly moved into guarded villages and detention camps to deprive the rebels of support from the local population.

On a grander scale, British colonies in Africa racially segregated the African and White populations through the establishment of reserves for African natives. South Africa, a dominion state, in 1913

55. Laurence James, *The Savage Wars: British Campaigns in Africa, 1870–1920* (New York: St. Martin's Press, 1985), 69.

"confined chiefdoms to small, barren reserves."[56] These discriminatory laws, which favored and protected white laborers at the expense of Africans, predated Apartheid by decades. Similar laws were passed in Southern Rhodesia in 1930. The colonial administration in Southern Rhodesia racially divided the whole country, with nearly 40 percent of land, the most fertile and valuable, being reserved exclusively for the white settlers, while the Africans were given barren land. These systems mirrored the "native reserves" established in Kenya that reserved the best lands for British settlers.

Nevertheless, how does the Japanese policy in Korea compare the Western experience? Keith Pratt, a British academic at Durham University, referred to the first decade of colonial rule in Korea as "a reign of terror."[57] Yet, was the "terror" that Koreans faced comparable to the forced labor, concentration camps, or racial policies discussed above? This study argues that it was not. First, Japan did not resort to forced labor as was found in the Dutch East Indies or in the British, French, Belgian, and Portuguese African colonies; second, the Japanese did not forcibly relocate Koreans into concentration camps as part of the pacification campaign from 1907 to 1910—something the Americans, Germans, and British had done in their colonies; and third, the Japanese expended greater efforts, mostly after the March First Uprising, than most other colonial powers to build Korea a modern infrastructure, education system, and economy.

---

56. *Encyclopedia of African History*, s.v. "South Africa: Capitalist Farming, 'Poor Whites,' Labor."

57. Keith Pratt, *Everlasting Flower: A History of Korea* (London: Reaktion Books, 2006), 213. Pratt is citing Andrew Nahm but does not provide a citation for the quote. Pratt also states that "Japan's colonialism needs to be understood . . . as a step toward the fulfillment of an age-old dream of continental domination." 213.

A Comparison of Colonial Modernization

Adherents of the national historical narrative seemingly are unable to acknowledge that anything positive came from the colonial era. For example, one study on Christianity in Korea maintained that Japanese "policies were thoroughly destructive" to Korean society and that the education system was designed to destroy Korea's social fabric.[58] Even Japan's contributions to modernization and industrialization are criticized by nationalist Korean historians; they "posit a disjuncture between colonialism and modernity because they assume that colonial rule either destroyed or distorted Korea's effort to modernize."[59] Many nationalist academics also discount Japan's introduction of modernity and social development into colonial Korea.

> Some scholars, especially those in Korea, are reluctant to examine modernity in the colonial context. For them, modernity signifies historical progress, and as such it cannot possibly be associated with such retrograde phenomena as colonialism; the latter hinders the creation of a "true" modernity or at best produces a "distorted" development.[60]

Colonial modernity is a contested area of academic discussion. Korea's introduction to the modern world, and all it offered, came largely while Korea was a colony. As a result, the colonial regime diluted and filtered, Koreans say warped and corrupted, the average Koreans' exposure to the modern age and contemporary social movements. Yet, a close appraisal of the Koreans' expectations from the colonial state, as well as the criticisms lodged by those same Koreans over how policies were implemented, reveal contradictions between what Koreans expected of Japan. On the one hand, Koreans

58. In Soo Kim, *Protestants and the Formation of Modern Korean Nationalism, 1885-1920* (New York: Peter Lang, 1996), 155-156.
59. Gi-Wook Shin and Michael Robinson, 5.
60. Ibid., 10-11.

charge that the GGK did too little to modernize Korea (in its offerings of public health facilities, educational facilities, and industrial financing), but on the other, criticize the colonial regime for bringing too much change to Korean culture. Within the nationalist historical narrative, Japan is condemned for every action and inaction.

To better understand Japan's colonial endeavor in Korea as moderate and proportional by global standards there is a need to compare Japan's educational record with the Western colonial powers and then move to examine Japan's other accomplishments in light of existing global practices. But before delving into Japan's educational accomplishments, it is necessary to establish the baseline from which the Japanese started. Korea had a sizable class of literate men. In traditional Korea, political power was held exclusively by members of the *yangban* (the hereditary elite) class who had passed the Confucian civil service exams. Boys and men preparing for the exams attended village Confucian academies (*sŏdang*) that taught them the Confucian classics as well as morals and ethics. Philip Jaisohn (Sŏ Jae-p'il) (1864–1951), a renowned Korean nationalist, condemned the educational efforts of the Yi dynasty. He wrote:

> The most cruel punishment a government can inflict upon its governed is to deprive them of the facilities of obtaining an education. Under the old Korean custom the government not only failed to provide the people with facilities of getting an education but actually discouraged them from having any. It was part of the scheme of the ruling classes to keep the people ignorant so that they could not complain about the unjust treatment which the government imposed upon them.[61]

The conservative Yi government clung to the old way of life and method of rule well into the 1890s; it even attacked progressive

61. Philip Jaisohn and Sŏn-p'yo Hong, *My Days in Korea and Other Essays* (Seoul: Yonsei University, 1999), 67.

elements within and outside the government. The result was that modernization was a low priority in Korea prior to 1905. Michael J. Seth, author of *Education Fever: Society, Politics, and the Pursuit of Schooling in South Korea* wrote that in 1904 "public education was confined mainly to Seoul" and that there "were only seven or eight primary schools operating in Seoul. . . ."[62] The total enrollment in modern public schools was around 500 pupils—for a nation of 12 million. To these numbers should be added hundreds of private schools, mostly run by Christian missions. All told, the GGK was essentially building a modern education system from scratch.

The colonial government moved at a steady pace to provide students a modern education that would prepare them for the new age of industry and technology. From these humble origins, the number of students registered in government-run primary schools grew from 20,100 in 1910 and to 901,200 in 1937. The total number of students attending all schools, excluding the Confucian academies, jumped from 110,800 in 1910 to 1,211,400 in 1937; one-fourth of all students were female. While these numbers show tremendous progress, only one in three school-aged children attended school. The Japanese regime had to account for the tax burden extensive school construction put on the average peasant, after all, it was the Korean peasantry that paid for the new schools. During the war the GGK had planned for the establishment of compulsory education in 1946.

Korean nationalists denounce the curriculum in schools for focusing on Japanese language, morals, and values; they note that education was a political tool to create loyal subjects of the emperor. And indeed, the tone of the curriculum borrowed heavily from the colonial tone of the day. Michael J. Seth states "Japanese ultranationalism and militarization pervaded the entire school system. . . ."[63] Students in the colonial education system were sub-

62. (Honolulu: University of Hawai'i Press, 2002), 16-17.
63. Ibid., 27.

jected to an education that told them that "factionalism was deeply engrained in the Korean political culture" and that "Korean society prior to annexation had been utterly stagnant."[64] The purpose of this education was to strengthen Japan's position in Korea, much like the hegemonic education systems in French Vietnam, the American Philippines, and even within the United States where Native Americans were forced to assimilate. An important purpose of education in all colonies is to promote loyalty, to solidify unity, and to strengthen the government. A word of caution is in order, however: care must be used against tossing around incendiary, emotion-laden terms such as "ultranationalism" and "militarization," words that cry out for precise defining, without which scholarly discussion is difficult.

Adherents of the national historical paradigm emphasize the discrimination against students within the classroom as well as the differences between schools for Japanese and Korean students. Seong-Cheol Oh and Ki-seok Kim, both of Seoul National University, note that "insufficient opportunities for secondary and post-secondary education [was] a serious social problem."[65] Koreans seeking a higher education often had to pursue their degree in Japan or a Western country. They also criticize the colonial education system for providing too few occupational opportunities for Korean graduates. The lack of employment opportunities, it must be acknowledged, is an area of legitimate criticism against Japan, even if Japan compares well to other colonial powers. For example, the highest-ranking Korean in the colonial railway system immediately after Japan's surrender was an assistant deputy stationmaster.

Japan, it must be remembered, unlike its Western counterparts had just become a colonial power. Still, the Japanese record for

---

64. Henry H. Em, 12.

65. Seong-Cheol Oh and Ki-Seok Kim, "Expansion of Elementary Schooling under Colonialism: Top Down or Bottom Up?" in *Colonial Rule and Social Change in Korea, 1910-1945*, eds. Hong Yung Lee, Yong-Chool Ha and Clark Sorensen (Seattle: University of Washington Press, 2013), 125.

secondary and higher education was comparable to Western colonial powers even when taking into account the small percentage of students that advanced beyond primary school. The GGK, in line with "gradualism," was consumed by providing a primary education to all villages before expanding secondary offerings. Colleges and teachers' seminaries had 6,313 registered students in 1939, plus another 206 students enrolled in Keijo Imperial University, Korea's only university (founded in 1925). In addition to these students, thousands of Koreans pursued their education in Japan. As of 1942, approximately 14,000 pupils were enrolled in secondary education schools in Japan and another 6,771 Koreans were enrolled in Japanese colleges and universities.

The record shows, in fact, that Japan had one of the best records of colonial education when compared against African and Southeast Asian colonies. Even granting that only one third of eligible Korean children attended school, this compares favorably to French Cambodia, where in 1944 "less than 20 percent of the male school-age population" was enrolled in schools; the percentage for female students was significantly lower. Secondary education in Cambodia *began* in 1933, but was still nominal as of 1944. Furthermore, there was no university in Cambodia, and by 1953 only 144 Cambodians had university diplomas.[66] These numbers are all the more dismal considering that the French had been in Cambodia since 1863, while Japan's Protectorate was established in 1905.

The French record in Vietnam is equally bleak. In Vietnam, modern "education reached one in every ten school-aged children"[67]

---

66. Thomas Clayton, "Restriction or Resistance? French Colonial Educational Development in Cambodia," *Education Policy Analysis Archives* 3.9 (1995): 5.

67. Gail P. Kelly, "Colonialism, Indigenous Society, and School Practices: French West Africa and Indochina, 1918–1938," in *Education and the Colonial Experience*, ed. Philip Altbach and Gail P. Kelly. (New Brunswick, NJ: Transaction Books, 1984), 12. Vietnam had an estimated population of 19 million, which

and, as in Korea, until the reforms of *bunka seiji*, the education system was segregated: one for children of the colonizer and one for the colonized. Predictably, the quality of the schools for Vietnamese was inferior; the "history and language curriculum of [these] schools pointed out that Vietnamese were unable to rule themselves . . . [and were] ignorant."[68] Also, the teacher salaries, like other French civil servant salaries, were triple those of their Vietnamese counterparts who performed the same tasks. Frenchmen were also provided housing allowances and leave with pay, benefits not available to the Vietnamese.[69] While benefits, such as pay bonuses, were used to entice Japanese from the homeland to go to work in Korea, the pay and benefits were modest when compared to those given to the French.

French West Africa's education system was worse than Vietnam's. In "West Africa, the schools accommodated 4.7 in every 1,000 children according to the most optimistic French estimates."[70] Also, in West Africa "the school system . . . lacked objective criteria for student selection" and the program "lacked centralization" and suffered as well from bureaucrati[zation] and was not "particularly based on meritocracy." Instead, the system "serve[d] almost exclusively the sons of chiefs and notables, and the school authorities were called upon to sustain this elite through the years of primary education."[71] Secondary education opportunities were extremely limited; there was only one university in of French West Africa, and even then, "more than half of the university students were French."[72]

---

was close to Korea's at that time.

68. Gail P. Kelly, "Conflict in the Classroom: A Case Study from Vietnam, 1918–1938," *British Journal of Sociology of Education* vol. 8, no. 2 (1987), 196.
69. Ibid., 194.
70. Gail P. Kelly, "Colonialism, Indigenous Society," 12.
71. Ibid., 11.
72. Walter Rodney, *How Europe Underdeveloped Africa* (Washington, D.C.: Howard University Press, 1981), 244.

As of 1937 there were only 631 students from West Africa enrolled in universities in Africa and Europe. In contrast, the British established four universities in its African colonies in 1948, but the student population at these universities was dominated by children of the white settlers.[73]

The British had a mixed educational record in her colonies. Most British colonies were governed through indirect rule, a system that left day-to-day power in the hands of the traditional elites. This meant education was largely in the hands of the indigenous rulers, who in turn left modern education to private organizations such as Christian missions. The education that emerged in English colonies catered to the elite classes, but did little for the peasants. In India, higher education was available, and in 1914 there were 50,000 university students out of the Indian population of over 300,000,000.[74] Yet, the literacy rate for the general population was an abysmal 12 percent.

British and French education in Africa both focused on molding students into subservient peasants, not laborers or active citizens. The schools instilled within the pupil a hierarchy that made the student feel inferior to the European ruler. A difference between the British and French education was that the French "made no sustained effort to prepare local people for self-sufficiency, higher education, free trade, . . . political participation, or independence." This education catered to the long-term goals of the colonial state, namely, it justified the subjugation of the colonial peoples and extoled the virtues of the overlord. For the French, this meant that the education "involved infantilizing their colonial protégés."[75]

The illiteracy rate in colonial Africa, as a continent, was between

73. *Encyclopedia of Western Colonialism since 1450*, s.v. "Education, Western Africa."

74. H.L. Wesseling, *The European Colonial Empires, 1815–1919*, trans. Diane Webb (New York: Pearson Longman, 2004), 62.

75. *Encyclopedia of Western Colonialism since 1450*, s.v. "French Indochina."

80 to 85 percent.[76] Among the worst colonial powers was the Portuguese.

> Portugal boasted that Angola, Guinea, and Mozambique have been their possessions for five hundred years, during which time a "civilizing mission" has been going on. At the end of five hundred years of shouldering the white man's burden of civilizing "African natives," the Portuguese had not managed to train a single African doctor in Mozambique, and the life expectancy in eastern Angola was less than thirty years.[77]

Portuguese colonial education, which also focused on cultural assimilation, had prohibitively high school fees that prevented nearly all children from attending school, and those who attended public schools received a low quality education.

The worst colonial educational system was Belgian Congo's. The Belgians neglected the human resources of their African colony and focused solely on extracting the colony's wealth. They made "the choice not to develop an indigenous elite." And "[s]econdary and university education were seriously neglected."[78] When the Congo gained independence in 1960, fewer than twenty in a country of 13 million had college degrees.

One of the best educational records was the United States in the Philippines, largely because America was preparing the Filipinos for self-rule. Schools in the Philippines offered an American-style education, which included an emphasis on the English language. There were no fees or tuition for primary school, and opportunities for secondary and higher education were readily available. Atop this system were five universities.

Let us now compare the educational records of three Southeast

---

76. Walter Rodney, 245.
77. Ibid., 206.
78. *Encyclopedia of Western Colonialism since 1450*, s.v. "Belgium's African Colonies."

Asian countries, "At the end of the colonial era only 8 percent of the Indonesian population were literate. In French Indochina this was 10 percent . . . but in the American Philippines the rate of literacy was no less than 50 per cent."[79] In comparison, the literacy rate among Koreans "was still below fifty percent" in 1945.[80]

A Comparision of Social and Economic Colonial Policies

A comprehensive comparison of Japan's accomplishments and shortcomings with the Western colonial powers is beyond the scope of this essay. Nevertheless, it is worthwhile to summarize a number of the major investments Japan made in Korean society to show that Japan was not an imperialistic vampire that sucked the lifeblood out of her colonies. Takashi Fujitani has stated that

> [W]hat we can perceive in an abundance of official documents and policies of the period, especially from 1937 on, is a new commitment to improve the health, education, and welfare of the Korean people. Whether the intentions of colonial administrators and others serving in unofficial organizations supporting the state were noble or sincere does not concern me here. For now, it is enough to note that *they acted as if their charge was to work harder to nurture the lives of the Korean people* and that when they noted improvements in indices measuring the health, wealth, and happiness of the Korean people, they argued for the necessity of doing more.[81]

The largest investment Japan made in Korea was in the railway system. Imperialists thought that railways were "*the* key to modernization, progress, and economic development."[82] Trains were

---

79. H.L. Wesseling, 60.

80. Carter J. Eckert et al. *Korea, Old and New*, 263.

81. Takashi Fujitani, 39. Italics ours.

82. Daniel R. Headrick, *The Tentacles of Progress: Technology Transfer in the*

critical to the economic development of Korea, Taiwan, and Japan, as well as to Japan's war effort in China. By 1940 there were 5,671 kilometers (compared at 24,955 for Japan) of railway spread throughout the Korean Peninsula; the rail system carried a total of 47.3 million passengers.[83] These statistics are negligible compared to British India which had 72,144 kilometers of railway (more than Germany, France or Britain) in 1940 that carried over 536 million passengers.[84] Of course, India's population and size were significantly greater than Korea's.

The GGK was constantly strapped for cash and operated with an ever-increasing debt. The GGK budget for 1940 was 564,657,000 yen, and the largest expenditure was railway construction at 178,848,000 yen (31.7 percent). Railway expenditures dwarfed education (3 percent), the police force (4.3 percent), and the courts and prisons (2.3 percent). A curious budgetary item was 48,000 yen for the encouragement of the Korean language. Much of the financing for the GGK budget came through tax receipts and debt. In 1941 the debt reached 1,035 million yen; this led one scholar to state that the "*welfare of Korea grew, so to speak, at the expense of the Japanese at home.*"[85]

The Japanese also invested heavily in Korean industrial development. From 1929 to 1938 the number of corporations in modern industry grew from 484 to 1,203, and the number of employees in these businesses jumped from 46,000 in 1922 to 231,000 in 1938. The largest numbers of businesses were in the chemical sector, followed by the food industry, then the textile and metal industries. If industry is more loosely defined to include mining, agricultural-re-

---

Age of Imperialism, 1850–1940 (New York: Oxford University Press, 1988), 49. Italics in original.

83. Andrew J. Grajdanzev, *Modern Korea* (New York: John Day Company, 1940), 185. The bus system in Korea carried an equal number of passengers.

84. Daniel R. Headrick, 55-56.

85. Andrew J. Grajdanzev, 210 and 217. Italics Palmer's.

lated factories, manufacturing, and modern construction, there were 2.1 million Koreans employed in these modern industries in 1938.[86]

Surveying the global scene, it is clear that Western colonial powers hindered or prevented the industrialization of their colonies because a colony existed to serve the economic needs of the metropole, not to compete with it. The French did not "encourage any manufacturing in Indochina that would compete with imported French goods."[87] Similarly, the United States, despite its benevolence in the Philippines, "promoted an intensely dependent, export economy based on cash-crop agriculture and extractive industries like mining."[88] Said more directly, industries in Indochina and the Philippines existed to serve the metropole's economy. Japan's record of industrialization in Korea was less exploitative when compared with that of other colonial powers. In short, the progression of Koreans into the modern age was altered, for the better, when Japan assumed control over the Korean nation.

The postulation of "colonial modernity" is a productive area to explore in colonial Korea, particularly outside the realm of economics and industrialization. It helps to expose the complexity of colonial life and to explain the ways that the Korean people transitioned into the modern world. As an academic tool, modernity moves beyond the nation as a unit of analysis and explores topics beyond the suffering/resistance of the "nation." In this way, historical analysis is expanded into areas that have been previously ignored.

On a basic level, modernity incorporates topics such as the urban landscape of Seoul transforming rapidly from dirt streets and single-story thatched roof homes into a concrete jungle that included "electric streetcars, grand architecture, and new forms of public entertainment."[89] Modernity even explores how the average

86. Ibid., Chapter 8.

87. *Encyclopedia of Western Colonialism since 1450*, s.v. "French Indochina."

88. Ibid., s.v. "United States Colonial Rule in the Philippines."

89. Katarzyna J. Cwiertka, "Dining Out in the Land of Desire: Colonial Seoul and

Korean had access to, and participated in, "baseball games, beauty pageants, exhibitions, display windows fronting new department stores, streetcars, street lights, and cafes."[90] These social changes affected people from all social strata:

> The colonial period saw the development of a modern civil service, a postal system, newspapers, banks, corporations, and trade associations as well as capitalism. . . . Korea during this period changed from a society largely dependent on the peasantry to one that became dominated by an industrial class and wage work. It saw the waning of a landed aristocracy and the rise of a middle class used to creating and running business enterprises.[91]

Consumerism, for example, grew in Korea as department stores became popular in the 1930s. During the colonial era, thousands of Koreans adopted consumerism. Women shopped at department stores, which offered an alternative to the traditional marketplace. In fact, a Korean capitalist owned the Hwasin Department Store. At the department stores, people dined out at restaurants and sampled the foreign foods being introduced.[92] One estimate claims that Koreans accounted for 60 to 70 percent of business done at the department stores in Seoul.[93] This sort of consumerism is important to understanding that urban Koreans had disposable income and engaged in modernity at multiple levels. The image of Korean housewives leisurely dining at a department store restaurant contradicts Pak Kyŏng-sik's declaration that Koreans lived in "inhumane slave-like labor conditions."

---

the Korean Culture of Consumption," *Consuming Korean Tradition in Early and Late Modernity: Commodification, Tourism, and Performance*, ed. Laurel Kendall (Honolulu: University of Hawai'i Press, 2011), 21.

90. Henry H. Em, 1.
91. Mark Peterson, *A Brief History of Korea* (New York: Facts on File, 2010), 174.
92. Katarzyna J. Cwiertka, 23, 28, 31.
93. Ibid., 31.

The GGK also allowed a variety of social movements related to gender and social status to develop during the 1920s. Foremost among these was an effort by the *paekchŏng*, an outcaste group with many similarities to the *burakumin* of Japan, to improve their social standing. Class distinctions had been abolished in 1894, but significant contempt for and discrimination against the group continued into the colonial era.[94] This social group successfully pushed for equality and human dignity. As a consequence of the colonial era reform movement, the *paekchŏng* have faced no significant prejudice in postwar Korea.

As part of the move toward modernity, the GGK invested in the public health of Koreans. For example, as of 1939, 12.5 percent of Korean families had electricity, a basic commodity of the modern era. In 1938 Korea had 149 modern hospitals; 95 of which were founded by private organizations. These hospitals treated 334,438 Japanese patients and 389,739 Korean patients.[95] Granted, these hospitals disproportionately favored the Japanese, who comprised only three percent of the Korean population; yet, Koreans were not excluded. Anyone with the financial means was able to avail themselves of these facilities.

In public health it is more difficult to ascertain the accomplishments of the various colonial regimes. As a common rule, medical care was provided first for the metropole's population, particularly soldiers and bureaucracy, then for the subaltern elites, followed by the peasant population—if enough resources were available, which was too often not the case. Take, for example, the British efforts of public well-being in India, which suffered chronically from famines. From 1874 to 1879 an estimated four million people starved

94. Joong-Seop Kim, "In Search of Human Rights: The *Paekchŏng* Movement in Colonial Korea," in *Colonial Modernity in Korea*, eds. Gi-Wook Shin and Michael Robinson (Cambridge, MA: Harvard University Asia Center, 1999), 312–326.

95. Andrew Grajdanzev, 260.

to death. When a commission recommended additional railways to help alleviate subsequent famines (and save lives), the British recommendation was rejected due to the expenses involved.[96] It is worth noting that through vaccinations and improved public health projects the life expectancy of Koreans increased from twenty-six years to forty-two years during the colonial era, and that there were no famines under Japan's rule.[97]

Heritage preservation is a fascinating field within colonial modernity because the Japanese sought to establish political and cultural hegemony through "a pedagogical endeavor in which [Koreans] would come to recognize the relative superiority of the colonizer."[98] To this end, the colonial government restored major Korean historical sites and symbols, such as the Sŏkkuram statue and grotto. Sŏkkuram, a Buddhist statue surrounded by stone reliefs within a cave temple, was built in the eighth century, but had fallen into serious disrepair. The colonial regime spent sixteen years, and significant financial resources, to rebuild the site.

Despite the colonial regime's investment in Sŏkkuram and the nearby Bulguksa Temple, Korean historical remembrance focuses on the Japanese plundering and looting of Korean cultural heritage as well as the failures of the colonial state in properly repairing the temple. As is discussed later, the illicit trafficking of Korean treasures took place, but the historical record cannot be reduced to Japan the exploiter. Instead, the Japanese nation made significant efforts to preserve Korea's past. Hyung Il Pai, one of the foremost scholars on the preservation efforts of Korea's cultural heritage, adds that she is "convinced that Japanese scholars were genuinely dedicated, interested, and fascinated by Korea's past."[99] It can be added that

96. Daniel R. Headrick, 74.
97. Mark Peterson, 174.
98. Henry H. Em, 10.
99. Hyung Il Pai, *Constructing "Korean" Origins: A Critical Review of Archaeology, Historiography, and Racial Myth in Korean State-Formation Theories*

colonial rule was undertaken largely by professionals.

Further highlighting this discussion on modernity and Sŏkkuram is the way the GGK utilized the Sŏkkuram as an educational tool. The restoration of the grotto (and other historical sites) had a pedagogical purpose; Japanese scholars, under the auspices of the colonial regime, interpreted the archeological evidence to "prove" that the Koreans were a subservient race that "had degenerated into a weak and ineffectual people by the time of the late Yi dynasty."[100] School children from Seoul and Pusan took fieldtrips to the grotto, and other historical sites from the Silla period (57BCE-935CE), as a way to inculcate in the students with a belief that Japan's control over Korea was a restoration of the ancient world—a world in which Korea had always been controlled by outside forces and that Japan and Korea had common racial roots.[101]

Still, the Japanese investment to restore and to promote Sŏkkuram, which is now a UNESCO World Heritage Site, shows the complexity of Japan's colonial legacy. The restoration displays the multifarious methods of control used by the GGK to secure hegemony over the peninsula as well as promote the well-being of the Korean people. The GGK did not utilize violence and terror alone, but instead diverted money into cultural projects that required patience (sixteen years to complete this project) and manpower. While scholars today may question colonial-era interpretations of the historical record as incorrect or disingenuous, it is important for us to see the multiplicity of forces in play. The colonial government had to balance between the budget (cost of restoring sites), educators (who disseminated information), colonial bureaucrats (who implemented policies), colonial politicians (who demanded hegemony), metropole politicians

---

(Cambridge, MA: Harvard University Asia Center, 2000), 286.

100. Hyung Il Pai, *Heritage Management in Korea and Japan: The Politics of Antiquity and Identity* (Seattle: University of Washington Press, 2013), 138. See also 128-130.

101. Henry H. Em, 10, 89-94, and Hyung Il Pai 2013, 138.

(who wanted peace and stability), and the Korean populace.

Korean nationalist historians largely reject colonial modernity and revisionist accounts that focus on the economic advancement of Korea and the durability of Japanese political institutions in the postwar era. Yong-Chool Ha claims that recent revisionist works "commit the error of 'reverse teleology,' or reading history backwards."[102] Yet, other nationalist Korean scholars have adopted the themes and topics of modernity and incorporated them into their censure of the colonial regime. For example, Hong Yung Lee, professor at the University of California, Berkeley, argues that Japan cannot be credited with the modernization of Korea because the arrival of modernization in Korea coincided with the Japanese colonial era. In other words, modernization was going to happen regardless of who controlled Korea.[103] However, much of this type of criticism is based on a view that colonialism is a zero-sum game, one in which every Japanese gain was at the expense of the Koreans. In other words, Korean nationalists claim their nation did not profit in any way from the entire thirty-five colonial experience.

Militarism and Militarists in Colonial Korea

A major and enduring indictment against Japanese colonial rule inhering in the nationalist historical narrative is that from the onset the GGK was militaristic because it was led by generals and admirals who, by nature of their military education, training and proclivities, led the charge to aggress against the Korean nation followed by their ironfisted rule to oppress the Koreans and snuff out their culture.

---

102. Yong-Chool Ha, "Colonial Rule and Social Change in Korea: The Paradox of Colonial Control," in *Colonial Rule and Social Change in Korea, 1910–1945*, eds. Hong Yung Lee, Yong-Chool Ha, and Clark Sorensen (Seattle: University of Washington Press, 2013), 40.

103. Hong Yung Lee, "Introduction," in *Colonial Rule and Social Change in Korea, 1910–1945*, eds. Hong Yung Lee, Yong-Chool Ha, and Clark Sorensen (Seattle: University of Washington Press, 2013), 16-17.

Andrew J. Bacevich, professor of International Relations at Boston University, notes that militarism includes "a romanticized view of soldiers, a tendency to see military power as the truest measure of national greatness, and outsized expectations regarding the efficacy of force," and that militarists "define the nation's strength and well-being in terms of military preparedness, military action, and the fostering of (or nostalgia for) military ideals."[104] It is worth noting that Bacevich argues that the United States has become a militaristic society.

We have the good fortune of having Professor emeritus Mark R. Peattie's precise and reasoned definition of these two terms.

> Militarism as a concept may perhaps be most succinctly defined here by identifying some of the attributes popularly subscribed to the "militarist": a glorification of war as an end in itself, an ever-increasing appetite for military adventures beyond the nation's borders, and a demand for complete control of the life of the nation by those of the military profession . . . that for some influential Japanese military men at least, the stereotype of the militarist in these terms needs a sharp qualification.[105]

Given Peattie's and Bacevich's definitions it would be hard to pigeonhole the governors-general of Korea as militarists. There is yet another pathway to clear them of the stain of being militarists and the blight that the office of the governor-general was militaristic. This is by seeing Meiji-Taishō Japanese military leaders as soldiers cum civilians.

Wonmo Dong is a staunch proponent of "Japan the militarist." He wrote that "we can safely state that military factors played a definite role . . . which led to the creation of a colony (sic) in Korea in 1905."

---

104. Andrew J. Bacevich, *The New American Militarism: How Americans Are Seduced by War* (Oxford: Oxford University Press, 2005), 2.

105. Mark R. Peattie, *Ishiwara Kanji and Japan's Confrontation with the West* (Princeton, NJ: Princeton University Press, 1975), 370-371.

He does not hesitate to name the names of the "militarists." He places Yamagata Aritomo among those in the "militarist" faction; one who justified Japan's acquisition of Korea on the ground that it was "a dagger pointed at Japan's heart."[106] Dong labels General Koiso Kuniaki as "one of the most powerful Army officers" whose appointment as head of the Colonial Ministry "undoubtedly meant a more positive control over colonial governments."[107] General Terauchi Masatake is called "a stubborn Samurai-turned-General" and a "typical Meiji militarist."[108] And General Minami Jirō is described as "this ultra-nationalist Governor."[109] Hardly anyone escapes Dong's scorn.

Dong's animus toward governors-general-cum-militarists knows no boundaries. He recites an incident based on Koiso's 1963 *Memoir* in which eight student leaders from high schools in Seoul protested that "the Government-General demanded from Koreans only duties without providing basic rights," and that "Koiso wrote later that he agreed with the students, and that he promised to do his best to abolish existing discrimination." Dong's judgment on Koiso's promise, a point raised earlier but one that deserves repeating: "Like *all* his predecessors, however, Koiso did not live up to his pledge."[110]

Ronald Dore gives what is still the best overview of this tradition by looking at the Tokugawa legacy. He emphasizes the vital role of *bun* [文] (learning) in the tradition by citing from the *Tokugawa Jikki* [徳川実記] (Official History of the Tokugawa Period):

> [Ieyasu] early recognized that the empire could not be ruled on horseback. He always had a great respect for the Way of

106. Wonmo Dong, 72-74. Itō Hirobumi, although a civilian, is also included among the expansionists.

107. Ibid., 183.

108. Ibid., 478.

109. Ibid., 383.

110. Ibid., 476. See page 774 of Koiso's *Memoir* for the incident.

> the Sages and knew that it alone could teach how to rule the kingdom and fulfil the highest duties of man. Consequently, from the beginning of his reign he gave great encouragement to learning.[111]

Dore follows the citation with his exegesis:

> There was, indeed, a tradition of the military class, that successful government required equal attention to *Bun* ("civil studies," "learning," "culture," "intellectual matters," "the literary arts". . .) and to *Bu*—the military arts.[112]

The inseparability of the *bun/bu* persisted into the Meiji and Taishō periods. I have seen, for example, that there are in the published and unpublished letters written to and by Yamagata Aritomo, a surprising number devoted to *waka* [和歌] (31 syllable Japanese poems) sent to and received from fellow practitioners for criticism. Itō Hirobumi, for his part, was justifiably proud of his *kanshi* [漢詩] (poems in the Chinese style). So powerful was the pull of this heritage that, as Devine has shown, Hasegawa's "academic abilities were . . . subject to [disdainful] comment" and that he was noted for his intellect, but seldom had a book in hand. Yet, he retained a measure of *bun* respectability by showing an "extraordinary ability for remembering flowery phrases."[113]

The significance of the samurai as administrator is that their success in office was measured by their ability to create and sustain the well being of those in their jurisdiction in a stable, secure, and peaceable political-social-cultural environment. And there was enough social turmoil in the Tokugawa-Meiji-Taishō periods to give

---

111. *Education in Tokugawa Japan* (Berkeley: University of California Press, 1965), 16.

112. Ibid., 16 and 95. Italics in original. This work, along with his other publications, have worn well over the decades, and reveal as well the high standards found in other publications by the early postwar Japan scholars.

113. Richard Devine, 525.

comfort to historians inclined to see a cup half-empty. Still, such was the persisting impact of this tradition that a failure almost certainly resulted in loss of position, demotion, or transfer, and, as we shall see in the section on Sprunger, one could be publicly flogged for his failure. The saving grace, even in the most egregious of failures, is that the perpetrator could redeem himself by self-reflection and attempts at remedy, as is illustrated by Hasegawa's "Recommendations."

Was Yamagata Aritomo a "Militarist"?

Wonmo Dong without qualification calls Yamagata a "militarist" who pushed for the acquisition of Korea as a colony. This charge demands challenge on two grounds. First, he is one of the chief architects in setting the ground rules for acquiring and maintaining Japan's non-contiguous territories. If he were indeed a militarist, then there is no merit in referring to him as a proponent of "realism," "moderation," "mutualism," and "proportionality"—a point we reject outright. And second, this perception of Yamagata as "militarist" persists among respected Anglophone scholars. This in turn taints the views of non-specialists, who depend on the highly regarded scholars who write about modern Japanese history and Japan's place in Asia for the wider general audience, including those in high places. If for no other reason, there is an urgency to clear the air.

In order to understand the origins of Yamagata's image as a militarist in the West, we shall limit ourselves to four sources in English; two of which were published during the War in the Pacific; and two in the recent past.

Gustav Eckstein was a well-known scientist, one who was sympathetic to Japanese cultural achievements and who spent time in Japan. Yet, in 1943, he published a work with a bilious tirade against Yamagata. He begins Chapter Thirty-eight, "Aritomo Yamagata, Soldier" with this unconditional indictment:

> If there is one Japanese more responsible than any other for the present Pacific war, the man is Yamagata, dead twenty-one years. In peace he planned war. In war he planned future war.[114]

Eckstein's book was given a priceless boost by the then pre-eminent Western scholar on modern Japanese history, E. Herbert Norman, whose works were influenced by Marxism. He was especially struck by Eckstein's portrait of Yamagata:

> The vignette on Field Marshal Yamagata Aritomo, in a few sharp strokes, characterizes that evil genius of modern Japan more deftly than I have seen elsewhere . . . ruthlessly striking down all opposition to aggression abroad or reaction at home.[115]

Norman also apparently agrees with Eckstein's basic notion that Yamagata was the chief architect of Japan's modern day aggression by describing Yamagata as, "This chilly bureaucrat, . . . was to be the key figure in Japanese reaction and aggression in the period which

---

114. *In Peace Japan Breeds War* (New York: Harper & Brothers, 1943), 228. I was puzzled by the 1927 copyright date in the 1943 First Edition, since Yamagata would have been dead only five years, not the "twenty-one." I asked Mr. David Flynn, Librarian for Business, Economics and Travel Industry Management, Hamilton Library, University of Hawai'i at Manoa to untangle the conundrum. After a yeoman effort, he concluded, and I have no reason to doubt his accuracy, that: ". . . Aside from the 1927 copyright date in the 1943 First Edition, the only mention I find is in a reference of the book in an appendix to the *Chrysanthemum and the Sword.* It lists it as Eckstein, Gustav (1943) (orig. 1927), *In Peace Japan Breeds War*. Of course, that does not necessarily mean that *it was never published before 1943. I find no trace of an actual 1927 printing of that title.*"

115. "Militarists in the Japanese State," A Review Article by E. Herbert Norman, *Pacific Affairs* 16. 4 (December 1943): 477-478. We cannot leave Eckstein without recounting another of his "vignettes," this one on Japan's soldiers, who with their "rough peasant faces, the squat bodies, the short legs, the animal alertness . . . make you think of chimpanzees." Eckstein, 233-234.

links the Japan of Saigō with the Japan of Generals Tanaka [Giichi (田中義一)], Tōjō [Hideki (東条英機)], and Koiso [Kuniaki]. . . . It is to him that the present warlords of Japan must look with a sense of political obligation. . . ."[116]

Given Yamagata's reputation and Norman's unparalleled standing as a scholar, I suspect that had Yamagata been alive at the end of December 1948, he would have been charged and hung as a Class "A" war criminal—a statement, naturally enough, that is not subject to proof.

If Eckstein's screed can be linked to wartime hysteria, and Norman's majestic prose to ideological fervor, the most recent incarnation by Frederick R. Dickinson cannot be so easily dismissed. The author is a Ph.D. from Yale; he has spent years in Japan; he has immersed himself in the Japanese-language literature on the subject; had his work published by Harvard; and is now a faculty member at the University of Pennsylvania, another Ivy League school.[117]

Dickinson, like McLaren, accepts the notion that a powerful Yamagata military-bureaucratic faction existed; that it was "the mightiest force for political conservatism." He also characterizes

---

116. E. Herbert Norman, "Feudal Background of Japanese Politics," *Secretariat Paper*. No. 9, IPR (January 1945) and Ottawa (December 1944), Chapter IV, 81. See also Norman's unpublished letter to Arundel Del Re, Civil Information and Education Section, SCAP, GHQ (2 March 1949). Arundel Del Re had written a manuscript on modern Japanese history and had asked Norman for his reactions. Norman criticized Del Re for not emphasizing Yamagata's pernicious role in the rise of militarism in the mid-1890s that choked Japan's ability to develop a freer political system. I am indebted to Dr. Harry Wray, now retired, who led me to this source. Del Re must have been dispirited by Norman's criticism since after a lengthy search, I find there is no record that Del Re ever published his manuscript.

117. Frederick R. Dickinson, *War and National Reinvention: Japan in the Great War, 1914–1919* (Cambridge, MA: Harvard University Asia Center, 1999). He has an M.A. and doctorate from Yale and an M.A. from Kyoto University; he is an Associate Professor of Japanese History at the University of Pennsylvania.

Yamagata as a dyed-in-the wool imperialist who had "a critical role in Japan's acquisition of an empire"; one who after the Russo-Japanese War regarded Japan's "continental expansion as an all-or-nothing proposition," that is, along with his faction "sought nothing less than complete regional hegemony."[118]

I have not met Dickinson, but I have had the good fortune of knowing the next Yamagata critic, Peter Duus, for over four decades.[119] I have the highest esteem for the sharpness of his intellect, his enviable narrative skills, and his indubitable scholarly integrity. He has published a deservedly well-acclaimed history of Japan's early involvement in Korea, *The Abacus and the Sword: The Japanese Penetration of Korea, 1895–1910* (1995). Akira Iriye praised it as the "best book in any language on Japanese expansion into Korea"; a sentiment echoed by professor emeritus Yong-ho Choe. It has been awarded three major prizes.

What follows is an attempt to underscore the pitfall of preconceived notions; the same trap that is also the basis of my critique of the nationalist historical narrative of Japan's Korean colonial policy.[120] Given that the perfect analysis or work on Japan's colonialism has yet to see the light of day, this is not an attempt to besmirch a superb monograph. In my response to these preconceived notions,

---

118. Frederick R. Dickinson, 41, 43, 217, and 246-247.

119. Duus is Professor emeritus, Japanese history, Stanford University.

120. Duus in his first monograph reveals that he already had a negative view of Yamagata. Yamagata, he asserts, was "the most influential and the one who clung most firmly to" the ideal "of 'transcendental government' . . . to perpetuate the benevolent bureaucratic authoritarianism" of the early Meiji period. He had, according to Duus, a widespread group of followers throughout the top echelon of the government whom he controlled as would a "watchful spider in the midst of the web he had spun so carefully, sensitive to every twitch in the net, scurrying forth whenever the threat of a domestic or international crisis joggled a strand." This is so well put except that it is wrong—a discussion that must await a later time. See, Peter Duus, *Party Rivalry and Political Change in Taishō Japan* (Cambridge, MA, Harvard University Press, 1968), 83-84.

I have the advantage of a three-decade long single-minded obsession in reading published and handwritten sources on Yamagata's thinking and actions.

A major theme found in Duus' work is his placement of Yamagata squarely among the military faction in opposition to the mostly civilian coterie. He also regards the former as consistently more inclined to take aggressive action against Korea. Duus in this instance positions some army leaders against "civilian leaders like Prime Minister Itō and Foreign Minister Mutsu Munemitsu," who were "worried about the possibility of foreign intervention" and therefore "were much more cautious and much less enthusiastic about a military solution."[121]

And again:

> Itō and Inoue [Kaoru] preferred to proceed cautiously, avoiding offense to the foreign powers, . . . while Yamagata, Matsukata, and Ōkuma wanted to pursue Japanese interests more aggressively, however the foreigners might react.[122]

And there is more:

> . . . a larger policy struggle that aligned Itō and Inoue Kaoru against more powerful advocates of annexation at the highest levels of the civilian and military bureaucracies, particularly among the members of the Yamagata faction.[123]

Given the above, the word, "interesting," in the following leaped off the page:

> It is interesting, however, that Yamagata's analysis [in his 1890 memorandum on "cordons of interest and sovereignty"] did not lead him to conclude that a preemptive military

---

121. Peter Duus, 65. Duus sometimes does not footnote his propositions, making it difficult for the reader to pursue the matter.
122. Ibid., 135.
123. Ibid., 202-203.

seizure of the peninsula was required.[124]

To this reader at least, "interesting" implies "unexpected," or "surprising."

The peril that inheres in postulating the Yamagata as militarist, aggressor, and hardliner is exposed by Duus himself. He begins with Hasegawa Yoshimichi's assertion, previously cited that "force was the only way to control the Koreans," and extrapolates from this that "The pessimism expressed by Hasegawa was shared by military leaders at a higher level." Duus then adds that Yamagata "expressed an equally gloomy view about the prospects for reform in Korea" and continues:

> It goes without saying that Korean politics are corrupt and disorderly, and its people lack the ability or the spirit to make progress. . . . Hoping that Korea will institute *sudden* changes as our country did during the Restoration is like trying to catch fish in a tree. At the time of our Restoration nearly all who took part in the most important affairs of state realized the need for the country to make progress, and knowledgeable men outside the government vied to introduce the country to Western things. . . . Korea has neither the basic knowledge nor sufficient capacity to absorb the new civilization. The Korean people, high and low, are indecisive and rather indolent.

He concludes from the above that "It was precisely such a view that licensed the iron hand tactics advocated by Hasegawa and other army leaders."[125]

Let me lay to rest the presumptions that Yamagata was an advocate of an iron-handed Korea policy, that he "wanted to pursue Japanese interests more aggressively, however the foreigners might

---

124. Ibid., 64.

125. Ibid., 196-197, citing from Yamagata's memorandum, "Sengo keiei ikensho" (戦後経営意見書), August, 1905 in Ōyama Azusa, 283-284.

react."[126] Yamagata can hardly be accused of being a hardliner. If the 1886 recommendations in Yamagata's *ikensho* that served as the blueprint for a realistic, moderate colonial policy undergirded by proportionality are without cogency, then this whole exercise is one of utter futility. I, naturally, do not accept that conclusion.

After working more than three decades on Yamagata's thoughts and behavior, I have no doubt that Yamagata was consistently moderate in his foreign policy positions; and, more than any other leader in the Meiji government, was filled with anxiety about the possibility that a weak Japan might antagonize Western powers and become isolated in a dog-eat-dog world. Let me support my position by going to three sources that address Duus' presumptions. The first one uses Yamagata's own words, and the others are those of longtime Yamagata watchers.

The first is the *ikensho* that Duus just cited. Immediately following the portion translated by Duus, Yamagata had added:

> Wouldn't it the height of absurdity [for us] to arbitrarily renovate with *one fell swoop* [Korea's] manifold institutions, and in the resultant confusion and consternation that Koreans feel, we undermine our good intentions and replace it with [their] ill-will and abhorrence [toward us]?
>
> Therefore, I propose that while we need to posthaste and strictly supervise Korea's foreign affairs, we must of necessity *gradually* [*italics*, Yamagata's] reform domestic affairs. It is not as if I have not repeatedly brought this to your attention. At present, despite the fact that Japan's management of Korea's foreign affairs is still a work in progress, Japan's meddling into the Korean Kingdom's domestic affairs has reached the point where it is practically hindering its self-reliance (*dokuritsu* [独立]). [For example, Japan] does not permit those whom the King trusts the most but who happen to have strong feelings of antipathy toward

126. Peter Duus, 135.

Japan to become prime minister and cabinet ministers. By taking such actions, we cause all the Koreans to hate Japan. Moreover, while it is natural to be concerned about Korea's fiscal reforms, is it too much to ask that as long as we can be assured that the [Korean Kingdom] does not surreptitiously borrow funds from nations other than Japan which would create troublesome situations for Japan, a guarantee [by the Koreans] that they would not do so should be sufficient. Can we say that it is a wise decision for us to suddenly and forcibly impose a fiscal system of an advanced civilization [on the Korean Kingdom] that at present possesses neither the will nor ability [to do so]. I believe that if we were to be true to the very meaning of administrative supervision, [we will] have Koreans who have the King's trust work in concert to handle the [Kingdom's] administration.

Our role will be [limited] to supervise [the ministers that the King himself has selected] and never fail to advise them on appropriate policies. And only when it becomes evident that what [the Koreans do] has no chance of succeeding, should we then involve ourselves in the reform. It will not be at this point too late to intervene. Again, [only] if the Koreans fail to recognize Japan's authority and morality (*tokugi* [徳義]) and merely indulge in movements to oust Japan, will it be necessary to take extreme measures. If without learning history's lessons, and by ignoring Korean culture and habits as well, we merely try to impose new laws and regulations on Koreans that have no prospect of success, this will [surely] invite the intervention of the Powers who are intently observing us (p. 284). I cannot warn Japan enough about [the folly] of such a policy (p. 285). In short, the danger of giving rise to the Powers' intervention in the face of the disorder in Korea is something that I earlier had pointed out. I earnestly desire that you will unceasingly focus your attention [on this possibility].[127]

127. Ōyama Azusa, 284-285. The last three sentences clearly are contrary to Duus' interpretation earlier cited.

The second source is a record of Christian minister Tamura Naoomi (田村直臣) of a five-hour conversation he had with Hara Kei in 1920 at which time Hara said:

> A war between the United States and Japan will not break out as long as Prince Yamagata is alive. Yamagata is weak kneed when it involves foreign countries. He is filled with anxiety vis-à-vis foreign countries. Depending on one's perspective, this is Yamagata's strength or weakness. It matters little how the young turks in the Army are acting up. As long as Yamagata is alive, nothing will happen.[128]

Finally, we turn to Tokutomi Iichirō (Sohō) [徳富猪一郎(蘇峰)], who had enjoyed a long time relationship with Yamagata, and who saw fit to write finis to Yamagata's anxiety filled life with this "epitaph" two days after Yamagata's death:

> [Yamagata] overestimated [the power] of foreign countries. He, for all his reputation, was never able to rise above his tremendous fear of foreign countries.[129]

PETER DUUS ON THE CONTENT OF JAPANESE TEXTBOOKS

I ask the readers' indulgence to let me digress. It would do Duus a grave injustice to leave the reader with the impression that his mistaken view of Yamagata explains the totality of Duus as a scholar. I reiterate my earlier comment on my esteem for Duus. He is without doubt a highly intelligent, articulate, and a fair-minded

---

128. Tamura Naoomi, *Waga mitaru Hara shushō no omokage* (Tokyo: Keiseisha, 1922), 21, 33-34.

129. "Yamagata Gensui (山県元帥)" in *Kokumin Shimbun* [国民新聞] (3 February 1922). A large number of letters written between Yamagata and Tokutomi over a period of years have been transcribed from *sōsho* [草書] (handwritten with brush) and translated that reveal the complex relationship that bound the two men. See, Itō Takashi and George Akita, "The Yamagata-Tokutomi Correspondence: Press and Politics in Meiji-Taishō Japan," *MN* 36.4 (Winter 1981): 391-423.

academic with a large measure of scholarly integrity. I offer the following example as support. The contents of the following have the added virtue of being directly relevant to our study.

The Shorenstein Asia-Pacific Research Center at Stanford University embarked on a three-year "The Divided Memories and Reconciliation" project to deal with memories of wartime Asia. The first year focused on high school history textbooks in Japan, China, South Korea, Taiwan, and the United States. Peter Duus participated in this study. The opening paragraph of an article in *The Daily Yomiuri*, 22 November 2008, sets the stage for his findings:

> For the past three decades, Japanese high school history textbooks have got bad press abroad. Some foreign critics say they do not pay enough attention to Japan's responsibility for the outbreak of the Asia-Pacific War or to the suffering the Japanese military wrought in occupied areas. Others argue that their content has become more and more nationalistic. . . .
>
> Far from being nationalistic, Japanese textbooks seemed the least likely to stir patriotic passions. They do not celebrate war, do not stress the importance of the military, and tell no tales of battlefield heroism. Instead they offer a chronicle of events without much interpretive narrative. . . .
>
> By contrast, national curriculum guides in most other East Asian countries assert the promotion of national pride and national identity as the primary function of history education. . . .
>
> [T]he South Korean textbooks focus almost exclusively on the wartime Korean resistance to Japanese colonial rule or on cultural developments in literature. In other words, the continuing national struggle for liberation is the plotline for Korean textbook narratives. Perhaps the most passionately nationalistic war stories are to be found in Chinese textbooks.[130]

130. Peter Duus, "Special on history textbooks / Japan's teaching on war doesn't deserve bad press" in *The Daily Yomiuri*, 22 November 2008.

Chapter Four

The Many and Varied Voices of Revisionism

Shortly after reading Brandon Palmer's writings on the Korean Volunteer Soldier System, I had a chance meeting at the Shōyū Kurabu [尚友倶楽部] in Tokyo with a young Korean scholar, Mr. Y., then a graduate student at a Japanese national university. I wrote to him asking about revisionism among Korean scholars on the subject of Japan's rule over Korea. He replied, naming names and pointing to Seoul National University in particular where there was an ongoing, bitter, vociferous debate between economic historians and historians that had been triggered by the former's "bold" assertion that their data reveal that the activities of the Japanese in 1910–1945 contributed to a measurable growth of Korea's economic progress, that, in turn, is directly linked to South Korea's current economic progress. The historians, however, persist in strongly emphasizing the depredation of the Japanese and the Koreans' forceful opposition to colonial rule. Those who hold to the "traditional" interpretation, he added, continue to be influential.[1]

Rhee Yong-hoon, a professor of economic history at Seoul National University, who has been introduced earlier, substantiates Mr. Y's descriptions. Professor Rhee's basic theme is that "objective" memory of the past is impossible because emotions color all remembrances. He continues, this is all the more reason for "fact based"

1. Undated letter postmarked 3 June 2005; with a second letter dated 23 June. Both are used with his permission.

analyses of the past. He states flatly that for the past sixty years, the nationalistic narrative that has *not* been supported by facts, but nevertheless has been taught in textbooks. This, he strongly asserts, is the reason for its hold on Koreans.[2] And in Chapter nine, he offers statistics-laden, detailed analysis and support for revisionism.[3] The points Rhee raises will be addressed later in a wider discussion of revisionist studies.

The State of Revisionism in South Korea

Brandon Palmer adds his voice to the debate that can be viewed by revisionists both with optimism and pessimism:

> The nationalist historical paradigm has lost much traction since the late 1980s. Nearly all Western historians of Korean history adhere to a revisionist approach and many younger Korean historians (in America and fewer in Korea) also are revisionists. However, the old guard and most Koreans in Korea cling to the nationalist paradigm.[4]

Palmer, excellent scholar as he is, is not one to be easily deterred by the minority position in which he and other revisionists find themselves. He describes scholars who challenge the nationalist historical paradigm and often advocate the colonial modernity narrative. I prefer to abjure the use of the term "theory" and go directly to the heart of the colonial modernity; that is, Japan's colonization of Korea was crucial to the modernization of the peninsula, or, put another way, a willingness to recognize the positive outcomes of the colonial era is the hallmark of this revisionism.

The advocates of this postulation or proposition move beyond a nationalist view of capitalism and explore the various ways that Korea and Koreans moved into the modern era under the leadership

---

2. Rhee Yong-hoon, 73, 76-77.
3. Ibid., 178-192
4. Letter dated 18 August 2009.

of imperial Japanese colonialists. These scholars, in sources cited earlier, examine the educational advancement, technical training, industrial development, modern infrastructure, and legal systems as Japanese contributions that helped Korea's postwar growth.[5] Among these works, *Kŭndae rŭl tasi ingnŭnda* (Another reckoning of modern times) and *Haebang chon-husa ŭi chae insik* (A rediscovery of history before and since liberation)[6] are valuable collections of essays, some translated from Japanese and English, that examine issues ranging from the economic and bureaucratic benefits Koreans received during the colonial era to the multilayered agendas of Koreans who cooperated with the Japanese. These studies evaluate the intricate relationship between the Korean people and the colonial regime, between colonialism and modernity, and between personal and national motives.

Yun Hae-dong, for example, postulates that Koreans are better off having been colonized by Japan because the colonial regime destroyed the hereditary elite, ended political corruption, and allowed modern businesses to operate. Like most scholars of this proposition, Yun exemplifies the mixed emotions that young Korean scholars feel about the colonial era. He acknowledges, for example, that the streets and roads, harbors, and railroads were used to exploit Koreans and the tools of empire flattened Korea's traditional cultural diversity. Nevertheless, Yun maintains that Korea, overall, benefitted from the colonial era.[7]

Despite the gradual trend toward revisionism in Korea, the dominant nationalist historical paradigm resists any reinterpretation of the past or claims that Japan had a positive impact on Korea's postwar success. A respected Korean scholar at Koryŏ University,

5. Chŏng Chae-jŏng, 39-49.
6. Yun Hae-dong et al. (2006), and Pak Chi-hyang (2006).
7. Yun Hae-dong (尹海東), *Singminji kŭndae ŭi p'aerŏdoksŭ* (식민지 근대의 패러독스) [The paradox of colonial modernity] (Seoul: Hyumŏnisŭtŭ, 2007), 62-63 and 238-239.

Kang Man-gil, continues to accuse the Japanese of depriving the Korean people an opportunity to modernize and democratize themselves. He points to the autocracy of the GGK as a major contributor to the postwar authoritarian regimes that emerged in north and south Korea.[8] Furthermore, other scholars have adopted the themes of modernity to find new areas where, in their estimation, Japan caused harm. Dong-No Kim writes,

> Social distortions in everyday life of Koreans people today are often attributed to the malicious heritage of Japanese colonial rule that ended more than half a century ago. The impact of colonial rule has thus been grave and everlasting on Korean society.[9]

Shin Yong-ha, Honorary Professor at Seoul National University, argues that revisionism makes the error of representing the plunder of Korean resources as modernization and falsely construes militarization as industrialization. In his opinion, scholars need to highlight the impoverishment and suffering of the Korean nation as part of the discontinuity between the colonial period and postwar state.[10] Scholars such as Shin adamantly "reject narratives suggesting that South Korea was influenced by economic, political, and other colonial legacies, and supports a historical narrative of the spirit of independence that existed before, during, and after the colonial period."[11]

At the foundation of this resistance to reinterpretation are the close ties between the legitimacy of the South Korean national founders and the colonial-era independence movement. The founders of the postwar Republic of Korea, and their successors, have benefitted by promoting the Japanese colonial regime as brutal: "the more the

8. Mark Peterson, 175.
9. Dong-No Kim, 140.
10. Translation found in Guy Podoler.
11. Guy Podoler, 237.

people suffered—the more brutal the colonizer was, and the more there have been people who suffered—the more heroic was the resistance."[12]

Terauchi Masatake: A Notorious Governor-General

We ask the reader to recall the statements made by Andrew Ou, who makes much of the fact that all the governors-general and an admiral were military officers, or, more to the point, "militarist[s]" who possessed "absolute power" and "unsurpassed political authority." He also unequivocally designates Terauchi Masatake, the first governor-general (1910–1916) "a typical Meiji period militarist."[13] We have also Kim Il Myŏn (金一勉) who resorts to "reverse anthropomorphism" by describing all the army generals who became governors-general as having "faces that remind us of leopards or tigers."[14] We start our revisionism with two of the governors-general who were especially disdained by the Koreans, remembering at the same time that positive developments did occur under others.

Governor-General Terauchi (1910–1916) is widely condemned by Koreans for instituting an era of military rule that resulted in the "dark period" [*amhŭkgi*]. Koreans accuse the Japanese of attacking Korean culture, appropriating Korean farmlands, and exercising power over the Korean people in a heavy-handed manner during the first decade of colonial rule. C.I. Eugene Kim and Han-kyo Kim claimed Terauchi established a "reign of terror" over Korea.[15] We concede that the Japanese wounded the national pride of Koreans,

12. Ibid., 124.
13. Andrew Hak Ou, 17, 18, 23-24.
14. *Chōsenjin ga naze 'Nihonmei' o nanorunoka: minzoku ishiki to sabetsu* [朝鮮人がなぜ「日本名」を名のるのか－民族意識と差別] (Tokyo: San'ichi Shobō, 1978), 57.
15. C.I. Eugene Kim and Han-kyo Kim, 214.

but argue that Japan's colonial rule was an improvement over the Yi dynasty (1392–1910) under King Kojong (r. 1863–1907): there was less corruption and more modernization, as well as greater opportunity for social and economic progress.

Even pro-Korean scholars within the nationalist historical narrative recognize the blatant abuses and shortcomings of the Korean government from the 1880s to 1905. C.I. Eugene Kim and Han-kyo Kim in *Korea and the Politics of Imperialism, 1876–1910* (1967), which is strongly critical of Japan's imperialism, cannot contain their disdain for King Kojong's regime. They note that "Agents sent out from the palace roamed the country selling public offices and exacting special taxes in addition to the regular land tax," and that the "palace attracted the greedy favor seekers who catered to the vanity of the emperor."[16] They also point out that progressive elements and opponents of the king were suppressed: "In this game for imperial favor, the most ruthless and cunning won. Against the abuse of power by the emperor and his infamous ministers, the commoners had no defense. Advocates of reforms . . . were hunted down and suppressed throughout these years." Korean society was also elitist; the richest three percent controlled all avenues to power and wealth. "The remaining 97 percent, especially the peasants, suffered from misgovernment, heavy taxation, illegal levies, and capricious administration of justice; and the rigid stratification of the society reinforced by orthodox Confucianism allowed little opportunity for them to seek redress. Common people were abused and forgotten."[17]

Contemporary Koreans, such as Philip Jaisohn (Sŏ Jae-p'il), complained that, under the Yi dynasty, the rich successfully skirted paying taxes, and illegally passed their tax obligation on to the poor. He estimated 90 percent of the Korean population in Chosŏn Korea lived in poverty. Consequently, the masses recognized that

16. Ibid., 116.
17. Ibid., 116 and 221.

the Korean government lacked concern for their well-being. Instead, King Kojong failed to protect the masses from corruption and abuse; Jaisohn claimed the king "believed that they [the Korean people] were his slaves and exploited them for his own gain and gratification."[18]

The corruption and misgovernance of the Korean government were also recognized by Western travelers in Korea. Isabella Bird Bishop, an Englishwoman who traveled the globe in the late 1800s, noted: "Though corruption has its stronghold in Seoul, every provincial government repeats on a smaller scale the iniquities of the capital, and has its own army of dishonest and lazy officials fattening on the earnings of the industrious classes."[19] She added, "Every man in Korea knows that poverty is his best security, and that anything he possesses beyond that which provides himself and his family with food and clothing is certain to be taken from him by voracious and corrupt officials." She continued,

> Among the modes of squeezing are forced labor, doubling or trebling the amount of a legitimate tax, exacting bribes in cases of litigation, forced loans, etc. If a man is reported to have saved a little money, an official asks for the loan of it. If it is granted, the lender frequently never sees principal or interest; if it is refused, he is arrested, thrown into prison on some charge invented for his destruction, and beaten until he or his relations for him produce the sum demanded.[20]

Philip Jaisohn explained the problem. He claimed that the "old Korean government never paid their public servants even a living salary, so the result was they were susceptible to bribery and corruption."[21] Academic sources also provide a bleak picture of

18. Philip Jaisohn, 83.
19. Isabella Bird, *Korea and Her Neighbors* (London: John Murray, 1898; reprinted Yonsei University Press, 1970), 263.
20. Ibid., 336 and 337.
21. Philip Jaisohn, 66.

life under the rigid and elitist Confucian bureaucracy. The government, which rejected human equality, demanded the conformity of the peasant farmers and tradesmen to the hereditary elite. In fact, the hereditary class system survived up until the Gabo Reforms of 1894, and lingering social prejudices survived into the colonial era. As Bird noted above, the legal system of Chosŏn Korea was too often abused by the powerful. Vipan Chandra, professor at Wheaton College in Massachusetts, adds that the

> Law was deliberately designed to leave room for the exercise of "wise" discretion. Hence abuses were not uncommon in practice. Such judicial discretion seemed not infrequently to have been an item for quiet sale to the highest bidder or to have been dispensed in favor of friends or relatives. …
>
> When purely judicial functions acquired prominence, it signified a failure of "virtuous" government. Because the modern democratic concept of separation of powers was alien to this dispensation, there were no civil liberties sacrosanct or unassailable. Freedom under egalitarian law—a prime secular value in the modern era—was not a political ideal in traditional Korea.[22]

By 1900 the Korean government had made progress toward loosening the control of the hereditary elite, the *yangban* class, but the conservative factions of the Yi government failed to allow political participation for the masses, to move toward popular participation in politics, or to correct widespread social inequalities.

Critics of the Japanese colonial regime are quick to forget that the Tonghak movement (an indigenous Korean religion that began in the 1860s) nearly toppled the Yi dynasty on the eve of the First Sino-Japanese War (1894) because the Korean government imposed excessive taxation on the peasants, was corrupt to the extreme,

22. Vipan Chandra, *Imperialism, Resistance, and Reform in Late Nineteenth-Century Korea: Enlightenment and the Independence Club* (Berkeley: University of California Institute for Asian Studies, 1988), 10.

and proved ineffective in responding to famine. It is logical to ask, 'Which government was better for the Korean people?' Were Koreans better off under the inept, brutal, capricious, and inefficient Yi dynasty that offered the rule of man, or were they better off under the modern, formidable, efficient, yet foreign GGK that offered the rule of law? The answers favor the governance under the GGK because the historical record is already there.

In 1910 Japan formally annexed Korea after five years of ruling Korea as a protectorate. Terauchi, governor-general from 1910 to 1916, had the Herculean task of removing traditional Korea's moribund ruling elite and replacing it with a professional Japanese bureaucracy. The long-term goal of the GGK was to repeat in Korea what the Meiji Government had accomplished in Okinawa, Hokkaido, and Taiwan. Namely, Terauchi aimed to implement policies to improve public health, eliminate antiquated cultural practices, rationalize the tax system, and, most importantly, establish complete control over Korean society; once these were complete, then Korea would be integrated into Japan's polity. The sudden transition from the Yi dynasty to the Japanese colonial regime must have confused and disturbed the Korean populace. Even though the Korean populace struggled to adapt to the new style of government, the Japanese were within global standards, as an imperial power, in their methods of establishing control over Korean society.

When the corrupt Korean government fell in 1905, there existed in Korea minimal investments in modernization, public health, and economic development. As a result, the GGK needed to invest heavily in infrastructure. Michael Robinson notes that "this early period inaugurated a sustained building boom as the Japanese invested millions of yen in the bricks and mortar of colonial rule," and that "Cumulatively the government buildings, shrines, railroads, motor roads, power and telephone lines, hydroelectric dams, barrages, and irrigation works" were constructed.[23] Critics of the colonial regime note that these were tools of empire that the Japanese used to dominate and exploit the Korean people. But these same critics seem to assume that imperial powers operate exclusively with altruistic motives.

It is not our intention to deny that the GGK under Terauchi censored the media, limited the freedom of speech, assailed Korean culture, weakened Christianity, detained innocent men, significantly expanded the police force, prevented Korean political participation, favored Japanese businesses over Korean, and suppressed Korean nationalism. These actions were part and parcel of a new imperial rule securing the foundations for long-term hegemony in a new colony. The Japanese bureaucracy was an imperfect instrument of governance, and the colonial regime was not popular among the Korean people. As has been discussed above, the Meiji leadership in Tokyo had lofty plans and good intentions for Japan's colonial endeavor in Korea, but the implementation of these policies was left to individual bureaucrats and policemen, some of whom looked down on the Korean people and had petty parochial issues. We maintain, however, that in the imperfect world, imperfect bureaucrats could not be expected to establish a Garden of Eden.

Take, for example, the Japanese response to the supposed assassination attempt of Terauchi in 1910 and the arrests that followed (more below). The colonial police arrested hundreds of Korean nationalists, many of whom were Christian, and put 123 of them on trial. Scholarly opinion is united that the charges were trumped up and the accused were not given a fair trial—yet, most sentences were commuted or reduced on appeal. Because many defendants were Christian, missionaries publicized the affair abroad, the trial brought international criticism of the prosecution of Japanese methods. This

23. Michael Robinson, *Korea's Twentieth-Century Odyssey* (Honolulu: University of Hawai'i Press, 2007), 42.

affair was clearly a move by the GGK to weaken the Korean nationalist movement and to establish hegemony over Korean society; it was, however, realpolitik in action, not a "reign of terror." Still, the implementation of Terauchi's policies was culturally insensitive, thereby contributing to the March First Independence Movement (1919).

We have noted that a member of Japan's House of Representatives, Inoue Kakugorō, told Hara that Koreans held Terauchi in low esteem. In relating the following involving Terauchi, Akita admits to subscribing to the old saw that "A single swallow does not spring make"—we cannot assume that the whole of Terauchi's time in Korea was deleterious. The following extremely short newspaper article caught my attention.

> South Korea's Constitutional Court ruled on Thursday that only the visually impaired can be licensed masseurs in the country, upholding a law set up a century ago despite arguments it infringed on free employment rights.
>
> The law was established in 1912 when Korea was under Japanese colonial rule to help guarantee the blind a livelihood.[24]

What especially caught my interest is that this social policy, so advanced for its day, was also given the imprimatur of South Korea's Constitutional Court. This, I suggest, contributed its bit to the theme of continuity between the colonial era and postwar Korean society.

Terauchi's administration also showed flexibility when dealing with Korea's poorest farmers. Early in the Terauchi administration, slash and burn agriculture, commonly practiced in the mountainous areas of the peninsula, was outlawed. However, this move toward "modern management practices" was at variance with the harsh realities of life in rural Korea where illiteracy and poverty were high and

---

24. Kim Junghyun, "South Korea court says only blind can be masseurs," in *The Daily Yomiuri*, 31 October 2008.

opportunities to make a living were low. When GGK administrators saw that the ban hurt the livelihood of many of Korea's poorest cultivators, the GGK "considered local conditions" and in 1911 issued permits to allow farmers to return to slash and burn cultivation.[25]

The Terauchi government also imposed laws that at the time were unpopular, but were necessary for a transition into the modern age. Many of these laws continued into postwar Korea. Among these laws were a prohibition on child marriages, a ban on gambling, and a requirement for Koreans to register household information (Koreans largely ignored this latter law). The colonial regime also actively pursued drastic measures to improve the public health among Koreans to prevent epidemics. Namely, policemen "visited homes to inspect and survey the health and sanitation conditions" of Koreans. Such visits were unwelcomed by Korean households partly because the state was reaching into their personal lives, but also because the police were heavy handed and arrogant.[26] Indeed, the *kempeitai* "was not the kind of organization that encouraged its members to sense the subtleties of popular feelings and adapt to change in circumstances."[26] These visits were the focus of many complaints by Koreans.

MINAMI JIRŌ: ANOTHER NOTORIOUS GOVERNOR-GENERAL

Andrew Ou aims his sharpest barbs at Minami Jirō, whose tenure as governor-general spanned the years 1936–1942. He calls Minami "colonial Korea's most notorious ruler" and "one of the most feared and despised figures in colonial Korea." Koreans dislike him because under his tenure the assimilation policies were intensified and the peninsula was mobilized for war.

The most hated of the assimilation polices was the name-change

25. Matsuda Toshihiko, 121.
26. Ibid., 146-147.

policy, introduced in 1939, that "allowed" Koreans to take Japanese names. In practice, coercion was exerted on Koreans to take a Japanese name; eventually, 84 percent of Korean households adopted a new name. Yet, a close examination reveals that this policy was not as intrusive as is commonly assumed because it largely dealt with the family registries (*koseki* [戸籍]) and governed the Koreans' bureaucratic interactions with the state (such as at school or city hall). The GGK also sought to bring Korean family registries in line with the Japanese to rationalize administrative procedures, not to suppress Koreans.[27] The Japanese name change policy was not intended to interfere with household matters.

Moreover, it must be kept in mind that Japan's defeat in August 1945 ended assimilation while most of the aspects were still works in progress. Mitarai asserts that "Minami succeeded in establishing the conscription system of Korean men."[28] Korean military service began with a volunteer system in 1938 and expanded as Japan's war fortunes declined. In May 1942 the Korean conscription system was announced, but was not implemented until August 1943, with the first Korean conscripts enlisting in December 1944. It is unlikely that conscription, and many of the assimilation policies, would have been aggressively pursued if Japan had not entered into war with China and the United States.

Education reform, a major plank in both Yamagata's *ikensho* and Hasegawa's "Recommendations," was still being worked on; "the GGK aimed to make no distinctions in the quality and curriculum afforded to Koreans and Japanese." In spite of substantial hurdles, Mitarai concludes that much was achieved.[29] Specifically, Minami,

27. Chōsen sōtokufu, *Kanpō* unnumbered (December 26, 1939), 1.
28. Mitarai Tatsuo (御手洗辰雄), ed., *Minami Jirō* [南次郎] (Tokyo: Minami Jirō denki kankōkai, 1957) *Hibaihin* [非売品] (private edition; copies are sent gratis upon request to other than those in the *denki kankōkai*), 471.
29. Ibid., 460-463, 472. Mitarai uses two terms *musabetsu* [無差別] and *byōdōka* [平等化] to describe the reforms.

as governor-general, doubled the enrollment numbers in elementary school during his tenure and attempted to eliminate the disparities and improve the quality and length of education being provided in the rural districts.[30] Nevertheless, Mitarai may be overly optimistic in this assessment of equality between the Japanese and Korean education.

Important advances were also made in reforming the colonial administration. The GGK under Minami "increased the number of Korean provincial governors." Minami also made "the Koreans the majority among the Directors of Industry (*sangyōbuchō* [産業部長]) and the Directors of Internal Affairs (*naimubuchō* [内務部長])." He also "opened up the post of chief of police stations (*keisatsushochō* [警察署長])" thus handing over more police powers to Koreans, who had direct, close involvement in the lives of fellow Koreans.[31]

Minami was a conservative so it is not surprising that "he opposed linking conscription with the granting of the franchise." Still, even here, there was forward movement. "The *fuin* [府尹] and the *menchō* [面長] remained appointees."[32] "The local assemblies, however, were given strong (*tsuyoi* [強い]) powers over the budget and other matters." In Japan, it is relevant to note, this power was the key to enable the opposition parties to gain power in the Diet and eventually to form party cabinets. Mitarai goes on to reveal that "for the Koreans, the franchise was the most important issue."

Moreover, "among them, the thinking was that even if complete independence was a chimera, they still nourished the hope that at an appropriate *time*, an Ireland-type self-government would be granted. This approach had support among some in Japan's general public as well as members of both Houses of the Diet." Minami supported "the gradual enfranchisement of Koreans" that would

30. Michael J. Seth, *Education Fever*, 23.

31. Mitarai Tetsuo, 472.

32. Ibid., 472. According to Professor Yong-ho Choe, *fuin* is "mayor of a city," and *mencho* is "chief of a sub-county."

lead to membership in both chambers, but "he rejected the notion of self-government." Still, that these hopes and dreams were not impossible reveal that under Minami, the political situation was not a totally unambiguously suffocating one for the Koreans. And long after his tenure as GGK, he was still working to widen the door to greater and freer Korean participation in Korea's political system as Privy Councilor (May 1942–March 1945).[33]

The description of Minami by Mitarai in a section entitled "The Most Liked Governor-General" can easily be dismissed as blatant panegyric propaganda. Mitarai, however, shows balance because he admits that Terauchi and Hasegawa were "without doubt the most feared." Mitarai notes that in the fourth year of Minami's tenure, he started the practice of holding bi-monthly meetings with Koreans. These were opened to anyone who signed up, and Minami, continues Mitarai, put the Koreans at ease by his unpretentiousness. There is another example of his attempts to reach out. In the November 1941 issue of the official GGK publication, *Chōsen* [朝鮮], there is a photo of Minami in a *hanbok* (*kanpuku* [韓服]) the traditional Korean garb, with the caption, "A smiling governor-general in a *kanpuku* and his granddaughter." These actions should not be dismissed out of hand. Our point is that for every effort and every expense expended to win over the Koreans there are that much less energy and funds used to suppress them.[34]

Despite the supposed efforts to eliminate Korean culture, there were examples of the persistence of aspects of Korean culture. In the late 1930s and early 1940s, many Korean movies showed Korean people (usually the elderly and woman) in *hanbok*. Prominent among these was a pro-Japanese movie released in 1941, "Volunteer Soldier" (Chiwŏnbyŏng [지원병, 志願兵]). In it, the Korean people

---

33. Ibid., 472-473.

34. Horiuchi Hiroo of Kensei Shiryōshitsu, the Diet Library furnished us with a copy of this issue.

are shown in traditional Korean dress. The movie is the story of Chun-ho, an ambitious young peasant who works as supervisor for an absentee landowner. Chun-ho is saddened that he cannot join the military even though the Korean people, in his mind, had been completely assimilated. Once Chun-ho learns that the Japanese army has established the volunteer soldier system, he excitedly submits his application for service and it is accepted. Throughout the movie, the landlord and Chun-ho's family are shown wearing Korean clothing and, more important, are speaking Korean. Moreover, in the background Koreans in their traditional garb are seen walking around.[35] I submit that this movie, even granting its propagandistic goal, is evidence that in 1941, the GGK is not systematically trying to suppress the Koreans by, in this case, obliterating their culture. Permit me to digress to buttress my point.

The year was 1955. I (Akita) had completed all the preliminary requirements for the doctoral program. All that remained to be done was to write the dissertation. I decided to go to Tokyo to do so. On my last day in Cambridge, as I was leaving the building where was located the Department of History and Far Eastern Languages, I happened to meet Professor Serge Elisséeff (1889–1975), the "Father of Far Eastern Studies in the United States." He was the first foreign graduate of Tokyo Imperial University, who by the way, wrote his dissertation in Japanese.[36] This was the first and last conversation I had with this great and deservedly honored scholar. I remember to this day, the core of this short conversation: "When in Japan, take every opportunity to go to the movies. They will teach you much about its history and culture, but more important, how they go about

---

35. Palmer watched this movie on a DVD copy found on-line as part of a package that included four Korean movies from the Japanese colonial era. At the time of publication, this movie and others can be watched on-line at http://mubi.com/films/volunteer for a small fee.

36. David Flynn provided the information found in "Serge Elisséeff: 1889–1975," *Harvard Journal of Asiatic Studies* 35 (1975): 12-13.

living their everyday lives without trying to make any specific point. Or, to put it inelegantly in contemporary jargon: 'You are getting no more no less than what you are seeing.'"

Therefore, it is significant that in the movie Palmer saw, there are scenes where Koreans are walking casually in their *hanbok;* and that in the GGK magazine *Chōsen*, Minami and his granddaughter are shown in *hanbok*. Therefore, to regard these pictorial events as "mere" propaganda is to miss the point that what is shown came naturally to those living at specific times and places. Moreover, the fact that in the movie the protagonists are speaking Korean is because, I suspect, even in 1941, many Koreans could not speak Japanese. So few Koreans spoke Japanese that the colonial administration was caught in a conundrum. If propaganda was in Japanese, too few Koreans would understand it; but if the propaganda was in Korean, then the language itself undermined the assimilation efforts.

In October 2012 my colleague and mentor for over thirty years, Professor Hirose Yoshihiro (広瀬順晧), told me of discovering among the collections of primary documents housed in the Kensei Shiryōshitsu the fifty-nine letters in *sōsho* under the rubric *Ōno Rokuichirō monjo* (大野緑一郎文書).[37] Ōno was the *Sōtokufu seimu sōkan* (総督府政務総監) under Minami Jirō (in Japan, this post would be the equivalent to the *Naikaku shokikanchō* (内閣書記官長 [Chief Cabinet Secretary]). Most of the letters are related to personnel items concerning Japanese bureaucrats in Korea and budget matters in reports to the Finance ministry or replies to questions from Diet members. All except one are written in matter of fact manner. The exception is one that appears to have been written from an *onsen* (hot spring). Within these letters, there is no evidence of bellicosity toward the Koreans.

It got interesting when Hirose noted that his main collaborator in

37. As another example of his unending help over the years, I am indebted to Horiuchi Hiroo of KSS for alerting me to Professor Hirose's work on Ōno.

this project is Kim Kyong-nam (金慶南), an archivist from Seoul National University and employee of the National Archives of Korea, whom he had met at an academic conference of archivists in Tokyo. She wanted to learn to decipher the *sōsho* into *kaisho* (楷書) [printed style] that she would then render into *hangul*, to deposit them in National Archives of Korea to make them available to scholars in Korea. This may just help to open a small window to clear the air in Korea from some of the misconceptions, not only about Minami Jirō, but also about Japan's Korea policy.

Gi-Wook Shin on Colonial Land Reform

I now turn to Gi-Wook Shin and Do-Hyun Han. The two provide insight into the colonial regime's preferred governance style, which was evident under Minami during his implementation of assimilation policies. The GGK utilized colonial corporatism, a methodology that emphasized "social harmony and hierarchy. . . ."[38] The Japanese regime operated through a plethora of "semiofficial, semivoluntary, intermediary associations for colonial control and mobilization." In addition to these, the bureaucracy reached the Korean masses through institutions that were traditional (such as village compacts) and modern police and educators. Shin writes that the Japanese sought the cooperation of Koreans and aimed to avoid outright coercion, but in the process, these methods led to "more direct state involvement in colonial affairs. . . ."[39] The GGK used its resources *to encourage* individuals to comply with state policies. Even though the GGK possessed unrestrained power within Korea, it used a carrot-stick approach with the Korean people to ensure compliance with colonial policies: the colonial bureaucracy and organizations

38. Gi-Wook Shin and Do-Hyun Han, "Colonial Corporatism: The Rural Revitalization Campaign, 1932–1940," in *Colonial Modernity in Korea*, ed. Gi-wook Shin and Michael Robinson (Cambridge, MA: Harvard University Press, 1999), 70-76.

39. Ibid., 76-77.

offered enticements. If inducements failed, the state then resorted to mildly coercive measures, which became increasingly persistent when individuals refused to comply.

To understand corporatism and the contributions of Minami to Korean society, it is useful to analyze the Rural Revitalization Campaign which was launched in 1932, but carried out largely under Minami. The colonial state set out to eliminate the food shortages and indebtedness that plagued rural Korea. To accomplish this goal, the GGK sought to reduce tenancy and "create owner-cultivators." This campaign offered agricultural, economic, and moral training to peasant farmers. Using the corporatist approach, the "government . . . provided tax breaks and mobilized financial co-operatives that offered low-interest loans for land purchases."[40] From 1933 to 1940, nearly a half million households availed themselves of this program's services. According to government surveys, the program had some successes: 21 percent of participants improved their economic status and 36 percent resolved food shortages; contrast this to only one percent reporting a decline in economic status.[41]

Since Gi-Wook Shin's analyses play such a major role in the discussion that will follow below, it is only proper that I introduce him to the non-specialist. Gi-Wook Shin burst into prominence with his well-received revisionistic study, *Peasant Protest and Social Change in Colonial Korea* (1996).[42] According to Shin, in the 1920s the GGK was concerned about the unrest and economic deterioration that infused Korea's agricultural regions. The GGK reacted by enacting the Tenant Arbitration Ordinance (*Kosaku Chōteirei* [小作調停令]) (1932) to benefit tenant farmers, and the Agricultural

40. Ibid., 86-89.

41. Ibid., 89.

42. Gi-Wook Shin earned his B.A. at Yonsei University, Seoul; his M.A. and Ph.D. at the University of Washington, Seattle (all in Sociology). He is currently Professor of Sociology, Stanford University, and Director, Walter H. Shorenstein Asia-Pacific Research Center.

Lands Ordinance (*Nōchirei* [農地令]) (1934) based upon the "moderate colonial policy" adopted after Hasegawa's tenure.[43] These actions, Shin writes, meant placing the GGK on the tenant farmer's side in their disputes with both Japanese and Korean landlords. Specifically, the tenant farmers now could demand reductions of their land rents and enter into binding contracts. In these ways, the tenant farmers gained the upper hand against the landlords. Two other consequences followed. The one was a decline of the landlord population until their numbers became practically nil after the Pacific War. The other was that a number of landlords who were unhappy with their future prospects poured their capital into industrial enterprises. This is further evidence that the GGK's actions contributed, in this case unforeseen, to the development of Korea's capitalistic economy.

Shin further illustrates the complexity of the situation in the agricultural regions by his revision of the standard view that the communist-tinged peasant union movement was energized by impoverished tenant farmers driven to revolt by the GGK's depredations. He shows, instead, that the tenant farmers were not involved; that the majority of participants were independent farmers who were extremely disaffected with land tax increases as well as with the local governments' interference in village administration. This led some to revolt, which in turn invited police retaliation, so that by the mid-1930s, the independent farmer populations had practically disappeared.[44]

Shin tackles another article of faith of the proponents of the nationalist historical paradigm: that the GGK carried out a cadastral

---

43. Gi-Wook Shin, *Peasant Protest and Social Change in Colonial Korea* (Seattle: University of Washington Press, 1996), 177-178. In another article, Shin points out that these Ordinances were patterned on Japan's 1924 model. Gi-Wook Shin, "Agrarian Conflict and the Origins of Korean Capitalism," *American Journal of Sociology* 103.5 (March 1998): 1327.
44. Gi-Wook Shin, *Peasant Protest*, 176-180.

land survey (1910–1918) to enable Japanese individuals and enterprises to expropriate land belonging to Koreans. He shows that, at least in specific cases, the Japanese through the medium of this survey, *did not radically alter Korean land tenure*. He shows that in a group of 9,256 parcels, only twelve went unreported, that less than one percent of the land was disputed during or after the survey, and that except for land owned by the palaces and government agencies, the survey brought little turnover in ownership.[45]

Shin argues convincingly in a lengthy article that the alleged postwar Korean "industrial transformation" or "'miracle' did not simply materialize due to forces operating after 1960; [but that] pre-1960 events such as colonialism, occupation, revolts, war, and reform" created the basis for the economic change that followed. He then without qualification stresses that "*colonial* industrialization and land reform [must be considered] to be *most crucial* in shaping postcolonial Korean development."[46]

Michael Robinson strongly supports Shin's conclusion.

> I have decided to write against the grain of nationalism, . . . and refocusing on Korea's early experience with modernity as a way to make sense of the present social and cultural conditions of South Korea. . . . The decisive truth of this matter . . . is that modernity arrived in Korea during the Japanese colonial period. . . . [47]

Herein we arrive at a critical point in our discussion of Korea's postwar inheritance of Japan's colonial legacy. Modernity in the forms of law, culture, industry, bureaucracy, land reform, public

---

45. Ibid., 39-41. See also Gi-Wook Shin, "Agrarian Conflict and the Origins of Korean Capitalism," 1326-1328.
46. Gi-Wook Shin, "Agrarian Conflict," 1311-1312.
47. "Narrative Politics, Nationalism and Korean History," *Papers of the British Association for Korean Studies* vol. 6 (1996), 36. Robinson is Professor, Department of East Asian Languages and Cultures, Indiana University, Bloomington.

health, and so forth shaped postwar Korea. It was only logical that once the Korean nation gained its independence, it would have been too much of a herculean task to reinvent the wheel and restructure the whole of Korean society and economy to one that eliminated all vestiges of the colonial era—particularly in the southern half that was occupied by the United States, which retained Japanese bureaucrats for a period before transitioning to Koreans who had cooperated with the Japanese.

Richard J. Smethhurst and Gi-Wook Shin on Land Reform

Gi-Wook Shin's passing reference that the GGK's enactment of the Tenant Arbitration Ordinance (1932) and the Agricultural Lands Ordinance (1934) were patterned on Japan's 1924 model brought to mind Richard Smethurst's and Penelope Francks' analyses of tenant-farmer reforms and their consequences in Japan.[48]

Richard J. Smethurst's *Agricultural Development and Tenancy Disputes in Japan, 1870–1940* (1986), is a detailed, closely reasoned, and convincing overview of prewar agricultural Japan. He starts with the premise that "Japan's rural economy expanded dramatically between 1868 . . . and the late 1930s," with both the government and the farmers responsible for this growth. The Meiji government's contributions lay in creating the framework of "orderly political, financial, educational, and technical institutions" and the encouragement of farmers to take advantage of the opportunities provided by the newly created infrastructure. It took little prodding for the farmers to do so and to commit themselves to improving agricultural techniques based upon "rational decisions and choices."

Smethurst also disagrees with the view that "a combination of landlord-government coercion and manipulation weakened the tenant movement in the late 1920s." In other words, the tenant

48. George Akita, *Evaluating Evidence*, 73-74.

movement's success in the 1920s "can be attributed to the national government's forbearance and even aid," which was, of course, welcomed by the tenant-farmers. This meant that the government, by its methods of mediating disputes, helped tenants to purchase land "inexpensively," while the police and courts, for their part, intervened infrequently in support of the landlords. Moreover, instead of faulting the government for its so-called miserly and slow-paced extension of the male franchise, Smethurst stresses that the expanding franchise enabled the tenant farmers to become a part of governance. They were able, he says, to gain seats on 27 to 32 percent of all village assemblies in Japan from 1925 until World War II, with positive results for their livelihood.[49]

In his review of Shin's *Peasant Protest and Social Change in Colonial Korea*, Vipan Chandra predicted that, Shin's "discovery of the colonial government's pro-peasant and anti-landlord stance is sure to vex both the Marxist and 'nationalist' historians on the peninsula."[50] Whether this came about is unclear, but Smethurst, indeed, faced a firestorm of criticism from "Marxist" leaning Japanese historians. A Japanese economic historian, Nishida Yoshiaki (西田美昭), could hardly contain his anger in a twenty-six page outburst: "Smethurst's book on modern Japanese agricultural history merits no serious consideration. Smethurst's biased use of the work of other scholars, his distortion of source materials, and the inevitably flawed conclusions that result render it wholly worthless."[51] This kind of critique has no

49. Richard J. Smethurst, *Agricultural Development and Tenancy Disputes in Japan* (Princeton, NJ: Princeton University Press, 1986), 3-4, 19-21, 27-32, 33-37, 40, 56, and 432-433. Smethurst is Professor, Department of History at the University of Pittsburgh. He received his B.A. from Dickinson College, and his M.A. and Ph.D. from the University of Michigan.

50. See, Chandra's review in *American Historical Review* 103.5 (December 1998): 1671-1672.

51. "Growth of the Meiji Landlord System and Tenancy Disputes after World War I: A Critique of Richard Smethurst, Agricultural Development and Tenancy Disputes in Japan, 1870-1940," *Journal of Japanese Studies* 15.2 (Summer

place in a scholarly world since it shuts down all avenues to scholarly exchange and mutual growth. There is irony in the positions taken by Smethurst and Nishida. Smethurst may be equated to the "revisionists" in Korean studies; whereas Nishida, a "progressive, Marxist-leaning, anti-nationalistic" scholar may be placed among those espousing the standard nationalist narrative that animates their works on Korea.

Let us now turn to the discussion of Penelope Francks' contribution. Francks' focus is on the roles of the village groups. She points out that large-scale cultivating landlords, usually village heads, were not necessarily significant everywhere in Japan, and some may have lost interest in rural agriculture, lured away by industrial and commercial opportunities. The "whole-village groups," in which medium-scale owner/tenant cultivators played a leading role, then assumed the functions of the large-scale cultivating landlords. The village groups could do this because the village itself had significant experience in group organization that had matured over generations and had developed the necessary institutions and skills required for group action.

This experience was put to use by the village groups in their role as "intermediaries" with the "outside world" that included government organs and extension services, and in their "tak[ing] over functions such as marketing and provision of credit that landlords had previously performed." Francks is particularly interested in the roles played by these village groups and the government in bringing about technological change and the completion of an irrigation project in the Saga Plain. The successes in these two areas of endeavor, she writes, transformed the agriculturalists there from "subsistence level production to sophisticated commercial farmers." In the process, the officials sometimes exercised "authoritarian" means, such as using the force of law to achieve their objectives. However, Francks con-

1989): 415.

cludes that officials and farmers worked together most of the time with a degree of mutual respect.

Another contribution by the government, according to Francks, was its long-term involvement in agricultural extension, that is, what Smethurst says is part of the infrastructure created by the government. Francks' emphasis is on the "balance between, the roles of governmental or research officials and farmers' organizations." This generally successful balance was possible because the government was represented by officials and workers "who had long experience and close contact with working farmers," who "consulted them or their representatives," who "backed up the adoption of technology," and who were "attuned to the structural changes" of the villages and could therefore also be "influenced by the farmers." The farmers' impact, in turn, was enhanced by the repository of local skills in the village groups and by the leaders' sensitivity to the "problems and potential" of their respective environments and their exercise of initiative in coping with the problems and potential.[52]

We cannot leave Shin without returning to his primary emphasis; that is, from a "sociohistorical perspective," he is persuaded that peasant political action must be understood in the context of how the peasants themselves acted on their own interests to better themselves; "Unless the ideas of leaders make sense to peasants on their own terms, peasants will not rise up in protest. . . . Korea from the 1920s to the 1940s witnessed not so much a Korean nationalist or communist peasant movement as a Korean *peasants'* peasant movement."[53] Put another way, Korean peasants (and Japan's tenant farmers) were not merely lumps of clay or sacks of potatoes. To believe otherwise is to deprive them of their humanity and their ability to act. Tessa Morris-Suzuki says it well:

---

52. Penelope Francks, *Technology and Agricultural Development in Pre-War Japan* (New Haven, CT: Yale University Press, 1984), 44-46, 245, and 277-285.

53. Gi-Wook Shin, *Peasant Protest*, 180. Italics in original.

> Even the smallest and most vulnerable indigenous communities were not just passive victims of state policy but shaped their own identity within the framework of empire, often participating with surprising vigor in colonial debates.[54]

Shin builds on this idea by describing Korean agrarianism as being strongly anti-capitalist, anti-urban, and anti-modern, with the goal of "reconstructing rural society as the core of a new Korea," in short, the rural should be "the center of economy and culture of a society" that would produce "a self-sufficient agrarian society."

He then states that Korean agrarianism appears to have been influenced by the Meiji era Japanese agrarianist philosophy. In fact, he sees "substantial parallels between Korean and Japanese agrarianism." For example, the Korean "*nongmindo* [농민도] (way of the peasant) . . . was a translation of the Japanese term *nōmindō* [農民道], which was in turn related to *bushidō* [武士道] (the way of the warrior)." The parallels do not surprise Shin, given that "leading Korean agrarianists were educated in Japan," including "Yi Sŏnghwan [이성환 李盛煥] . . . [who] attended an agricultural school in Japan" as well as the fact that "many village leaders . . . [who represented] the twenty-seven model villages" that had "achieved self-reliance while fighting against commercial and urban forces" toured villages in Japan in order to "find ideas and examples for building their own 'utopian'" societies.

Shin points to colonial modernity as a major difference between Korea and Japan in spite of these similarities; namely, Korean agrarianism developed under the tutelage of Japanese colonial rule. Still, the linkage between Korean and Japanese agrarianism is yet another example that the binary "them" (the Japanese) versus "us"

54. "Becoming Japanese: Imperial Expansion and Identity Crises in the Early Twentieth Century," in *Japan's Competing Modernities: Issues in Culture and Democracy, 1900–1930*, ed. Sharon A. Minichiello (Honolulu, University of Hawai'i Press, 1998), 159.

(the Koreans) explanation of the colonial experience is much too simple, and cannot stand up in the light of documentary evidence.[55]

Industrialization in Colonial Korea

Soon Won Park's (朴淳遠) contributions to revisionism can be divided into two large issues. The first is found in her article, "Making Colonial Policies in Korea: The Factory Law Debate, Peace Preservation Law, and Land Reform Laws in the Interwar Years."[56] She takes note of the "*conventional view* of a powerless colonial Korean labor force oppressed by an authoritative and exploitative Japan." She argues, however, that "Japanese colonial policies were not always authoritative" and that colonial "legislation resulted from a complex decision-making process" that included "a need to balance the interests of different leaders, shifting policy priorities in Japan, and local pressures." She disagrees with the premise that the Korean workers were "silent, passive victims" or "surplus colonial workers . . . who had no legal protection or channels for [their] grievances."

She then points to recent studies that are quite critical of the workers for being "silent, passive victims" without recourse to escape from their deplorable state of affairs. In other words, these studies, representing the standard (nationalistic) postulations, are "totalizing, politically biased narratives that repress and cover up the richness and complexities" of the colonial experience, and replace it with "a simple, binary exploitation-resistance theme [black

---

55. Gi-Wook Shin, "Agrarianism: A Critique of Colonial Modernity in Korea," *Comparative Studies in Society and History* 41.4 (October 1999): 794, 796, and 800-802. Italics in original.

56. *Korean Studies* 22.1 (1998): 41-61. Park received her B.A. from Ewha Women's University in Seoul and her M.A. and Ph.D. from Harvard University. She is most recently listed (2015) as Adjunct Professor, Department of History and Art History, George Mason University. She has taught at Howard University and Keiō University in Tokyo.

or white; good vs. bad] onto colonial Korea." She further argues that "the colonial government handled each piece of social legislation case by case, *cautiously* selecting and modifying them for [the requirements of] the colonial situation."[57]

Park also divides the application of Japanese legislation in Korea into large groups. One is the "liberal principle of the 'extension policy' (*naichi enchōshugi* [内地延長主義] . . .)"; and the other the "'cultural policy' (*bunka seisaku*)" that was adopted as a response to the March First Movement.[58] She seems to be of two minds on *bunka seisaku*. First, she writes that it was "clearly *authoritarian* " and had "a more sophisticated, divide-and-rule [aspect in its] implementation," but second, she later describes the "relatively relaxed sociopolitical atmosphere in Korean society during the cultural policy of the 1920s."[59] Be that as it may, Park's great contribution is to bring into the open the complexity of the colonial government's approach to factory workers.

I reiterate my position that Park continues to emphatically reject the "dichotomizing" and "binary" approaches that see colonial Korea as a narrative featuring "resistance" (the good Koreans) vs. "collaboration" (the bad Koreans) or, Korean "martyrdom and nationalism" vs. Japanese "oppression."

Park, like other revisionists, sees clear "continuity" between colonial and modern Korea, saying that "understanding the nature of colonial modernity . . . [is] a prerequisite for understanding the increasingly complex and diverse modernity of present-day Korea." In chapter 4 of her monograph, titled "Workers in Liberated Korea: The Onoda Samch'ŏk [오노다삼척] Factory," she takes up in detail, the "larger historical questions relating to the impact of the colonial legacy on twentieth-century Korean labor." The basic thrust

57. Soon Won Park, 41 and 45.
58. Ibid., 45. Italics in original.
59. Ibid., 45 and 49.

of this legacy is that "Japanese colonialism and its cultural policy [*bunka seiji seisaku*] produced *multiple possibilities* for cultural adaptation." Park's workers, as with Shin's peasants, were not passive lumps of coal. They had choices and acted on them. Some decided to learn Japanese and participate in Japanese-owned companies or Japanese dominated bureaucracies. Others gained intensive work experience that made them *valuable human assets* in "*liberated Korea.*" In short, "[b]y the end of the colonial period, a number of Koreans," many of them "ambitious Korean youth[s]," "had established themselves as responsible, independent, and skilled workers . . . [who had] reached the top layer of the labor hierarchy open to Koreans." This statement, of course, points to the existence of "openings" available only to Japanese.

Park is generally positive in her judgment of the rather open-ended environment in colonial Korea. She points out that the "*upward movement* was not limited to the workforce in factories, mines, and construction sites"; it "was *widespread* in other modern-sector jobs in schools, companies, banks, and even government offices." And then there were others who struck out on their own to become "small and medium-scale Korean capitalists."[60] All in all, Park strikes a heavy blow for the revisionist agenda.

The Expropriation of Korean Lands and Artifacts

One of the most sensitive issues that divide the Koreans and Japanese is that the GGK, by conducting surveys in the 1910s of landownership, enabled rapacious Japanese to expropriate lands owned by the Koreans. Edwin H. Gragert questions this charge by doing what a scholar should do: he went to the primary documents.

Gragert selects three GGK sources: Tochidaichō (土地台帳) (1914), Tochi shoyūken shōsho (土地所有権証書) (1917), and Chisekizu

60. Soon Won Park: *Colonial Industrialization and Labor in Korea: The Onoda Cement Factory* (Cambridge: Harvard University Asia Center, 1999), 2-3, 5, 6, 9, 188, and 190.

(地籍図) (1910–1918). Using the information contained in these land surveys, he uses five villages as case studies to trace the changes in landownership from the late Yi dynasty to the end of the colonial period. His conclusion is that from the annexation to 1918 *there were no great changes in ownership* from Korean hands to Japanese individuals and enterprises. Moreover, through 1935 in the same villages less than 10 percent of lands of all kinds changed hands from Koreans to Japanese. He then points to the impact of the worldwide Great Depression as a major factor for changes in ownership. He writes that during the 1920s, Korean and *Japanese* landowners used their land as collateral for loans from institutions such as Chōsen Shokusan Ginkō (朝鮮殖産銀行) and Tochi Kaihatsu Kaisha (土地開発会社). Then came the Depression, and the borrowers who could not repay their loans lost their lands to these institutions.[61] In other words, nothing nefarious was involved.

This is such a sensitive, contentious subject, however, that it bears noting and repeating what Gi-Wook Shin wrote about the same subject, only on a smaller scale:

> The Japanese [through the medium of this survey] did not radically alter [Korean] land tenure . . . [of a group] of 9,256 land parcels only 12 . . . went unreported . . . less than 1% of the land . . . [was] disputed during or after the survey . . . the survey brought little turnover of landownership.[62]

In summary, the change in ownership from Korean to Japanese hands was not a direct result of the land survey or unscrupulous actions by the GGK.

---

61. *Landownership Under Colonial Rule: Korea's Japanese Experience, 1900–1935* (Honolulu: University of Hawai'i Press, 1994), *passim*. Gragert is Director Emeritus with iEARN-USA. iEARN stands for International Education and Resource Network that facilitates on-line collaborative project-based learning in elementary and secondary schools in 130 countries worldwide.
62. Gi-Wook Shin, *Peasant Protest*, 39-41.

The Japanese are accused of not only stealing Korean lands but, even worse, of "indiscriminately plundering Korean cultural relics as part of an elaborate conspiracy to deprive Koreans of their national heritage and, thus, racial identity." Hyung Il Pai (裵炯逸) in a study earlier used by Palmer, also points out that another consequence of this anti-Japanese rhetoric is that the Koreans are portrayed as "unwitting victims of superpower politics so as to absolve them from any hint of collaboration in the contentious issue of 'who is to blame for the plunder of Korea.'"[63]

Her answer will not comfort the proponents of the nationalist historical narrative. Her charge is that those who did the "actual looting, digging, delivery of items, and even theft from CSTF [the Chōsen Sōtokufu] museums were . . . *locals*, including peasants, smugglers, and merchants connected to the many antiquity dealers." Their customers were "Japanese such as Itō Hirobumi and Yanagi Sōetsu [柳宗悦] . . . but by the late colonial period, there arose a class of rich and urbane Korean colonial elite . . . [that] accumulated their own antiquity collections, patronizing the same shops and competing with the Japanese for the best deals and bargains."[64] The "culpability" of both the Japanese and Koreans on this issue may suggest a way to look at the comfort women/"sex slave" question; that is, the matter is more complicated than one that is seen simply as a bifurcated "white vs. black" matter, with one side being "obviously black or bad." Moreover, while Pai stresses that the founders of the Office of Cultural Management, established in 1961, earnestly maintain that

63. "The Creation of National Treasures and Monuments: The 1916 Japanese Laws on the Preservation of Korean Remains and Relics and Their Colonial Legacies," *Korean Studies* 25, no.1 (2001): 76. Pai received her B.A. in History from Sogang University, Seoul, and her M.A. and Ph.D. in Anthropology from Harvard University. She is currently Associate Professor, Department of East Asian languages and Cultural Studies, University of California, Santa Barbara.

64. Ibid., 76

the "Korean independent spirit . . . was *solely responsible* for the preservation of the Korean national heritage." She, however, is also most emphatic about the colonial government's legacy in the "preservation of the Korean remains and relics;" in short, there existed continuity between colonial Korea and the present in the face of all the anti-Japanese vitriol.[65]

She raises three points to support this contention. First, she draws attention to the fact that in the matter of "how authenticity" of the artifacts is established and "displayed for public consumption has *not fundamentally changed since the beginning of the Japanese colonial era*"—this, in spite of the upheavals resulting from independence [from Japan], the Korean War," the emergence of the two Koreas, and successive "military regimes."[66]

Second, Pai notes that the "structure and administration of the OCP [Office of Cultural Properties itself] and the collections of national museums today . . . continue to reflect colonial-era preferences in their ranking of cultural properties."[67] To this can be added that the laws related to the preservation of Korea's cultural heritage are strongly impacted by their colonial origins.[68]

And third is that the "current rankings of Korean cultural properties" as sequentially numbered is in the *same order* "of colonial registries dating between 1934 and 1941." And, starting "from the first South Korean national properties registry dated 1962 to the present day, newly registered items *continue to be appended to the 1943 list.*"[69]

Pai, however, is not without criticism of the GGK on the issue of preserving Korean artifacts. On the one hand, she emphasizes that the GGK's funding for scholarly research on Korea's heritage was

65. Ibid., 72 and 76.
66. Ibid., 77.
67. Ibid.
68. Hyung Il Pai, *Constructing "Korean" Origins*, Introduction.
69. Hyung Il Pai, "Creation of National Treasures," 86.

anchored on its promotion of the "common racial origins theory" aimed at justifying its rule over Korea. Moreover, she asserts that the archeologists funded by The Committee on the Investigation of Korean Antiquities (CKKK) established in 1916 by the GGK conducted "haphazard surveys" in which the novices among them sharpened their skills in Korean sites. This led to the destruction of many historically important sites in Korea.[70] Still, the lasting impression conveyed by the article on this issue is that colonial and present-day Korea are tied at the hip like Siamese twins, as articulated by Pai herself:

> [I]t is still indispensable that we recognize the enduring legacies of state-[established] authenticity in the bureaucratic origins of heritage-management practices, for *there remain undeniable Japanese cultural, aesthetic, and legalistic continuities*. It is about time that South Korean scholars and OCP bureaucrats in particular address this colonial inheritance in a more systematic manner if they are indeed serious about the task of decolonizing the ethics and aesthetics of collecting state cultural properties.[71]

Henry H. Em writes a study quite similar to Pai's in that he examines the use of Japan's cultural preservation efforts, but in a different light. He looks at the restoration of cultural sites as a pedagogical endeavor, one in which the colonial state was "successful in terms of producing detailed studies of Korean art, customs, language, religion, and history" with the "goal of transforming . . . peasants into *Chōsenjin* (Koreans)." In other words, by promoting Korea's ancient past, the colonial state was able to "reconstitute (disparate) Korean identities into a homogeneous *Chōsenjin* that became both a bureaucratic and a derogatory classification for all Koreans regardless of gender, regional origin, or class background."[72] Em raises an

70. Ibid., 87-89.
71. Ibid., 89.
72. Henry H. Em, 10-12.

important point that highlights the nuances at play in this subject. He notes that the Japanese state promoted a single, coherent Korean identity from all the regional differences, a move that contradicts nationalist accounts that the GGK sought to eradicate Korean culture. Yet, Em points out that the Korean subject was constructed to be an inferior subject to be ruled over. His analysis moves beyond the binary or simplistic portrayal of Japan the oppressor and Korea the victim.

The Persistence of the National Historical Narrative

Alexis Dudden's *Japan's Colonization of Korea: Discourse and Power* (2005) has drawn high praise from scholars of esteemed Ivy League universities such as Princeton and Brown as well as from Stanford.[73] They all agree that Dudden's great contribution is in showing that the Meiji leadership used "Euro-American concepts of international law" to justify "imperialism in general," which in turn "legitimize(d)" Japan's colonization of Korea.[74]

Strewn throughout her monograph, however, are unscholarly, puzzling, one-sided statements, and simplistic, questionable conclusions sometimes based on non-evidence. The lack of respect for scholarly apparatus is harshly criticized in a book review by James C. Baxter, then of the International Research Center for Japanese Studies (*Kokusai Nihon Bunka Kenkyū Sentā* [国際日本文化研究センター]) in Kyoto:

> The strikingly handsome dust jacket features effusive blurbs by three distinguished senior historians, one of whom (James L. McClain) states, "Her work will surely be compared favorably with other landmark studies on Japanese colonialism by Hilary Conroy, Mark Peattie, and

73. Dudden has a Ph.D. from the University of Chicago and is Professor of History, University of Connecticut.

74. See book jacket.

> Peter Duus." . . . But should Dudden's work be compared "favorably" to its predecessors? Not, in my judgment, until a good deal of tidying up has been done.

Baxter gives her credit for showing "how imperialism worked in the international system that prevailed in . . . [the] years" she covers. Baxter proceeds to go into great detail about her errors and concludes: "But Dudden and the University of Hawai'i Press set a bad example for younger researchers by going to press when such a large number of problems remain in the academic apparatus. . . . To earn regard as the professional peer of her predecessors in this field, Dudden needs to get the details in order, not just to make a spirited argument for a stimulating thesis."[75] No one should doubt the inextricable link between scholarly apparatus and the narrative. Therefore, Dudden's sloppiness (there is no other word for it) in comporting with the nitty-gritty of scholarship leads to, as stated above, questionable statements and conclusions.

Dudden has a one-sided view of the Meiji leadership and Korea's colonial government. Her discussion of Itō Hirobumi is an example. She mocks those who "maintain an elitist reverence for Itō Hirobumi [by] subscribing to notions of his benevolent hand (i.e., that Itō would *never* have annexed Korea), [yet] overlook the fact that he authorized torture in the Korean penal codes under his rule, and that such legacies endured throughout the colonial period and arguably beyond."[76]

I would like more support for the statements that there were those who maintain that "Itō would *never* have annexed Korea" or that he "authorized torture." Moreover, since Dudden says that the Korean penal code Itō authorized started a legacy of torture that "endured throughout the colonial period and arguably beyond," she must be

---

75. *MN* vol.60, no. 3 (Autumn 2005), 409-412, esp. 411-412.

76. Alexis Dudden, *Japan's Colonization of Korea: Discourse and Power* (Honolulu: University of Hawai'i Press, 2005), 117. Italics in original.

equating torture with "flogging," a connection, as we shall see, that should not be made.

Dudden also denigrates Japanese legal specialists with highly respectable reputations as Itō's judicial missionaries and legal scions, as if they were his Potemkin Village-like puppets.[77] Sprunger, in the context of his study on penal reform, appears to agree with my negative reaction to Dudden's statement on "judicial specialists." He states, "Dudden portrays men like Ume Kenzaburō (sic) (梅謙次郎), and Kuratomi Yūzaburō (倉富勇三郎) as 'legal missionaries' on the surface only. They self-consciously helped to construct a façade of legal modernity . . . behind which a national project of state aggrandizement operated. In the context of this argument, she contends that their legislative efforts in Korea were nothing more than 'performative displays.'"[78] Sprunger found most colonial bureaucrats within the penal system to be competent professionals.[79]

Dudden then moves on to the year 1911 when General Terauchi Masatake began to "'round up . . . suspects,' investigating an alleged (or wholly fabricated) attempt to kill him [in 1910]."[80] She says that "Hundreds of Koreans were imprisoned, tortured, and in some cases beaten to death, yet the whole affair would probably have remained unnoticed—*as similar events most likely did. . . .*"[81] The italicized portion is such an unscholarly conjecture, it requires no comment. Yet her charge that, "Hundreds of Koreans were imprisoned, and tortured, and in some cases beaten to death" is so vague that I checked her footnote reference. What I found was a note of archival materials available on the subject. This, to me, shows a lack of professional courtesy. The incident to which she refers is the "105

77. Dudden, 117, 126, and 177 fn. 58.
78. Michael L. Sprunger, 104, fn.33. Sprunger should have listed Kenzaburō as Kenjirō.
79. Ibid., 12, 15.
80. Alexis Dudden, 120.
81. Ibid., 121.

Persons Incident," also known as the "Korean Conspiracy Case." Between 600 and 700 Koreans were arrested, including Christians and Korean nationalist leaders. In the end, the Japanese tried 123 and convicted 105, but most sentences were reduced or overturned on appeal.

In another instance of questionable scholarship, Dudden asserts that "it is important to draw attention to this first decade [1910–1919] of Japanese colonial rule—especially its first few years, 1910–1914—because it *appears* to have been an *exceptionally brutal period*."[82] A check of footnote 65 on page 177 gives us no source for her charge of "extreme brutality" but instead directs the reader to the issue of "collaboration"; Hildi Kang's *Under the Black Umbrella*, a collection of oral histories, largely contradicts Dudden's claims. This is an example of "bait and switch" and is inexcusable.

We move from her unsustained generalizations to the specific: she makes the unqualified proposition that the comfort women were "sexual slaves."[83] This is a charge that cannot be swept under the rug because it is a complex issue that must be addressed.

Nationalist histories on the comfort women focus on the unscrupulous recruiters' use of deceit and kidnapping to fill Japan's military brothels. Koreans have nationalized the comfort women issue in such a way that all sexual encounters between Korean military prostitutes and Japanese soldiers are extrapolated to the rape of Korea (the woman) by Japan (the soldier). In this sense, all Koreans were terrorized and shamed. Given this sort of distorted academic coverage, it is worth our time to note that revisionist histories are challenging this nationalistic narrative.

The recruitment of women for prostitution and the operation of brothels have a particular history that is critical to understanding why the comfort women cannot be categorically classified as mili-

82. Ibid., 118.
83. Ibid., 115, 144-145.

tary sex slaves. Revisionists note that the system of military prostitution (the comfort station system) was an expansion of licensed prostitution that existed in Japan and Korea. C. Sarah Soh, professor of Anthropology at San Francisco State University, discredits claims that most of the women were tricked into prostitution by recruits; in most cases, the process was open and the woman (and her family) knew she was headed to a brothel because thousands upon thousands of Korean women were often sold into brothels by their fathers, husbands, or went willingly as a way to rescue their family from poverty. The Confucian patriarchy in Korean society relegated women to an expendable resource.[84]

The academic pendulum that, early on, cast blame on the Japanese military and government has lost momentum and is now beginning to swing in the direction of placing greater accountability on Korean society and families. The Japanese military certainly played a major role in sustaining the comfort stations, but—as revisionist studies show—they were not solely responsible.

Comfort women were purchased by middlemen who were most often Korean, although many Japanese were also recruiters.[85] Herein we see that Koreans were critical in every phase of the recruitment process; Korean men sold their female family members to Korean recruiters who sold them into brothels. Soh accurately notes that Korean women were victims of structural violence: the patriarchal nature of Korean society gave them no voice at home, and the colonial system left them little chance to resist their plight.[86]

---

84. See C. Sarah Soh, *The Comfort Women: Sexual Violence and Postcolonial Memory in Korea and Japan* (Chicago: University of Chicago Press, 2008), 1-27. Other academic works point out that the comfort stations were an expansion of the prewar brothel system.

85. Song Youn-ok (宋連玉), "Japanese Colonial Rule and State-Managed Prostitution: Korea's Licensed Prostitutes," *Positions: East Asia Cultures Critique* 5.1 (Spring 1997): 181.

86. C. Sarah Soh, "The Korean 'Comfort Women' Tragedy as Structural Violence," in *Rethinking Historical Injustice and Reconciliation in Northeast*

Yet, the nationalist historical narrative portrays all sexual encounters as outright rape. We do not deny that some comfort women suffered sexual slavery; however, almost all accounts related to the comfort stations note that the Japanese soldiers paid the brothel proprietor, who was Korean or Japanese, for the sexual encounter. Some proprietors paid the prostitutes for their work and some did not; some comfort women left the comfort station when their debts were paid and some were detained against their will. There is no universalizing story; therefore it is inaccurate and misleading to project slavery as the master narrative of the comfort women.

Too often ignored in this discussion are the thousands of Japanese comfort women. "Korean activists and researchers consider it important to make a distinction between Korean comfort women as forced sexual slaves and Japanese comfort women as voluntary participants for commercial purposes."[87] Yet, Japanese prostitutes experienced the same victimization as their Korean counterparts: most were from impoverished families that sold them into a brothel. Yet, there is no international outrage over the plight of these Japanese women because they are of the "wrong" nationality. Victimization of any group of people is wrong, regardless of their country of origin.

Varying Perspectives of Flogging in Colonial Korea

The foregoing discussion may be tiresome to some and trivial to others, but it serves my principle purpose: to bring up the charge of the cruel and unusual practice flogging of prisoners that Dudden appears to equate with torture. This is an especially sensitive, heated matter for Koreans as it proves to them the unusually cruel nature

---

Asia: The Korean Experience, ed. Gi-Wook Shin, Soon-Won Park and Daqing Yang (London: Routledge, 2007), 20.

87. Pyong Gap Min, "'Korean Comfort Women': The Intersection of Colonial Power, Gender, and Class," *Gender & Society* 17.6 (December 2003): 939.

of colonial rule.

Dudden begins her narrative with, again, another unsubstantiated statement meant to be semi-humorous. She starts with the premise that a "healthy ratio" of 151 Japanese to 160 Korean jailers in 1908 meant that "a Japanese warden would *always* have had a Korean jailer available to flog a Korean inmate," and thus perpetuating the Japanese insistence that flogging was, after all, "demonstrabl[y]" in "fact and memory" an "old Korean custom" and therefore, a justifiable form of physical punishment.[88]

She then turns to Edward J. Baker's "The Role of Legal Reforms in the Japanese Annexation and Rule of Korea 1905–1919."[89] She states that Baker has "*demonstrated* that torturing Korean prisoners in Japanese-run jails not only remained a practice throughout the colonial period, but became . . . [as Baker cleverly puts it] 'a policy objective.'" She cites Baker's assertion that "Flogging was an extremely cruel form of punishment. Victims suffered as many as ninety strokes on the buttocks with a bamboo rod while tied in a prone position. . . . In *a number of cases*, death resulted."[90]

To ascertain where and how Baker had concluded that "In a number of cases, death resulted," I went to my colleagues at the

---

88. Alexis Dudden, 116-117. A recent article on present day education in Korea has this to say: ". . . the [South Korean] government hopes to reduce the strain on students [caused by corporal punishment]. Corporal punishment, an *entrenched and formalized* ritual in South Korean schools, is now prohibited (although students told me it still happens occasionally)." Amanda Ripley, "Teacher, Leave Those Kids Alone." in *Time*, 5 December 2011. Ripley is an Emerson fellow at the New America Foundation, and sent this report from Seoul.

89. Ibid., 173. Baker's article is found in the *Harvard Law School: Studies in East Asian Law: Korea*, reprinted from *Studies on Korea in Transition,* Harvard Occasional Papers, no. 9 (Cambridge, MA: Harvard University Press, 1979) (sic). Baker received his law degree from Yale, and his M.A. from Harvard. He is currently an associate and consultant, Executive Committee, Harvard-Yenching Institute. He has spent most of his life as an administrator.

90. Alexis Dudden, 116.

University of Hawai'i's Center for Korean Studies. In a fine spirit of collegiality, Ms. Mercy Labuguen the Administrative Assistant, and Dr. Michael E. MacMillan, the Publication Specialist, made me a copy of *Studies on Korea in Transition, Occasional Papers No. 9*.[91] So here again, we note another example of Dudden's carelessness. Baker's paper that she credits as being published by Harvard University Press had in fact been published in Hawai'i.

I noted from Baker's contribution that he had depended as his source on Henry Chung, *The Case of Korea* (1921).[92] Baker admits that Chung's work "is an emotional attack on Japanese rule and obviously contains exaggerations." Still, he justifies using Chung because "[he] could find no other description of flogging," and he adds, because official reports also so state.[93] Baker, furthermore, continues to protect himself from possible criticism by qualifying his description of flogging. He does this by admitting that "The *only* descriptions I have discovered were of floggings administered in 1919 in connection with the Independence Movement. These beatings, administered by *alarmed* and *angry* Japanese officials, *may not have been representative of those of the preceding nine-year period*."[94] Baker's remarks are more like a lawyer's brief (he is a lawyer) for supporting circumstantial "evidence," but his standards are, at least, higher than Dudden's.

We are now left only with Chung's assertion that "a number of deaths occurred." I therefore again asked my colleagues at the Center for Korean studies for Chung's book. They did not have it, but in another example of collegiality, they took the trouble to reproduce it

91. Edited by David R. McCann, John Middleton, and Edward J. Shultz (Honolulu: Center for Korean Studies, University of Hawai'i, 1979).
92. Henry Chung passed away in 1985. He was born to a wealthy family in Korea. He was a very bright student, earning his Ph.D. from American University. He served at one time after the liberation as Korea's Ambassador to Japan.
93. Edward J. Baker, 223, fn.109.
94. Edward J. Baker, 223-224, fn 112.

from Google (with no charge for the paper!) This was a better result since I now had my own copy in which I could scribble notes.

Chung makes the following points about flogging. One, that flexible bamboo strips are used on the premise that it is "desirable" to *avoid tearing of the buttock's flesh*. Two, the prisoner is first examined "by the police doctor, but this does not often happen."[95]

Chung follows with the example of the flogging of eleven young men and repeats the words of one of the eleven, a Mr. Sur. According to Mr. Sur, each of them had been sentenced to ninety blows to be delivered over three days. Sur says that "[b]lood was drawn at the *first beating*"; after the second, the "flesh was like jelly"; and the pain was "frightful" after the third. Sur goes on to say that they could have gone to a Japanese hospital in town but, "we would [have] just as soon go back to jail as to go there." Instead, they elected to use Korean medicine, which proved ineffective. So they decided then to go to a Mission Hospital some two hours away by train. Chung then repeats Mr. Pak's and Mr. Kim's experiences as related by the nurses. The nurses said that they removed "large pieces of gangrenous tissue" from Mr. Pak whose "[d]eath was due to *septic peritonitis and exhaustion from excessive pain*." Mr. Kim, continuing the nurses account, died from peritonitis because his "buttocks were frightfully infected."[96] Chung says that he saw and photographed the remaining four boys. All of "their backs were raw and bleeding" and "large areas of the skin and underlying tissue had [been] sloughed away." One of the four was "awfully sick" and "*peritonitis was evident*, and he being a weak lad, had little chance to fight his way through."[97] According to Chung's account, then, there are two "confirmed" deaths and one "probable" demise. And from this, I assume, he bases his conclusion that "In many cases

95. Henry Chung, *The Case of Korea* (New York: Fleming H. Revell, 1921), 76-77.

96. Ibid., 78-79.

97. Ibid., 81.

they [the Koreans] were flogged to death."[98]

It is *not*, I repeat, *not* my intention to belittle the worth of a single Korean's death. Yet, using Chung's own narrative, from 1 March to 20 July 1919, 10,592 Koreans were flogged.[99] Baker and Dudden, who follow Chung's narrative, would be hard pressed to explain away the fact that this comes to 0.028 percent of the total flogged—assuming there are no other deaths from flogging. Moreover, Chung, earlier in his narrative, went beyond exaggeration when he charged that "God only knows the hundreds who have been beaten, shot and bayoneted, to crawl home and die unattended and *unknown*."[100]

What of Chung's indictment that the prison authority's flogging led to the tearing of the flesh which in turn caused sepsis that led to peritonitis and death. My enquiry into the question leads me to the conclusion that the cause and effect stated by Chung is difficult to ascertain. I first went to *The Johns Hopkins Medical Handbook: The 100 Major Medical Disorders of People Over the Age of 50*.[101] The descriptions of peritonitis are brief: "inflammation of the lining of the abdominal cavity," and "infection of the abdominal cavity."[102] I then asked Dr. Gerin T. S. Chun, MD, an anesthesiologist, who also happens to be a neighbor. He appeared to be an appropriate consultant since he is required to be present at a wide range of surgical procedures. He helpfully sent me the definition of "peritonitis" from the *Britannica Concise Encyclopedia*. According to this source, there are two types of peritonitis. The one is "primary peritonitis" that usually stems from a "perforated gastrointestinal tract, as with rupture with appendicitis." The other is "acute peritonitis," the consequence of

98. Ibid., 87.
99. Ibid., 83.
100. Ibid., 80. We have not located any other reliable accounts of Koreans dying from flogging.
101. Prepared by the editors of the Johns Hopkins "Medical Letter, Health After 50" (New York: Medletter Associates, Inc., 1992).
102. *The Johns Hopkins Medical Handbook*, 198 and 203.

inflammation "from elsewhere." His reply to my question whether sepsis caused by flogging can lead to peritonitis was: "Peritonitis caused by flogging of the buttocks is a *remote possibility*, given that the gastrointestinal tract includes the stomach, small intestine, large intestine, and *rectum*."

Let me add my personal experiences with life-threatening episodes. I owe my life to Dr. Naoto Yagi (八木直人) at the Yagi Clinic (八木医院). Over a decade ago he suspected that the excruciating pain in my right leg was caused by a blood clot: He prescribed Warfarin (also known as Coumadin) which I understand is used as rat poison. I survived.

On 2 April 2012 I suffered excruciating pain in my right thigh. I could not stand or lie on the floor. Dr. Naoto Yagi instantly recognized that it was the result of the Coumadin working too well and insisted that I go immediately to the nearest hospital, where the diagnosis was that the pain was caused by deep vein thrombosis, an extremely dangerous condition. Having been treated for seventeen days I was released on 19 April. During my hospitalization Dr. Yuzawa Hisanori (湯沢久徳) and Dr. Tōgi Toshinori (東儀季功) both, in conversations held separately on different days, told me that the cause and effect of death from sepsis-induced peritonitis as described in Chung's book is "plausible" but "rare."

Again, in early October 2012, extreme pain in my right leg sent me to the hospital at Dr. Naoto Yagi's urgent recommendation. After careful examination, including X-rays, Dr. Yuzawa concluded that it was caused by tendonitis. He gave me a steroid injection but the pain moved to another part of the leg, so at the next visit he injected steroid on the affected part. On this second visit I asked him about sepsis and peritonitis. He said that once sepsis enters the blood stream, the danger will not be limited to the peritoneum, but will affect all the major organs. There is a protective shield, however, that protects the brain from sepsis. Still, sometimes sepsis can penetrate the shield. To make a long story short, he should be credited for enlightening me on the danger of sepsis, and as with Dr. Naoto Yagi, for saving my life.

Given all of the above, it is justifiable to question the odds that *three* out of the *eleven* young men involved in the beating had died from sepsis induced peritonitis. Therefore, what we have here is *more* than the "exaggeration" that Baker has said of Chung's book.

Crime and Punishment in Korea

Adherents of the national historical narrative criticize the Japanese for the use of flogging as a form of punishment. Yet, they seem to ignore the precedence for its use throughout the Yi dynasty. Foreigners who lived in and visited Korea prior to 1905 frequently noted in their writings the prevalence of flogging. Isabella Bird Bishop, who visited Korea on four occasions between 1894 and 1897, wrote that Korean "methods of punishment" were known for their "brutal flagellations by *yamen* runners, [and] its beating of criminals to death," adding that the "howls of anguish penetrat[ed] the rooms of the adjacent English mission. . . ."[103] Bishop's account of Korea was filled with Orientalism, but she was fair-minded in her treatment of Korean society.

Homer H. Hulbert, a longtime resident of Korea and personal friend to the Korean king, wrote: "The penal code is filled with directions for administering beatings." He noted that often the flogging was "done with a huge paddle, which falls with crushing force, frequently breaking the bones of the leg and rendering the victim a cripple for life."[104] But this was just one aspect of punishment in Korea before it was colonized. Hulbert added:

> The other forms of punishment in vogue are imprisonment,

103. Isabella Bird Bishop, 33.

104. Homer B. Hulbert, *The Passing of Korea* (1906; reprint Yonsei University Press, 1969), 64-65.

> beating and impressment into the chain-gang. Men that are slightly suspected of seditious ideas are kept under lock and key. . . . Nothing can be proved against them, and they are simply held in detention, awaiting a promised trial which in many cases never comes off. One man has lately been released from prison who remained a guest of the government in this way for six or seven years without trial. He was suspected of too liberal ideas.[105]

As noted above, Hulbert and Bird based their writings on their experiences in Korea *before* the Japanese took control of Korea. Both accounts testify to the brutal nature of flogging and criminal justice under the indigenous Korean regime. Thus, Japan's claim that they brought back an existing Korean practice is correct. Yet, the Japanese continued to use flogging because they thought it was more effective than incarceration and because they underestimated the capabilities of Koreans to understand the civil code.[106] I now move to Sprunger's discussion of flogging.

Michael L. Sprunger's examination of flogging is wide-ranging, but detailed and balanced. Sprunger introduces the reader to flogging with exact and minute description of the flogging platform that, he says, consists of "two inter-locking boards" with the "longer piece measuring 227 centimeters in length." So too his portrayal of the whip: it is "made of bamboo with the joints removed" and is "just over 54 centimeters long, .75 centimeters thick," etc. The flogging, he continues, is "likely administered by the substation chief . . . within the confines of the substation, with the audience limited to a doctor (if available) and . . . a few [others]." He continues that the prisoners "[i]deally" would be "examined by the doctor to *ensure* that . . . [the prisoner] was physically capable of withstanding . . . [the] flogging." He notes that "the number of strokes . . . in a single

105. Ibid., 64.
106. Chulwoo Lee, 33.

session was limited to thirty."[107]

In a longer description, he cites colonial government sources that justified flogging in terms of it being "'civilized,' 'humane,' and 'scientific.'" Before dismissing out of hand the following as self-serving, it is incumbent on us to at least see how flogging was justified. We do so in the detail Sprunger gives us.

> First, they [the Japanese] emphasized that great care should be taken for both the physical and emotional health of the person being flogged. The penalty was only to be applied to Korean *men* between the ages of sixteen and sixty. . . . a doctor was to be present (if available) to check the convict's physical and mental condition. If either was found lacking, the punishment could be delayed up to thirty days. In addition, the officer applying the penalty was to observe the convict's physical and emotional state while delivering the lashes, watching for signs of *injury* or distress. To further *prevent serious injury,* the number of strokes delivered in a single day was limited to thirty, to be evenly distributed between the right and left buttocks, and *ice* was to be provided at the conclusion of the "procedure." Finally, to *minimize the convict's discomfort,* authorities were to ensure that the convict had not eaten for at least an hour before being flogged, and were to *provide water* for the convict *during the punishment.*
>
> Officials delivering the flogging were also to *pay close attention* to the convict's *emotional* state. Floggings were to be delivered *in private,* with only an official or two in attendance, and other prisoners were not to be present—these were *not to be shameful or fearful spectacles.* Thus, despite the corporal nature of the punishment, "*unnecessary pain*" could purportedly be *avoided* "as far as possible."
>
> [Moreover] [t]he detail of these instructions . . . left very little to chance, turning the flogger into a precision

---

107. Michael L. Sprunger, 91-94. Sprunger is Assistant Professor of East Asian History, Hendrix College, Conway, Arkansas.

> instrument delivering an exact measure of pain to the convict, purportedly *in direct correspondence to the crime he had committed.*[108]

Sprunger then leads the reader to a significant factor involved in flogging; i.e., that Japanese officials used bamboo whips and *never* the "*inhumane, flesh-tearing whips* [as] in the West"; and that "*piercing the flesh was prohibited.*"[109] Furthermore, he adds that the Japanese authorities were not only concerned about easing physical pain, but in reducing psychological stress as well. He notes that in the Chosŏn era (1392–1910), in the Japan's Tokugawa period (1600–1868), as well as in the West, flogging was a "public spectacle, meant to incur shame. Even high officials in the Board of Justice [in Japan] could be flogged for dereliction of duty!" Sprunger re-emphasizes that the "'new' flogging, of course, was carried out in private, sparing the convict such dishonor and preserving his dignity to the degree possible."[110] In short, the penal system in Korea was created with modern judicial practices in mind.

Sprunger ends his discussion with the words that "Despite these various efforts, colonial authorities were *never very successful in selling* flogging as a scientific, humane, and efficient punishment." And partly as a result of international criticism that followed the March First Independence Movement the colonial government "abolished flogging in April 1920."[111] It is necessary, however, to repeat our proposition that the colonial government did not stubbornly dig in its heels, and was willing to change.

Despite his criticism, he still acknowledges that the colonial authorities continually tried to reform the penal system that included flogging. In fact, his work outlines the "various and often competing

---

108. Ibid., 145-146. We see here an example of the Japanese penchant for proportionality, a major theme of our study.

109. Ibid., 150.

110. Ibid., 151. Exclamation point in original.

111. Ibid., 156.

political and economic interests" at play in the creation of a modern penal system in colonial Korea.[112] Moreover, he stresses the undeniably pivotal point that even if the colonial government did not fully match their civilizing rhetoric with achievements, their progressive reform efforts "were *rarely, if ever, accomplished in prisons around the world.*"[113]

This last statement is the kind that makes Sprunger's work a model achievement The success of a doctoral dissertation and the book that may follow is measured by the light it shines into areas previously unknown. The greater probability is that it brings fresh perspectives, helps to revise, or leads to the rejection of previously strongly held "truths." Sprunger accomplishes both standards with this scholarly, fair-minded, and balanced study.

The proof is in the pudding, so I here list seven points that to me underpin the strengths of his study. One, he gives due credit to the colonial bureaucrats who appear to him "to have *truly believed* in their *moral responsibility* as civilizers," and who "*earned* a reputation throughout the empire for their *professionalism* and *competence*."[114] Bruce Cumings, professor at the University of Chicago, agrees. "Japan did not send to Korea conquerors like Cecil Rhodes, but chose the civil service bureaucrat as the model overlord."[115]

Two, the strength and persistence of the national historical narrative is due to the fact that "many" such narratives are "focused *solely on the experiences of well-known Korean nationalists* who were incarcerated in colonial prisons."[116]

Three, Sprunger wryly points out that what is *entirely ignored* is that the "vast majority of those punished during the colonial era"

112. Ibid., viii.
113. Ibid., 174-175.
114. Ibid., 12, 14; also, 28.
115. Bruce Cumings, *Korea's Place in the Sun: A Modern History* (New York: W.W. Norton, 2005), 150.
116. Michael L. Sprunger, 23, also 233.

were "common criminals,"[117] not political prisoners, as most nationalist accounts seem to assume.

Four, that the "vast majority" of prisoners were concerned, as "most human beings are, with their own safety and health." Their primary goal, in short, lay in satisfying "quotidian" or daily needs, such as "food, sanitation," and in general to make "prison life [more] bearable" rather than in "ideological" purposes.[118]

Five, the prisoners were not "passive" objects of an oppressive "colonial regime," but resisted by "riots, work stoppages, hunger strikes, [and] escapes." They helped their own causes by "working *within the rules of the penal system*" and by engaging "the press, lawyers, and the general public," they "*negotiate[d] significant changes* in both penal practice and policy."[119] He cites Theodore Jun Yoo, who makes clear that the negotiators included "*colonial administrators* and researchers, *Japanese* and Korean social reformers, and actual Korean families."[120] Let it be said again that the ability of prisoners to negotiate, granting that sometimes they resorted to hunger strikes, and the involvement of a wide-ranging scope of negotiators make it difficult to picture an oppressive colonial government at work.

Six, Sprunger, in contrast to those who espouse the national historical narrative, believes that the transition to the cultural rule (*bunka seiji*) following the March First Movement resulted in real changes in areas of "speech, publication," and in the ability of Koreans to organize. The result was a "more vocal Korean colonial

---

117. Ibid., 233.

118. Ibid., 17, 233, 234, and 267.

119. Ibid., 235 and 257. This is further proof that the colonial officials were not interested in, and in fact, did not create a suppressive, suffocating environment in Korea.

120. *The Politics of Gender in Colonial Korea: Education, Labor and Health, 1910–1945* (Berkeley: University of California Press, 2008), 169-176; in Michael L. Sprunger, 9-10.

public" that prompted penal officials to "redoubl[e] efforts to attain the reformative potential of penal confinement."[121] In fact, Sprunger goes further by asserting that even *before* the advent of *bunka seiji,* colonial officials "*clearly did care about public opinion*, and, . . . *took actions to temper criticism* from both the *Korean* public and the international community in Korea *throughout the colonial period*."[122]

And seven, Sprunger raises a point that explains the limitations faced by the colonial government and penal reformers: the budget played an "*outsize role in colonized societies*."[123] The implication is that the availability or lack of funds constricted reform agendas. As a political historian, I have long believed that the budget is the most crucial document in governance. Read the budget and it will reveal what is important to the administration and whatever organ or institution that shares with it the burden of governance. The budget will expose their priorities, their values, and how they visualize the problems it faces in achieving their goals.

I read an article by David Broder over fifteen years ago in which he introduced *Mirage*, by George Hager and Eric Pianin. He cites them, and their words have made me refine my views on the central play of the budget in a polity:

> The budget is not just some arcane and indigestible collection of dollar figures but a detailed statement of what the nation cares about and what its priorities are. . . .[124]

Professor Banno Junji (坂野潤治), formerly of the University of Tokyo, recently published a general history of modern Japan. In it he touched on what had been the accepted wisdom on Article 71 of the Meiji Constitution: "When the Imperial Diet has not voted on

121. Michael L. Sprunger, 170, 174, 264, 267, and 273-274.

122. Ibid., 262.

123. Ibid., 12.

124. *Japan Times*, 17 April 1997.

the Budget, or when the Budget has not been brought into actual existence, the Government shall carry out the Budget of the preceding year." This was taken at that time by most if not all Japanese as well as foreign political historians to mean that the Article strengthened the Government's hand since it could ignore the political parties' attempts to control the budget by voting down the Government's budget for the forthcoming fiscal year. Banno goes on to say that, "43 years ago, the American scholar, Professor George Akita made it clear that this Article should not have pleased the Government, since, to this very day expenditures have been rarely below that of the previous year."[125]

It now appears that Sprunger and I share the same insight on the budget's role in a polity, since his references to budget-related prison reforms are abundant.[126]

I quote at length his final judgment on Korea's penal system and the colonial officials' role in it.

> [I]t is not necessary to assume that colonial punishment was a simple instrument of political suppression, that colonial prisons were mere warehouses . . . penal administrators had no interest in the high-minded principles . . . many colonial penal officials were dreamers, even if they dreamed in paternalistic, racially informed terms; and Korea was the setting where they tried to make their dreams real. . . . [They

125. *Nihon Kindaishi* [日本近代史] Chikuma Shinsho 948 (Tokyo: Chikuma shobō, 2012) 193-194. I made the argument on Article 71 in my dissertation and later book, *Foundations of Constitutional Government in Modern Japan, 1868-1900*, (Cambridge, MA:. Harvard University Press, 1967), 81-82. It was translated by Arai Kōtarō (荒井孝太郎) and Banno Junji as *Meiji Rikkensei to Itō Hirobumi* [明治立憲政と伊藤博文] (Tokyo: University of Tokyo Press, 1971). The Marxist-leaning scholars that influenced academia at that time completely ignored the book and it sank beneath the waves with nary a ripple, so it pleases me that Banno has called attention to it.

126. Michael L. Sprunger, 12, 13, 137, 138, 141, 158, 159, 160, 170, 173, 232, 236, and 267.

> believed] in the promise of punishment to bring about a significant transformation in both individual criminals and society in general. They embraced internationally circulating penological and criminological theories . . . Indeed, a major theme of . . . [the colonial government's document on penology] is not just that colonial penal administrators had managed to incarcerate unruly and backward Koreans, but that *they had created a penal system at least on par with that in Japan*. . . . Penal reform in Korea was a colonial project *par excellence* [italics in original], exhibiting contradictions, ambiguities, and tensions that have *characterized colonialism around the world*. . . .
>
> One of the goals of this study was to examine colonial punishment not as a simple imperial imposition, a system superimposed *onto* (italics in original) a thoroughly oppressed, colonized society; but rather as a complex, compromised institution bearing all the markings of the vibrant, dynamic society *into* (italics in original) which it was grafted. *Like colonial Korea in general*, the colonial penal system was neither a site of utter colonial domination, *nor one of absolute anti-colonial resistance*.[127]

This is as usual for Sprunger, well put, but in the process he also rescues, without intending to, the reputation of a governor-general. He writes that the impact of total mobilization began "in the *late 1930s*." This *coincided* with the time the "colonial penal administrators were unveiling their *showcase* policy, their *progressive-stage system*, and *celebrating their progress*" in penal reform. This means that the "*showcase policy*" worthy of being celebrated overlapped in part with the tenure of the most despised "governor-general, Minami Jirō" (5 August 1936 to 29 May 1942).[128]

This is, we submit, at the heart of Japan's assimilation; to create in

127. Ibid., 273-275.

128. Ibid., 28 and 275. He also reveals that prisoners in colonial prisons were recruited for military service with the promise of parole. (Ibid., 276, fn 106.)

the colonies what had been achieved in Japan. That is, structures and institutions infused by the values of an open and pluralistic polity—granting the caveat that all matters touched by human hands are at best imperfect. We have only to recall Zhao Ziyang's final testament to support this proposition: his conviction that postwar Taiwan and Korea made the transition to a parliamentary system: multi-parties; active press; independent judiciary—all matters I have covered up to this point as being modern Japan's achievements. Colonial Korea was making great progress in all of these areas during the colonial rule, but wartime restrictions undid much of that progress.

A much younger compatriot is equally convinced that China's future depends on accepting the ideals enunciated by Zhao. Chen Guangcheng (陳光誠), the blind Chinese activist who caused a diplomatic incident by fleeing to the U.S. Embassy in Beijing in 2012, made several points in his first public appearance in New York. One is that like Ai Weiwei he believes that the internet has loosened the grip of China's leaders over the country; and he counters the argument that "China, with its different culture and history, should not copy Western-style democracy" by pointing out that "Japan, South Korea, and Taiwan" had succeeded in achieving "eastern democracy." It may be a function of a generational gap, but Japan has finally been given its due. It is admirable that Chen goes beyond Zhao and adds Japan to the list; but, unfortunately, he neglects, as does Zhao, to point out that Japan had led the way.

Chen is also more positive in his evaluation of the central government that is "moving in the right direction," and is critical of the "lawless" actions of local officials.[129] On this point, Japan, particularly Yamagata's words and actions, may offer lessons for China: that is, "bottom up governance" based upon the free, active, voluntary participation of the citizenry.

---

129. Sebastian Smith, "Democratic reform irreversible in China: Chen," in *The Daily Yomiuri*, using (AFP-Jiji), 2 June 2012. Chen was also awarded the 2012 Tom Lantos Human Rights Prize. *Honolulu Star-Advertiser*, 30 January 2013.

Customary Law in Colonial Korea and Its Legacy

I begin with an apologia. I am an outlier in matter of law and modern Korean history. This said, we need to review a quote from Chulwoo Lee's article titled, "Modernity, Legality, and Power in Korea under the Japanese." Lee's article adopts elements of the colonial modernity model, while retaining elements of the national historical narrative. Speaking of Japan's legal contributions to colonial Korea and the new modality of power exercised by the GGK, he states:

> My account may not appear different from conventional accounts, which hold that although modernization may have taken place in form, in the sense that law and justice were systematized, *no modernization occurred in content, since power was exercised in a "brutal" way* and the people did not enjoy democratic protections. However, I suggest that we sensitize our inquiry to changes in the modality of domination behind the facade of this so-called distorted modernization.[130]

In response to the above claims, we turn to Marie Seong-Hak Kim's lengthy article and her interpretations on customary law. My selections may be seen in parts to appear arbitrary, biased, and even mistaken. The fault is mine, more so since Kim writes with clarity, precision, and fluidity as befits her legal background.

In Marie Seong-Hak Kim's Abstract[131] is a birds-eye view of her article, but one that also compels reading the whole to flesh it out. Given the constraint of space, I limit myself to those parts that may shine light on our own study.

Kim begins her Abstract with her basic conclusion: "The colonial

---

130. Chulwoo Lee, "Modernity, Legality, and Power," in *Colonial Modernity in Korea*, eds. Gi-Wook Shin and Michael Robinson (Cambridge, MA: Harvard University Asia Center, 1999), 35.

131. Marie Seong-Hak Kim, "Customary Law and Colonial Jurisprudence in Korea," *The American Journal of Comparative Law* 57.1 (Winter 2009): 205.

construction of customary law has crucially shaped modern Korean civil law and jurisprudence." The questions are: Why did the colonial authorities feel compelled to "construct" customary law? Who did the "construction"? And how was this achieved?

Kim discusses these points in the body of her study. She writes that shortly after the 1910 annexation, the GGK declared that Japan's Civil Code and Code of Civil Procedure would be the "general law in Korea" and then "decreed that most private legal relations among the Koreans [would] be governed by Korean Custom."[132] Yet, Chosŏn Korea "did not have a body of written private law." This compelled the authorities to "rely on the concept of customary law" to implement "private law in family and succession matters" and thereby entrusted colonial judges to discover customary rules of law. In short, "it was through jurisprudence and doctrinal activities that old usages and practices . . . were collected, redefined, and turned into customary law." Kim then reverts to her basic conclusion: "A *substantial part of postcolonial Korean civil law* is grounded in this colonial custom."[133] She later poses this as a question "If colonial customary jurisprudence was *merely a pernicious* byproduct of the Japanese imperial agenda, why did the postcolonial civil law system continue to rely on so many of the precedents and on the legal reasoning of the colonial courts?"[134] She answers her own question: "The legacy of colonial customary jurisprudence appears to be more profound and widespread than has been acknowledged."[135]

Legal transplantation involves a process that "lawmaking elites" have been making "*throughout history*"; that is, "reshaping [of] existing legal order with rules and concepts originating *in other legal systems*."[136] She asserts that "Evidence shows that there were

132. Ibid., 205.
133. Ibid., 207.
134. Ibid., 209-210.
135. Ibid., 210.
136. Ibid., 207.

genuine efforts by the courts and among jurists to reconcile Korean customs with the Western legal concepts and principles."[137] She had earlier argued that "Korea's legal historiography *can benefit* from a broadly conceived *comparative approach, untrammeled by the nationalist paradigm*."[138] She then informs the reader that in Korea's case, "Colonial customary law was created with the specific goal of *reshaping Korean laws and practices in line with modern legal concepts and principles [already] contained in the Japanese Civil Code*."[139] Even Chulwoo Lee acknowledges that "Japanese laws did not simply 'extend' to Korea," but rather, Japan left room for Korean customs, such as customary property rights, to survive.[140]

Why would the colonial regime retain customary law? If the GGK was as malicious as the national historical paradigm claims, why did it not transplant Japanese legal codes carte blanche? Were the Japanese bureaucrats fearful of Korean reactions, or were they pragmatists who respected Korean culture? Yong Chool Ha, professor at the University of Washington, provides an explanation for why the colonial state made allowances for Korean culture. He writes:

> Colonial authorities were extremely cautious about changing Korean customs. Japanese authorities were wary of possible reactions and resistance from conservative forces in Korea. Therefore, they decided to take a *gradual* approach that was particularly visible in the introduction of new civil codes. The guiding principle was that Korean customary laws were permitted to continue to operate with very few exceptions.[141]

Marie Seong-Hak Kim returns later to legal transplantation by noting that "*Creation* of custom as a tool to push colonized societies toward a desired goal was *shared by colonial powers almost univer-*

137. Ibid., 231.
138. Ibid., 209.
139. Ibid., 207, See also 222 and 224.
140. Chulwoo Lee, 27.
141. Yong Chool Ha, 67.

sally." She then briefly touches on the experience of British colonies in Africa.[142]

Kim first raises the issue of how "the dominant trend in Korean legal historiography" has been concerned primarily to prove that "*indigenous Korean law and custom was intentionally suppressed* and *altered* by the colonial judicial authorities for the purpose of assimilation." She disagrees with this postulation on two grounds. One, it assumes mistakenly that "customary law as a coherent legal order existed in premodern Korea." Two, by pointing out that "[it] is *beyond dispute*" that, "Korea's first civil code" that was "promulgated in 1958" and "took effect in 1960" was "*crucially based* on the Japanese Civil Code." This is to be expected, she seems to say, but wisely so, because, "The first generation of judges and lawyers in postcolonial Korea, including the drafters of the Civil Code, were educated and trained during the colonial period."[143] I remind the reader that this was equally true for the immediate post-independence South Korean military force. Kim succinctly closes this argument by noting that "remnants of colonial jurisprudence are more ubiquitous than commonly believed"; and that "[m]odern Korean civil law was solidly grounded in the colonial jurisprudence on customary law."[144] Before concluding my essay on Kim's study, I point to another example of continuity.

The reader will recall that Hyung Il Pai made the point that the "structure and administration of the OCP [Office of Cultural Properties itself] . . . continue to reflect colonial-era preferences." Kim, in line with this, writes that Itō Hirobumi, the first resident-general asked Ume Kenjirō, then a Tokyo Imperial University professor of civil law, who helped to draft Japan's Civil Code, to come to Seoul

142. Marie Seong-Hak Kim, 246. She is critical of Caprio because his work has no analysis of colonial policy in French West Africa or British East Africa. See Marie Seong-Hak Kim, review of Mark Caprio, 437.

143. Ibid., 236-237, See also, 240, 241, and 243.

144. Ibid., 244.

to help create the "formation of a modern legal system in Korea." One result was the Court Organization Law of December 1907; and, as Kim tells it, "The structure and organization of the Korean courts built at [that] time remain largely the same today."[145]

Kim, just before the mid-point of her article, asserts a point that is precisely on target and warrants a full quotation:

> In colonial Korea, it was doubly important to avoid the appearance that Japanese judges were making up rules *to control* the private relations of the Korean people. The courts *had to take public opinion into account*, and the judges were *mindful* of the *reception of their decisions by the colonial population*. Even under a colonial regime, *they had to seek* some degree of *public legitimacy*, and their implementation of "customary law" rationalized their decisions.[146]

Well put, but a reminder as well that the Japanese authorities put the matter positively—here is Hasegawa Yorimichi precisely on that point: the "universal affliction stemming from despotic government (or *sensei seiji*) is that it impedes (*sosoku*) the concerns of the lower ranks from reaching those in power." I reiterate Sprunger's declaration that "colonial penal officials clearly did care about public opinion, and, . . . took actions to temper criticisms from both the Korean public and the international community in Korea throughout the colonial period." Whatever the GGK's motives for responding to public pressure, it exhibits malleability and adaptability. Still, it is only proper that we yield to Kim for the final word:

> It seems that an attempt to understand Korea's legal past should start with the acknowledgement that the colonial courts in Korea were *more than* an instrument of *self-serving* colonialism. It is beyond dispute that the main aim of the colonial legal institutions was to bring about the integration

---

145. Ibid., 211.
146. Ibid., 228-229.

> of law between Korea and Japan that would *secure colonial domination*. But treating law merely as a product of *colonial politics is undesirable* and studying legal history strictly as a national history less than satisfactory. . . .The *impact* of legal modernization in Korea seems to *transcend the nationalist paradigm lingering in historiography*.[147]

I remind the reader again that he/she should not be put off by the length of an article on law, for Kim indeed does write well and persuasively, and is fair and balanced.[148]

Japan's Role in Korea's Capitalistic Development

A few paragraphs can do no justice to Carter J. Eckert's "turning point" contribution to understanding Japan's role in Korea's capitalistic development.[149] Eckert starts with the premise that the 1919 founding of the giant enterprise *Keijō Bōshoku* [京城紡織] (shortened as *Keibō* [京紡]) marks the inception of Korea's industrial capitalism. He then shows how much *Keibō*'s management structure, capitalization (including no collateral loans), distribution system, procurement of raw materials, and transfer of Japanese technology stemmed from its intimate ties with Japanese enterprises and the GGK. Hasegawa, we should recall, had also stressed that one of the "lessons to be learned from the recent [March First] uprising" is that "we should . . . strengthen the economic ties linking Koreans and Japanese [and] . . . facilitate investment in Korea by removing all barriers that may presently hinder it, [and] encourage the growth of

147. Ibid., 247.

148. After writing these words, David Flynn unearthed another reason for her narrative skills; i.e., she was a staff writer at *The Korea Times*.

149. *Offspring of Empire: The Koch'ang Kims and the Colonial Origins of Korean Capitalism, 1876–1945* (Seattle: University of Washington Press, 1991). Eckert is Yoon Se Young Professor of Korean History, Department of East Asian Languages and Civilizations at Harvard University. He was the director (1993-2004) of the Korea Institute at Harvard University and is now Acting Director as well as a member of the Institute's executive committee.

business enterprises by expanding subsidies to them. . . ."[150]

I omit a detailed repetition of Eckert's themes, given that the book has been published in English and widely read. It is also available to the Japanese audience in a fine translation.[151] The translation, moreover, contains two attractions unavailable in the English version. The first is Eckert's response to the *Koreans*' reactions to his book. He writes that he is *encouraged especially by the young Korean scholars* who informed him that his work has enabled them *to go beyond the nationalistic narrative*. The reactions of other Koreans are hardly benign and range from the accusation that he is "sugarcoating" Japan's colonial rule to the *ad hominem* charge that he is "contemptuous" of Korean history. He believes that the accusation that his work is a vindication of Japan's colonial rule is based on *a deeply rooted misunderstanding of that rule, compounded by Korean translations that are "dogmatic," "selective," "inaccurate," and some that are based on "hearsay."*[152]

The other attraction is the review by Professor Kimura Mitsuhiko (木村光彦) of Tokyo's Aoyama Gakuin Daigaku. He points to the unshakeable fact that in the waning days of Japan's colonial rule, 90 percent of the capitalization of Korea's enterprises was Japanese, in a word, that Korean capitalists were being overwhelmed under Japanese rule, thereby, seemingly nullifying Eckert's primary contention of growth of Korean enterprises. Kimura notes approvingly, however, that Eckert had turned that percentage figure on its

150. Richard Devine, "Japanese Rule in Korea," 530.

151. 日本帝国の申し子：高敞の金一族と韓国資本主義の植民地起源1876-1945, Nihon teikoku no mōshigo: Kōshō (Kochian) no Kin (Kimu) ichizoku to Kankoku shihonshugi no shokuminchi kigen: 1876-1945 (Tokyo: Sōshisha, 2004), trans. Kotani Masayo (小谷まさ代). The Korean version is제국의후예: 고창김씨가와한국자본주의의식민지기원 (Cheguk ŭi huye: Koch'ang Kim Ssi ka wa Han'guk chabonjuŭi ŭi singminji kiwŏn, 1876-1945) (Seoul: P'urŭn Yŏksa, 2008), trans. Chu Ik-chong.

152. Carter Eckert in Kotani Masayo, 3-4 (of five page commentary). See previous footnote.

head by his assertion that the Koreans had a 10 percent share of the capitalization. Kimura then declares that *if* Korea had *not experienced the undeniable postwar economic growth*, then the argument that Japanese capital had a stranglehold on pre-1945 Korean economic development becomes valid. He adds that Eckert is correct in pointing out that in the final days of colonial rule, the majority of enterprises were Korean, including the engines of Korea's postwar miracle, Samsung and Hyundai.[153]

Gi-Wook Shin provides somewhat different data than those cited by Eckert and Kimura, but this may reflect different periods of time involved. He nonetheless argues in support of the postulation of active Korean participation in colonial industrialization. He notes that "[b]y the early 1940s, industry accounted for about 40% of national production" and agriculture was also at 40 percent; and as well, over fifty percent of Korea exports were industrial.[154]

Shin also argues that "by 1937 Korean firms constituted about 40% of all firms and the Korean share of total capital formation . . . was about 13%." And, he adds, since "30% of all firms" were "jointly owned by Koreans and Japanese," then "Korean participation in colonial industrialization was *even more substantial*." Shin puts it this way: "This colonial activity bequeathed a *significant industrial legacy to postcolonial Korea*." Others, Shin adds, write of the "*human/cultural* legacy . . . to postcolonial entrepreneurship" since this human/cultural legacy evolved during "colonial industrialization."[155] He cites fellow scholar Jung-en Woo, who argued that "the 1930s bequeathed a set of patterns, a model, that could be the silent companion of Korean development."[156] Shin then concludes: "Although one can debate the extent and nature of this

153. Kimura Mitsuhiko in Kotani Masayo, 441 (of a six-page review).

154. Gi-Wook Shin, "Agrarian Conflict," 1312.

155. Ibid., 1312-1313.

156. Ibid., 1313. Shin is citing from Woo's work, *Race to the Swift: State and Finance in Korean Industrialization* (New York, Columbia University Press, 1991), 41.

colonial legacy . . . , *there seems little question that colonial industrialization shaped subsequent industrial transformation*."[157]

I conclude this segment by reiterating what Sprunger wrote about the impact of *bunka seiji* (cultural rule) and even the years before it was officially expounded. He maintains that *bunka seiji* did create "*real changes*" in Korea's environment and the relationship between Koreans and Japanese that made penal reform possible. This is, it seems to me, what Woo described as a "silent companion" of patterns and a "model" for Korean industrial and capitalistic development. Japan's colonial authorities were not in Korea to suppress Koreans and to expedite their exploitation. This is why Hasegawa Yoshimichi's "Recommendations" (1920) and the 1886 Yamagata *ikensho* should be read and re-read, for there in these two documents for all to behold are the standards and actions the Japanese authorities tried to follow as much as humanly possible in their governance of their colonies.

157. Gi-Wook Shin, "Agrarian Conflict," 1313.

Concluding Remarks

If a primary emphasis of this study is the continuity between colonial and present-day Korea, what of Japan's experience? The conviction among the victorious Allied powers in 1945 was that Japan, in every aspect of its society, economy, culture, religion, and governance was completely flawed; they felt that a root-and-branch reform program was needed to create a Japan that could take its place among civilized nations. These views of Japan spilled over into perceptions of the Japanese as brutal colonial overlords. In American eyes, and perhaps the eyes of other Anglophone writers, the effort was successful; with a recent United States president declaring flatly that the United States made Japan "democratic." The first question that needs to be answered by those who still hold to the "bad prewar Japan" belief is how to explain the existence of "pluralistic, progressive" elements in prewar Japan. In Smethurst's telling, land reform was being carried out and the women's suffrage movement had a long prewar pedigree; Krämer shows that prewar "fascistic" education did not exist since a lively debate on education reform was being carried out from 1925 to 1945; Teters proved through the *Ōtsu jiken* that Japan had a strong and independent judiciary, as did Mitchell by looking at the *Teijin* Incident. The parliamentary system continued to work—elections were held and the results respected. Tojō Hideki became the only leader of the warring nations to have been dismissed from his post in the midst of the world conflict. The list goes on. In short, just as Japan's governance of Korea was not totally bad, neither was Japan's prewar past as bad as depicted; and just as present-day Korea is joined at the hip to colonial Korea; Japan has built upon the positives it inherited from the years before its defeat in 1945.

COLLABORATION IN KOREA

I need to confront as well the highly sensitive question of collaboration that was raised by Hyung Il Pai as well as by the Shanghai family who had befriended, because of shared humanity, the detective who had been assigned to keep watch for possible subversive acts; but was then charged with collaboration after the war. There is also the position taken by the general history of Korea earlier cited:

> In the 1930s, the line between political purity and *collaboration* became blurred, as *everyone* was *forced* to participate in some measure. The *great tragedy* of the colonial period was that at its end *so many had been compromised.*[1]

I would prefer to drop the word, "forced" since it denies the Koreans free agency and it goes against all the findings of the revisionists so far cited. The words, "everyone" and "so many" imply that 1930s Korea was populated by no one else but victims and collaborators. This is surely unprovable, but also a particularly harsh judgment on the Koreans themselves. In point of fact the historical record shows that many of Korea's greatest nationalists during the 1910s and 1920s ended up as collaborators in the 1930s. A shortened version of this list includes the writer Yi Kwang-su, the statesman Yun Ch'i-ho,[2] the historian Ch'oe Nam-sŏn, the educator Helen Kim, the industrialist Kim Yŏn-su, and many members of the Korean

1. In Carter Eckert et al., *Korea Old and New*, 320; also, 319.
2. Yun was one of the 105 Korean Christian nationalists arrested in 1911 as part of the Terauchi assassination plot.

imperial family (especially Yi Ŭn). The success of the Japanese in winning the support of many Korean nationalists cannot be solely explained as the result of coercion; one must also take into account free will.

Historical Remembrance in Korea

If Japan's colonial record was, as we claim, moderate by global standards, why do North and South Koreans continue to harbor deep animosity toward the Japanese? Other than the reason given by Pyon and Tsukagoshi in which they maintain that the Japanese who are "barbarians" invaded Korea, a much more "highly civilized" country, Michael Seth posits several explanations. The first is "that governments in North and South Korea have made anti-Japanese sentiment a rallying point for patriotism."[3] The founding fathers of North Korea (Kim Il-sung) and South Korea (Syngman Rhee) based their legitimacy on their anti-Japanese activities, and their respective regimes continue to distort the overall nature of Japan's colonial presence in such a way as to represent Kim and Rhee as national heroes in their respective nations.

A second explanation offered by Seth is that the "bitterness toward the Japanese was also a result of the intense nature of Japanese rule." By this he means that the GGK's "vast bureaucracy and police system penetrated down to the village level." Most colonial regimes had little interaction with the average subject and ruled through the indigenous elites; the Japanese, on the other hand, had police, bureaucrats, and educators in nearly every village, as was the case in Japan. This made colonialism a personal matter to nearly every Korean.[4]

Another explanation is offered by Adrian Buzo in *The Making of Modern Korea*. He writes:

3. Michael J. Seth, *A Concise History of Modern Korea: From the Late Nineteenth Century to the Present* (Lanham, MD: Rowman & Littlefield, 2010), 79.
4. Ibid., 79.

> The experiences they remembered were of individual and collective contempt and ill-treatment, denial of civil liberties, strict censorship, expropriation, new taxes and fines on wines and tobacco, the forced cultivation of new cash crops, and an avalanche of new regulations covering animal slaughtering, common cemeteries, firewood gathering and the licensing of traditional medicine (*hanyak*) practitioners. In the words of one Korean quoted in a Japanese report at the time, "It is better to lead a hard life with real parents than to enjoy a comfortable life with stepparents."[5]

This strikes a chord with us. If Buzo is correct, the anger and animosity is not so much over the actions of the colonial regime, but is tied more closely to the humiliation of being subjugated.[6] The fact that the Japanese were an alien ruler mattered more than the policies that were implemented. If the GGK had been an ethnic Korean government, then the historical remembrance would be completely different.

Japan hoped its colonial endeavor in Korea would, in the long run, be of mutual benefit to both peoples, but war with China and then America led to an intensified mobilization that touched nearly every Korean. From 1938 until the end of the war, the gradual and moderate approach was replaced by haphazard and coercive assimilation policies that have become the focus of the national historical narrative.

The lingering, visceral animosity toward Japan is currently passed from the older generation to the younger. Korean schools teach their students the most extreme version of the national historical narrative. Anti-Japanese sentiments are also publicized in museums, in movies [*Hanbando* (한반도) and *Modern Boy* (모던 보이)], and on television [*Immortal Admiral Yi Sun-sin* (불멸의 이순신) and *Eyes*

5. Adrian Buzo, *The Making of Modern Korea*. (New York: Routledge, 2002), 21.
6. Guy Podoler, 125.

of Dawn (여명의 눈동자)]. An anecdote may help convey this point. In 1995, Palmer was teaching English to a group of middle school students in Seoul. During a discussion on food, one student stated that he did not eat kimchee, a traditional Korean food. When asked why, he claimed it was a food of Japanese origins; luckily, the rest of the class quickly corrected this student.

On the national stage in Korea, the Independence Hall of Korea claims to promote better Korean-Japanese relations. Yet, the museum, which cost $118 million U.S. dollars (in 2007), includes graphic reminders, snapshots really, of Japan's more brutal moments in Korea. The curators took "special care to emphasize the cruelty of, and the specific atrocities committed by, the Japanese."[7] Life-sized mannequins show Korean nationalists being tortured in prison, paintings show villages being burned, and dioramas play out the forcible recruitment of comfort women. We do not deny that Japanese authorities sometimes were guilty of these activities; we do wonder about the impact and impression this leaves on the schoolchild who walks through the Independence Hall. What does the student learn from at an interactive exhibit that allows the student to shoot Japanese police with a play machine gun?

Even more serious than these anecdotes are the forced resignation of Koryŏ University professor Han Sŭng-jo for making public statements much akin to those found in this essay. Professor Han made three claims that angered the Korean public. First, he stated that Japan was not the only nation to utilize military prostitutes during war; second, that Korean culture prospered during the colonial era; and third, that Korea was blessed to be colonized by Japan rather than Russia.[8] The public outrage against these statements was so great that Han resigned his position at Koryŏ. It is this sort of vitriol that prevents an open discussion of the colonial era in Korea.

---

7. Guy Podoler, 84.
8. *Yŏnhap News*, 6 March 2005, and *Tong-a Ilbo*, 7 March 2005.

The warning posited by Amos Oz, the Israeli author and literary critic, should be heeded:

> . . . there are differences among states. Some are almost fair, some are bad, some are lethal. And since writers are, or at least they ought to be, in the subtleties department and in the precision department, it is our job to differentiate. Whoever ignores the existence of varying degrees of evil is bound to become a servant of evil . . . the *moment we put things into words, our words are promoted into evidence. Hence our responsibility for precision, for nuances, for subtleties.* [This is why I put so much emphasis on the words used in the volume edited by Eckert.] Hence our duty to map evil, to grade it, to measure its degrees . . . Let us not give in to the temptation of simplification. We ought to be telling the bad from the worse from the worst.[9]

More than a decade later, an *Arkansas Democrat Gazette* journalist wrote a superlative article on the importance of differentiating distinctions among words. It is so well put and relevant that I share it with the reader:

> To lie should mean to tell a deliberate falsehood. That is, to tell a falsehood conscious that it is one, and so attempt to deceive. To say something false believing it to be true is not a lie; it is only an error. . . . Nor is a failure to fulfill a promise a lie. . . . [If a politician] said he'd lower taxes but he didn't [do so,] [t]hat's not a lie but a broken promise. . . . There is a distinction between a lie and a mistake. And one of the functions of language is to make distinctions, not muddle them. . . . The preservation of language, like that of liberty, requires eternal vigilance. Words are the currency

---

9. *The New Republic* 194, 3710 (24 February 1986), 28. Oz was born in 1939 and is a novelist and journalist. He has written 18 books in Hebrew and about 450 articles and essays. His works have been translated into some 40 languages, including Arabic. He is also Professor of Literature, Ben-Gurion University in Be'er Sheva.

> of thought, and when they are debased, so is how we think, feel, and soon enough act.[10]

I have attempted to follow throughout this study the dicta laid down by Oz and Paul Greenberg, and should any reader note lapses on my part, I would be pleased to stand corrected.

Colonial Korea as a Place of Hope

Before I rank colonial Korea in Oz's hierarchy, one last building block to support this study's thesis must be put in place. This is that Japan and the GGK gave the Koreans the intangible but nevertheless palpable sense of hope that was lacking in Chosŏn Korea. Hildi Kang alludes to it: "As Korea, . . . rushed forward into the modern world, life became a time of multiple possibilities."[11] In short, one could improve his place in Korean society under Japanese governance. Soon-Won Park also addresses this point:

> . . . [workers] were eager to learn and readily adapted themselves to the routines and regulations of factory life. . . . [the] factory site was *popular* because it was a place where work was always available and a full-time worker could afford rice and beef and live in a heated room or house, all of which were rare in other areas. . . . [a]n elementary school diploma … qualif[ied] a teenage boy for a job as a clerk in local government, a clerical position in a Japanese store, or a local police post. And these jobs increased the status not only of the young man himself but also of his family.[12]

It is Kang's stalwart, Hong Ŭlse, who puts a human stamp on this with two stirring comments:

> . . . it gave me confidence that if Japan could do things, then we could do them, too.

---

10. Paul Greenberg, "Lies" in the *Chicago Tribune*, cited in *The Daily Yomiuri*, 11 November 2008.
11. Hildi Kang, 3.
12. Soon Won Park, *Colonial Industrialization*, 75, 78-79.

> . . . "Where there is a will there is a way."[13]

There in Hong's words are Japan's justification for assimilation: if we [Japanese] can do it, so can you [Koreans], but more important, let us work together to make it happen. The highest-ranking Japanese authorities in Tokyo embarked on the colonial endeavor to lift the Korean nation up; as has been shown, assimilation was intended, over time, to bring equality, enfranchisement, and progress to the Korean people.

I iterate that in the process of assimilation there was suffering, pain, humiliation, and anger among Koreans. Many of the problems resulted from colonial authorities who deviated from the agenda outlined in Tokyo. Colonial authorities often confronted a disparity between Japan and Korea's economies, educational accomplishments, and social standards. Through it all, Japan exhibited a plurality of voices, most of which sought the betterment of the Korean people. What is striking are the good intentions and actions of Japan's leadership and the GGK so that, despite the blemishes, their Korean colonial policy may be judged as being, "almost fair."

---

13. Hildi Kang, 27 and 31.

Bibliography

Japanese-Language Sources

Akita, George. *Taikoku Nihon: Amerika no Kyōi to Chōsen: Ribijyonisuto no Shikō to Kōdō* [Japan as a Great Power: The Threat and Challenge to America: The Ideas and Conduct of the Revisionists] Tokyo, Nihon Hyōronsha, 1993.

Banno Junji. *Nihon Kindaishi* [History of Modern Japan]. Chikuma Shinsho, 948. Tokyo: Chikuma shobō, 2012.

Eckert, Carter J. *Nihon teikoku no mōshigo: Kōshō (Kochian) no Kin (Kimu) ichizoku to Kankoku shihonshugi no shokuminchi kigen: 1876–1945* [Offspring of Empire: The Koch'ang Kims and the Colonial Origins of Korean Capitalism, 1876–1945]. Translated by Kotani Masayo. Tokyo: Sōshisha, 2004.

Hara Keiichirō, ed. *Hara Kei Nikki* dai 3 kan [The Diary of Hara Kei Volume 3]. Tokyo: Fukumura Shuppan, 1965.

Ichikawa Kunitoshi, Ichihara Yasuhisa, and Yoshida Eiji. *Kojima Iken (Koreka-ta) no Kōseki* [Impact of Kojima Iken]. Suita-shi: Kansai Daigaku Hōgaku Kenkyūjo, 1996.

Ienaga Saburō and Kojima Iken. *Ōtsujiken nisshi* [The Record of the Ōtsu Incident]. Tōyō bunko, 187. Tokyo: Heibonsha, 1982.

Inoue Kaoru kankei monjo [The Inoue Kaoru Documents]. Kensei Shiryōshitsu, National Diet Library.

Inoue Kowashi denki hensan iinkai. *Inoue Kowashi den, Shiryōhen daini* [Biography of Inoue Kowashi, Documentary Sources Volume 2]. Tokyo: Kokugakuin daigaku toshokan, 1968.

Kaneko Kentarō. *Itō Hirobumi den chū-kan* [Biography of Itō Hirobumi Volume 2]. Tokyo: Tōseisha, 1943.

Kang Tŏk-sang. *Chōsenjin gakuto shutsujin: Mō hitotsuno wadatsumino koe* [Korean Students Go to War: Another Voice of the Sea]. Tokyo: Iwanami shoten, 1997.

Kim Il Myŏn. *Chōsenjin ga naze 'Nihonmei' o nanorunoka: minzoku ishiki to sabetsu* [Why Do Koreans Change Their Names Into 'Japanese Names'?: Racial

Consciousness and Discrimination]. Tokyo: San'ichi Shobō, 1978.
———. *Tennō no guntai to Chōsenjin ianfu* [The Emperor's Military and Korean Comfort Women]. Tokyo: San'ichi Shobō, 1976.
Liu Mei-shū. *Taiwan tōchi to ahen mondai* [The Taiwan Governance and Opium Problem]. Tokyo: Yamakawa shuppansha, 1983.
Mitarai Tatsuo, ed. *Minami Jirō* [Minami Jirō]. Tokyo: Minami Jirō denki kankōkai, 1957.
Ōta Masao, ed. *Ienaga Toyokichi to Meiji kenseishiron* [Toyokichi Iyenaga, Essays on Japanese Constitutional History]. Translated by Ōta Masao. Tokyo: Shinsensha, 1996.
Ōyama Azusa. *Yamagata Aritomo ikensho* [The Position Papers of Yamagata Aritomo]. Tokyo: Hara Shobō, 1966.
Pak Kyŏng-sik. *Chōsenjin kyōsei renkō no kiroku* [The Record of the Forced Displacement of Koreans]. Tokyo: Miraisha, 1965.
———. *Nihon teikokushugi no Chōsen shihai* 2 [Japanese Imperialistic Domination of Korea, Volume 2]. Tokyo: Aoki shoten, 1975.
Rhee Yong-hoon. *Daikan minkoku no monogatari: Kankoku no "kokushi" kyōkasho o kakikaeyo* [The Narrative in Republic of Korea: "National History" Textbooks of South Korea Must Be Revised]. Translated by Nagashima Hiroki. Tokyo: Bungei Shunjū, 2009.
Tamura Naoomi. *Waga mitaru Hara shushō no omokage* [This Is the Image of Prime Minister Hara That I Possess]. Tokyo: Keiseisha, 1922.
Tanaka Tomoyoshi, ed. *Hara Kei Zenshū ge-kan* [The Complete Works of Hara Kei Volume 2].Tokyo: Hara Kei Zenshū Kankōkai, 1929.
van Wolferen, Karel. "Nihon seiji saisei o meguru ken'ryoku tōsō no nazo [The Enigma of the Power Struggle over the Resuscitation of Japanese Politics]." Translated by Inoue Minori in *Chūō Kōron* (April 2010), 182-197.
Yakabi Osamu. "Kindai Okinawa chishikijin no senjika no genron: Iha Fuyū to Shimabukuro Zenpatsu" [The Wartime Debate Between Two Okinawan Intellectuals: Iha Fuyū and Shimabukuro Zenpatsu] *Hongō* 86 (March 2010): 16-18.

KOREAN-LANGUAGE SOURCES

Pak Chi-hyang et al., eds. *Haebang chŏn-husa ŭi chae insik* [A Rediscovery of History Before and Since Liberation]. Seoul: Ch'aek sesang, 2006.
Yi Ki-dong. "Ilbon cheguk gunŭi Hangukin changgyodŭl" [Korean Officers in the Japanese Army] *Sin Tong-a* 299 (August 1984): 452-499.
Yun Hae-dong et al., eds. *Kŭndae rŭl tasi ingnŭnda: Han'guk kŭndae insik ŭi saeroun p'aerŏdaim ŭl wihayŏ* [Another Reckoning of Modern Times: A New Paradigm for Modern Korea]. Seoul: Yŏksa Pip'yŏngsa, 2006.
Yun Hae-dong. *Singminji kŭndae ŭi p'aerŏdoksŭ* [The Paradox of Colonial Modernity]. Seoul: Hyumŏnisŭtŭ, 2007.

English-Language Sources

Akita, George. *Evaluating Evidence: A Positivist Approach to Reading Sources on Modern Japan*. Honolulu: University of Hawai'i Press, 2008.

Altbach, Philip G., and Gail Paradise Kelly, eds. *Education and the Colonial Experience*. New Brunswick, NJ: Transaction Books, 1984.

Bacevich, Andrew J. *The New American Militarism: How Americans Are Seduced by War*. Oxford: Oxford University Press, 2005.

Baker, Edward J. "The Role of Legal Reforms in the Japanese Annexation and Rule of Korea 1905–1919." *Harvard Law School: Studies in East Asian Law, Korea,* no. 1.

Baldwin, Frank P., Jr. "The March First Movement: Korean Challenge and Japanese Response." Ph.D. diss., Columbia University, 1969.

Bender, Gerald J. *Angola under the Portuguese: The Myth and the Reality*. Berkeley: University of California Press, 1978.

Bird, Isabella. *Korea and Her Neighbors*. London: John Murray, 1898; reprinted Yonsei University Press, 1970.

Buzo, Adrian. *The Making of Modern Korea*. New York: Routledge, 2002.

Caprio, Mark E. *Japanese Assimilation Policies in Colonial Korea, 1910–1945*. Seattle: University of Washington Press, 2009.

Chandra, Vipan. *Imperialism, Resistance, and Reform in Late Nineteenth-Century Korea: Enlightenment and the Independence Club*. Berkeley: University of California Institute for Asian Studies, 1988.

Chung, Henry. *The Case of Korea*. New York: Fleming H. Revell, 1921.

Clayton, Thomas. "Restriction or Resistance? French Colonial Educational Development in Cambodia." *Education Policy Analysis Archives* 3.19 (1995): 19 pages.

The Constitution of the Empire of Japan, With the Speeches Addressed to Students of Political Science in the Johns Hopkins University, Baltimore, April 17, 1889. Baltimore: The Johns Hopkins University. 1889.

Devine, Richard. "Japanese Rule in Korea after the March First Uprising: Governor General Hasegawa's Recommendations." *Monumenta Nipponica* 52.4 (1997): 523-540.

Dickinson, Frederick R. *War and National Reinvention: Japan in the Great War, 1914–1919*. Cambridge, MA: Harvard University Asia Center, 1999.

Dong, Wonmo. "Japanese Colonial Policy and Practice in Korea, 1905–1945: A Study in Assimilation." Ph.D. diss., Georgetown University, 1965.

Dore, Ronald. *Education in Tokugawa Japan*. Berkeley: University of California Press, 1965.

Dudden, Alexis. *Japan's Colonization of Korea: Discourse and Power*. Honolulu: University of Hawai'i Press, 2005.

Duus, Peter. *The Abacus and the Sword: The Japanese Penetration of Korea, 1895–1910*. Berkeley: University of California Press, 1995.

Eckert, Carter J. *Offspring of Empire: The Koch'ang Kims and the Colonial Origins of Korean Capitalism, 1876–1945*. Seattle: University of Washington Press, 1991.

Eckert, Carter J., Ki-baek Lee, et al. *Korea, Old and New: A History*. Seoul: Ilchokak, 1990.

Eckstein, Gustav. *In Peace Japan Breeds War*. New York: Harper and Brothers, 1943.

Em, Henry H. *The Great Enterprise: Sovereignty and Historiography in Modern Korea*. Durham: Duke University Press, 2013.

Fallows, James M. *More Like Us: Making America Great Again*. Boston: Houghton Mifflin, 1989.

Francks, Penelope. *Technology and Agricultural Development in Pre-War Japan*. New Haven, CT: Yale University Press, 1984.

Fujitani, Takashi. *Race for Empire: Koreans as Japanese and Japanese as Americans during World War II*. Berkeley: University of California Press, 2011.

Gragert, Edwin H. *Landownership Under Colonial Rule: Korea's Japanese Experience, 1900–1935*. Honolulu: University of Hawai'i Press, 1994.

Grajdanzev, Andrew J. *Modern Korea*. New York: John Day Company, 1940.

Hackett, Roger F. *Yamagata Aritomo in the Rise of Modern Japan, 1838–1922*. Cambridge, MA: Harvard University Press, 1971.

Hardacre, Helen, and Adam L. Kern, eds. *New Directions in the Study of Meiji Japan*. Leiden: Brill, 1997.

Headrick, Daniel R. *The Tentacles of Progress: Technology Transfer in the Age of Imperialism, 1850–1940*. New York: Oxford University Press, 1988.

Hulbert, Homer B. *The Passing of Korea*. 1906; reprint Yonsei University Press, 1969.

Itō Hirobumi. *Commentaries on the Constitution of the Empire of Japan*. Translated by Itō Miyoji. Tokyo: Igirisu-Hōritsu Gakkō, 1889.

Jaisohn, Philip, and Sŏn-p'yo Hong. *My Days in Korea and Other Essays*. Seoul: Yonsei University, 1999.

James, Laurence. *The Savage Wars: British Campaigns in Africa, 1870–1920*. New York: St. Martin's Press, 1985.

Joe, Wanne J. *A Cultural History of Modern Korea: History of Korean Civilization*. Elizabeth, NJ: Hollym, 2000.

Kajiyama, Toshiyuki. *The Clan Records: Five Stories of Korea*. Translated by Yoshiko K. Dykstra. Honolulu: University of Hawai'i Press, 1995.

Kang, Hildi. *Under the Black Umbrella: Voices from Colonial Korea, 1910–1945*. Ithaca, NY: Cornell University Press, 2001.

Kelly, Gail P. "Conflict in the Classroom: A Case Study from Vietnam, 1918–1938." *British Journal of Sociology of Education* 8.2 (1987): 191-212.

Kendall, Laurel, ed. *Consuming Korean Tradition in Early and Late Modernity: Commodification, Tourism, and Performance*. Honolulu: University of Hawai'i Press, 2011.

Kim, C.I. Eugene, and Han-Kyo Kim. *Korea and the Politics of Imperialism, 1876–1910*. Berkeley: University of California Press, 1967.

Kim, In Soo. *Protestants and the Formation of Modern Korean Nationalism, 1885–1920*. New York: Peter Lang, 1996.

Kim, Marie Seong-Hak. "Customary Law and Colonial Jurisprudence in Korea." *The American Journal of Comparative Law* 57.1 (Winter 2009): 205-248.

Krämer, Hans Martin. "The Prewar Roots of 'Equality of Opportunity': Japanese Educational Ideals in the Twentieth Century." *Monumenta Nipponica* 61.4 (Winter 2006): 521-549.

Lee, Hong Yung, Yong-Chool Ha, and Clark W. Sorensen, eds. *Colonial Rule and Social Change in Korea, 1910–1945*. Seattle: University of Washington Press, 2013.

Linn, Brian M. *Guardians of Empire: The U.S. Army and the Pacific, 1902–1940*. Chapel Hill: University of North Carolina Press, 1997.

———. *The U.S. Army and Counterinsurgency in the Philippine War, 1899–1902*. Chapel Hill: University of North Carolina Press, 1989.

Matsuda Toshihiko. *Governance and Policing of Colonial Korea, 1904–1919*. Kyoto: International Research Center for Japanese Studies, 2011.

McCoy, Alfred W. *Policing America's Empire: The United States, the Philippines, and the Rise of the Surveillance State*. Madison: University of Wisconsin Press, 2009.

Miliukov, Paul. *Russia and Its Crisis*. New York: Collier Books, 1962.

Min, Pyong Gap. "'Korean Comfort Women': The Intersection of Colonial Power, Gender, and Class." *Gender & Society* 17.6 (December 2003): 938-957.

Minichiello, Sharon. *Japan's Competing Modernities: Issues in Culture and Democracy, 1900–1930*. Honolulu: University of Hawai'i Press, 1998.

Mitchell, Richard H. *Justice in Japan: The Notorious Teijin Scandal*. Honolulu: University of Hawai'i Press, 2002.

———. *Thought Control in Prewar Japan*. Ithaca, NY: Cornell University Press, 1976.

Myers, Ramon Hawley, Mark R. Peattie, and Jingzhi Zhen. *The Japanese Colonial Empire, 1895–1945*. Princeton, NJ: Princeton University Press, 1984.

Najita, Tetsuo. *Hara Kei in the Politics of Compromise, 1905–1915*. Cambridge, MA: Harvard University Press, 1967.

Nihon Zaijū Gaikokujin Shinpojūmu, Toshihiko Matsuda, and Sadami Suzuki. *Korea Under Japanese Rule: Past and Current Research Results and Issues for Future Research*. Kyoto: International Research Center for Japanese Studies, 2009.

Nishida Yoshiaki. "Growth of the Meiji Landlord System and Tenancy Disputes after World War I: A Critique of Richard Smethurst, Agricultural Development and Tenancy Disputes in Japan, 1870–1940." *Journal of Japanese Studies* 15.2 (Summer 1989), 389-415.

Norman, E. Herbert. "Feudal Background of Japanese Politics." *Secretariat Paper*. No. 9, IPR, 1945.

———. *Soldier and Peasant in Japan: The Origins of Conscription*. Vancouver, Canada: University of British Columbia, 1943; 1965 ed.

Nzongola-Ntalaja, Georges. *The Congo from Leopold to Kabila: A People's History*. New York: Zed Books, 2002.

Oh, Andrew Hak. "The Japanese Policy of Cultural Assimilation in Colonial Korea Under Governor-General Minami Jirō (南次郎)." M.A. Thesis, University of Hawai'i, 2001.

Ōkuma Shigenobu. "Japan's Policy in Korea," *The Forum* 37.4 (April–June 1906): 577-580.

Oppenheim, Robert. "'The West' and the Anthropology of Other People's Colonialism: Frederick Starr in Korea, 1911–1930." *The Journal of Asian Studies* 64.3 (August 2005): 677-703.

Pai, Hyung Il. *Heritage Management in Korea and Japan: The Politics of Antiquity and Identity*. Seattle: University of Washington Press, 2013.

———. *Constructing "Korean" Origins: A Critical Review of Archeology, Historiography, and Racial Myth in Korean State-Formation Theories*. Cambridge, MA: Harvard University Press, 2000.

———. "The Creation of National Treasures and Monuments: The 1916 Japanese Laws on the Preservation of Korean Remains and Relics and Their Colonial Legacies." *Korean Studies* 25.1 (2001): 72-95.

Palmer, Brandon. "Japan's Mobilization of Koreans for War, 1937–1945." Ph.D. diss., University of Hawai'i, 2005.

Park, Soon Won. *Colonial Industrialization and Labor in Korea: The Onoda Cement Factory*. Cambridge, MA: Harvard University Asia Center, 1999.

———. "Making Colonial Policies in Korea: The Factory Law Debate, Peace Preservation Law, and Land Reform Laws in the Interwar Years." *Korean Studies* 22.1 (1998): 41-61.

Peattie, Mark R. *A Historian Looks at the Pacific War*. Stanford: Hoover Institution on War, Revolution, and Peace, Stanford University, 1995.

———. *Ishiwara Kanji and Japan's Confrontation with the West*. Princeton, NJ: Princeton University Press, 1975.

Peterson, Mark. *A Brief History of Korea*. New York: Facts on File, 2010.

Podoler, Guy. *Monuments, Memory, and Identity: Constructing the Colonial Past in South Korea*. New York: Peter Lang, 2011.

Pratt, Keith. *Everlasting Flower: A History of Korea*. London: Reaktion Books, 2006.

Pu Bao, ed. *Prisoner of the State: The Secret Journal of Zhao Ziyang*. Translated and edited by Pu Bao, Renee Chiang, and Adi Ignatius. New York: Simon & Schuster, 2009.

Robinson, Michael. *Korea's Twentieth-Century Odyssey*. Honolulu: University of Hawai'i Press, 2007.

———. "Narrative Politics, Nationalism and Korean history." *Papers of the British Association for Korean Studies* 6 (1996): 26-40.

Rodney, Walter. *How Europe Underdeveloped Africa*. Washington, DC: Howard University Press, 1981.

Rokuhara, Hiroko. "Local Officials and the Meiji Conscription Campaign." *Monumenta Nipponica* 60. 1 (Spring 2005): 81-110.

Rubinger, Richard. "Who Can't Read and Write? Illiteracy in Meiji Japan." *Monumenta Nipponica* 55. 2 (Summer 2000): 163-198.

Rubinstein, Murray A., ed. *Taiwan: A New History*. Armonk, NY: M.E. Sharpe, 1999. Expanded ed., 2007.

SarDesai, D.R. *Southeast Asia: Past & Present*, 5th ed. Boulder: Westview Press, 2003.

Schmid, Andre. *Korea between Empires, 1895–1919*. New York: Columbia University Press, 2002.

Seth, Michael J. *A Concise History of Modern Korea: From the Late Nineteenth Century to the Present*. Lanham, MD: Rowman & Littlefield, 2010.

———. *Education Fever: Society, Politics, and the Pursuit of Schooling in South Korea*. Honolulu: University of Hawaii Press, 2002.

Shin, Gi-Wook, and Michael E. Robinson, eds. *Colonial Modernity in Korea*. Cambridge, MA: Harvard University Asia Center, 1999.

Shin, Gi-Wook. "Agrarian Conflict and the Origins of Korean Capitalism." *American Journal of Sociology* 103.5 (March 1998): 1309-1351.

———. "Agrarianism: A Critique of Colonial Modernity in Korea." *Comparative Studies in Society and History: An International Quarterly* 41.4 (October 1999): 784-804.

———. *Peasant Protest and Social Change in Colonial Korea*. Seattle: University of Washington Press, 1996.

Shin, Gi-Wook, Soon-Won Park, and Daqing Yang. eds. *Rethinking Historical Injustice and Reconciliation in Northeast Asia: The Korean Experience*. London: Routledge, 2007.

Shin Yong-ha. *Modern Korean History and Nationalism*. Translated by N.M. Pankaj. Seoul: Jimoondang Publishing Company, 2000.

Smethurst, Richard J. *Agricultural Development and Tenancy Disputes in Japan, 1870-1940*. Princeton, NJ: Princeton University Press, 1986.

Soh, C. Sarah. *The Comfort Women: Sexual Violence and Postcolonial Memory in Korea and Japan*. Chicago: University of Chicago Press, 2008.

Song Youn-ok. "Japanese Colonial Rule and State-Managed Prostitution: Korea's Licensed Prostitutes." *Positions: East Asia Cultures Critique* 5.1 (Spring 1997): chapter 6.

Sprunger, Michael L. "Grafting Justice: Crime and the Politics of Punishment in Korea, 1875–1945." Ph.D. diss., University of Hawaii, 2011.

Staubitz, Richard. "The Establishment of the System of Local Self-Government (1888–1890) in Meiji Japan: Yamagata Aritomo and the Meaning of 'Jichi' (Self-government)." Ph.D. diss., Yale University, 1973.

Uchida, Jun. "A Sentimental Journey: Mapping Interior Frontier of Japanese Settlers in Colonial Korea," *The Journal of Asian Studies* 70.3 (August 2011): 706-729.

Wakabayashi, Bob Tadashi. "Comfort Women: Beyond Litigious Feminism." *Monumenta Nipponica* 58.2 (Summer 2003): 223-258.

Wesseling, H.L. *The European Colonial Empires, 1815–1919*. Translated by Diane Webb. New York: Pearson Longman, 2004.

Wurfel, David, ed. *Meiji Japan's Centennial: Aspects of Political Thought and Action*. Lawrence, KA: University Press of Kansas, 1971.

Yoo, Theodore Jun. *The Politics of Gender in Colonial Korea: Education, Labor and Health, 1910–1945*. Berkeley, University of California Press, 2008.

Newspapers and Encyclopedias

The Asia-Pacific Journal: Japan Focus
Associated Press
Chicago Tribune
Daily Yomiuri
Encyclopedia of African History
Encyclopedia of Western Colonialism since 1450
Honolulu Star-Advertiser
Japan Times
Kanpō
Kokumin Shimbun
The Korea Times
New Republic
New York Times
Newsweek
Newsweek International
Pac Net Newsletter
Reuters
Time
Tong-a Ilbo
Yŏnhap News

INDEX

About the Authors

George Akita was born to immigrant parents from Hiroshima, Japan; attended public schools in Honolulu, including the University of Hawai'i (1941–1942; 1948–1951). Drafted into the U.S. Army, attended Army language school at Fort Snelling, Minnesota. Stationed in Tokyo, 1946–1947, and employed as a Department of Army Civilian (Tokyo). He returned to attend the University of Hawai'i (1948–1951, BA) and Harvard University (1951–1953, M.A.; and Ph.D. in 1960). Employed at University of Hawaii (Assistant Professor, Associate Professor and Professor) from 1960 to 1985 when he took early retirement to work with Japanese colleagues in deciphering documents in the cursive (*sōsho*) form of writing.

Professor Akita began this journey when, in the summer of 1977, he joined a team of graduate students and young professors at the urging of Itō Takashi, then a professor at the University of Tokyo. He continued to spend the next few summers in Japan when he realized that the only way to make real progress was to spend more time in Japan. Thus in 1985, he began to spend eight months of the year in Japan. In the meanwhile, he was invited (at an event sponsored by both Houses of the Diet) to give an address in Japanese at the National Diet to celebrate the 100th anniversary of its founding.

Thirty years of deciphering holographs with different teams of Japanese scholars added fifteen volumes of such documents to his curriculum vitae. This was followed by the unique and unprecedented distinction of being honored with a *festschrift*, with articles contributed by ten Japanese scholars.

He is currently working at age eighty-eight on two more works in English before he begins his lifework of five to six volumes of translated and annotated writings of Yamagata Aritomo and other Meiji Era leaders.

Professor Akita's publications include 明治立憲政と伊藤博文 *Meiji Rikkensei to Itō Hirobumi (translation of Foundations)*, Tokyo, University of Tokyo Press, 1971; *Taikoku Nihon: Amerika no Kyōi to Chōsen: Ribijionisuto no Shikō to Kōdō (*大国日本アメリカの脅威と挑戦リビジョニストの思考と行動 [Japan as a Great Power: The Threat and Challenge to America: The Ideas and Conduct of the Revisionists], Tokyo, Shin Hyōronsha, 1993; *Evaluating Evidence: A Positivist Approach to Reading Sources on Modern Japan*, Honolulu, University of Hawai'i Press, 2008.

Brandon Palmer is an Associate Professor of History at Coastal Carolina University, where he teaches Asian history. Palmer received his Ph.D. in Korean History from the University of Hawai'i. His research interests include Japan's mobilization of Korea during the Asia-Pacific War (1937–1945) and Korean immigrants in the United States.